RAISING
A
SELF-DISCIPLINED
CHILD

★ ★

Help Your Child Become More Responsible, Confident and Resilient

Robert Brooks PhD & Sam Goldstein PhD

New York   C   Mexico City
Milan   Toronto

Raising a Self-disciplined Child
Help your child become more responsible, confident and resilient

Robert Brooks & Sam Goldstein

ISBN 13: 978-0-07-711742-9
ISBN 10: 0-07-711742-5

 **Professional**

Published by:
McGraw-Hill Publishing Company
Shoppenhangers Road, Maidenhead, Berkshire, England, SL6 2QL
Telephone: 44 (0) 1628 502500
Fax: 44 (0) 1628 770224
Website: www.mcgraw-hill.co.uk

British Library Cataloguing in Publication Data
A catalogue record of this book is available from the British Library.

Since the case illustrations in this book are taken from both authors' clinical and
consultation practices and workshops, these examples refer to us in the plural (as
we and us), not only to simplify the writing style, but also to acknowledge the
contributions of material from both authors' professional activities. The names of the
patients are fictional to respect confidentiality.

Printed in Great Britain by Cromwell Press Ltd, Trowbridge, Wiltshire

With love to my grandchildren, Maya, Teddy, Sophia, and Lyla. I wish you a self-disciplined life filled with joy, love, and compassion.
—R.B.

As always, for Janet, Allyson, and Ryan.
—S.G.

We wish to thank Judith McCarthy, our editor, for her patience, encouragement, and support in guiding this book, our fourth with McGraw-Hill. Thanks also to our agent, James Levine, and to Kathleen Gardner, our editorial jack of all trades.
—R.B.
—S.G.

Contents

Preface

In a recent *Psychology Today* article, Hara Estroff Marano suggests that parents are raising a generation of "wimps" because their children are overprotected and their lives carefully planned. Marano's concern is that children rarely have to fend for themselves or experience even minor setbacks because parents rush forth to protect them and direct their lives. But as author and child psychologist David Elkind of Tufts University notes in the article, "Kids need to feel badly sometimes. We learn through experience and we learn through bad experiences. Through failure we learn how to cope." As we noted in our book *Raising Resilient Children*, mistakes are important challenges in helping children manage obstacles and become resilient.

For every overprotected child, there are many others who either are left to fend for themselves or are harshly treated by parents who punish every misstep. At one extreme, countless youngsters are exposed to too much too soon. They have free access to television and computer screens, where they are bombarded by images they cannot understand or absorb. More and more, their knowledge comes from cyberspace rather than from their parents. At the other extreme are angry, arbitrary parents who rob their children of opportunities to take the initiative and become effective, thoughtful problem solvers. When children are overprotected, neglected, or harshly treated, they miss out on experiences that will help them establish a comfortable sense of self-discipline, a key requirement for coping with life's challenges.

In the 1950s and '60s, television portrayed children as innocent though sometimes mischievous scamps whose antics invoked humor and entertained viewers. Their families were mostly intact, headed by parents who had been married for several years. Even when a mother or father was not present, these television families had two parent figures, as in the program "My Three Sons," which cast Uncle Charlie as a surrogate mother to his three great-nephews. In fact, more often than not, Charlie was cooking and wearing an apron!

Fast-forward to the new millennium. Television, movies, and music videos portray today's children as confused if not disturbed, angry, and chronically dysfunctional. More often than not, the children are raising themselves or ensconced in fragmented families with equally impaired, clueless parents. In their defense, the creators of popular programs in today's entertainment media point out that their work simply reflects trends in our culture. Though we question whether the tail is wagging the dog, they are correct in many cases. True, many families are finding ways to raise healthy, resilient children in response to today's stresses, but well over one-third of children today live in single-parent homes, a situation that often places additional stress on the parent and the children. Also, many children are growing up in homes beset by at least one significant stressful life problem. Over the past twenty years, there has been and continues to be an increase in the severity of problems among youth, such as obesity, mental illness, and victimization. In this environment, no child is immune. The number of children facing adversity and the number of adversities they face continue to dramatically increase. Even children fortunate to avoid significant hardship or trauma and the burden of daily intense stress or anxiety experience the pressures around them and the expectations placed upon them.

In our previous work, we have suggested that children have a high potential to experience serious problems in a complex,

technologically advanced culture. Parents therefore must prepare their children to cope with this ever-challenging world. To
accomplish this goal, parents must become educators, guiding
their children to develop what we call a *resilient mindset.* When
parents nurture this mindset, their children learn to handle stress
and pressure, cope with everyday challenges, and bounce back
from disappointment, adversity, or trauma. Children with a resilient mindset can set goals, solve problems, relate to others, and
develop empathy, altruism, and self-discipline. To raise resilient
children, parents don't focus on building walls and stronger locks
to keep the world out; rather, they help their children develop
the skills and abilities to handle what life brings.

In his fascinating book *The Eternal Child*, Clive Bromhall
writes that long after humans developed the ability to walk on
two legs and their brains became larger than those of any other
species on this planet, our species was still limited in thinking
and development. Our ancestors' brains grew larger, but humans
appeared to reap few intellectual benefits. However, within the
past fifty thousand years, something happened in the human
brain that transformed the already large brains of our ancestors
into what they are today. At some point, brain circuitry changed.
Our human ancestors developed the ability to think. As Bromhall
notes, the brain became "partitioned," permitting the capacity
for subjective experience. In other words, we can simultaneously
experience internal thoughts and the external world.

This fascinating capability described by Bromhall is significantly influenced by our capacity for self-discipline. The skills
associated with self-discipline give us the ability to stop, think,
generate strategies, consider alternatives, and most importantly,
act while consciously and critically analyzing the effects of our
actions. These skills are not just in the genes but must be nurtured as we grow. Thus, it is neither surprising nor unexpected
that the capacity for self-discipline has played and continues to
play such a critical role in our everyday lives.

Since the publication of our first book, *Raising Resilient Children*, it has become increasingly apparent that for today's youth, knowing what to do and doing what they know are not necessarily synonymous. We have become acutely aware that opportunities to develop a resilient mindset are necessary but not sufficient to ensure that the processes of resilience will play a central role in our children's lives. We have come to realize that one of the components of a resilient mindset may also be a central force in driving that mindset. That influential component is self-discipline. To be resilient requires the ability to think before acting, rather than allowing our actions to be dominated by our emotions. To survive in a world that is often chaotic and unpredictable, children must learn to negotiate life in a reflective, efficient manner.

With this goal in mind, we have created a road map for parents to become more effective disciplinarians so that you will be better prepared to raise self-disciplined children on what has become an increasingly uncharted path. We hope the road map will help you navigate this very important parental journey.

Talent without discipline is like an octopus on roller skates. There is plenty of movement but you never know whether it is going to be forward, backwards or sideways.
—H. JACKSON BROWN JR., AUTHOR OF
LIVE AND LEARN AND PASS IT ON

If we don't discipline ourselves, the world will do it for us.
—WILLIAM FEATHER, AUTHOR AND PUBLISHER

It has gotten to the point that my belief in the importance of discipline borders on an "invariant prescription" for children's problems. Of course it is hardly earth-shattering news that discipline and limits are important for healthy children.
—LAWRENCE H. DILLER, DEVELOPMENTAL PEDIATRICIAN AND AUTHOR OF
THE LAST NORMAL CHILD

1

Developing Self-Discipline in Our Children

Recently, while dining at a popular restaurant, we were confronted by the powerful role children play in shaping the world around them. A few moments after we arrived, a young couple with an eleven-month-old boy entered and sat down two tables away. We soon learned that this boy was their first child. Within a few moments, this child had managed to engage everyone around him. Waitresses were stopping to pat him on the head. If you looked in his direction, he was sure to make eye contact and smile before looking away. His level of engagement, pleasant temperament, and mood were infectious. For his first-time parents, parenting (as they told us upon learning of our work) wasn't very difficult. In fact, they proudly reported that they were planning on having many more children.

About halfway through our meal, another young couple came in with a child of about the same age and sat nearby. Perhaps this child was having a difficult day or struggled with a difficult temperament in general. Even while the family was waiting to be seated, this young boy was squirming and kicking in his mother's arms. As she turned, his outstretched foot knocked over a glass of water on an adjacent table. The mother admonished him to stop wiggling, and the family's dining experience went rapidly downhill from that point. The child's irritable behavior quickly annoyed the other diners. This child showed no interest in engaging others in a positive way, and if he hadn't been so young, we might have guessed that he had an agenda to disturb his parents. Perhaps this would remain a one-child family!

We suspect that if we had investigated, we would have found little in the parenting strategies and personalities of these two young couples that could predict the significant difference in the children's self-control at such an early age. While we have long advocated that biology is not destiny, it does significantly affect probability. In other words, parents can influence how their child turns out, but only within limits determined by their child's genetic makeup. In the restaurant, the first child seemed to have a strong genetic endowment for good self-control and likable demeanor, so his early interpersonal experiences were positive. In contrast, the second child's lack of self-control had already triggered in his parents a chain of ineffective efforts to manage what may have been his biological vulnerability. Even at this young age, differences in self-discipline produced significant consequences.

The Power of Self-Discipline

The need to develop and harness self-discipline at an early age, while critical in any culture, may take on greater importance in a society filled with complex demands, challenges, and stresses. Having self-discipline and using it effectively pave a successful road into adulthood. In our fast-paced, seemingly chaotic world, children who can exercise self-discipline at young ages appear to negotiate the maze of family, school, friends, and community more successfully than those who struggle to control themselves. A child with self-discipline has internalized a set of rules so that even when no parent or caregiver is around, the child will act in a thoughtful, reflective manner.

Self-discipline is a vital component of a person's sense of responsibility for his or her behavior. A large body of research has demonstrated that children who can resist temptation (a simple application of self-discipline at all ages) fare significantly better than their more impulsive peers when they enter their adolescent years. For example, one research team measured preschool children's ability to resist an attractive snack when requested to do so. Those who resisted better as preschoolers

> *Children who can exercise self-discipline at young ages appear to negotiate the maze of family, school, friends, and community more successfully than those who struggle to control themselves.*

were significantly more likely to do better as adolescents in terms of measures such as school success, mental health, and avoiding the juvenile justice system. The power of self-discipline to affect the course of a child's and adult's life should never be underestimated. Self-discipline is so significant because it helps us develop qualities that together form resilience.

Several of our previous books have focused on helping children develop resilience by teaching parents and educators the components of a resilient mindset in children. A *mindset* consists of assumptions or attitudes we possess about ourselves that shape our behaviors and the skills we develop. Parents who raise resilient youngsters understand—explicitly or intuitively—what they can do to nurture a resilient mindset and behaviors in their children. These parents follow a blueprint of important principles, ideas, and actions in their day-to-day interactions with their children. They help their children learn to communicate, experience empathy, be accepted, feel appreciated, learn to solve problems, make decisions, and develop a social conscience. These lessons and experiences determine the steps necessary for parents to reinforce resilience, as well as the obstacles that often prevent parents from helping their children develop resilience.

Among the most important of the obstacles to developing resilience is a lack of effective self-discipline. Many parents have limited ideas of how to instill self-discipline in their children. Yet all the qualities associated with resilience mean little if children lack the necessary self-discipline to put them into effective practice. Knowing what to do (for example, possessing empathy) does not guarantee that children will do what they know (act on their feeling of empathy). To do what they should, children—like adults—need self-discipline.

> *Knowing what to do does not guarantee that children will do what they know. To do what they should, children need self-discipline.*

The Role of Parents

To nurture the development of self-discipline in their children, parents have a key ingredient to contribute: discipline. One of the most important roles that parents play is that of a disciplinarian, regardless of the nature of a child's inborn temperament. However, parents fulfill this role in vastly different ways, as the following examples illustrate.

Among the participants in a parenting workshop we offered were two couples: Bill and Samantha Ewing and Tom and Jennifer Franklin. Each of the couples had three children, and in both families, the oldest child was a twelve-year-old boy. As these parents described their twelve-year-olds, we suspected that both boys had been born with more challenging or "difficult" temperaments. Compared with their younger siblings, they were harder to soothe, more irritable and argumentative, and less likely to be cooperative, especially when they felt frustrated.

A lively discussion ensued when the topic turned to disciplinary practices. Bill Ewing stated, "The only thing that Jim responds to is a spanking. You can try to reason with him for hours, and he will wear you down. He never does what you ask. There's always an argument. When I spank him on his rear, it gets him to do what I want. I don't have to spank my other kids, because they do what Samantha and I ask them to do. I guess the only way some kids learn is if you spank them. To be honest, my parents spanked me, and I turned out OK." As Bill said this, we couldn't help but notice the anger in his voice.

His wife, Samantha, added, "While Bill grew up in a home where his parents spanked him, my parents never spanked me. Before we had kids, I would have sworn that I would never yell or spank my kids, but having Jim changed all of that. I have to agree with Bill that Jim only seems to respond to being spanked. The only thing that bothers me is that we've been spanking him for years and he keeps doing the same things. He's almost a teenager. I'm not sure if we can keep spanking him much longer."

Jennifer Franklin jumped into the discussion. "My parents spanked me, just as Bill's parents spanked him. I really don't think it did much good. I still resent what they did. I know I wasn't the easiest kid, but each time they spanked me, I became angrier. To this day, I don't have a very good relationship with them. I must admit that when Stevie was born, there were times I really felt like hitting him. He made me so mad. But each time I came close to slapping him or was ready to yell at him, I thought back to what my parents had done to me. I didn't want Stevie to feel about me the way I feel about my parents."

Tom Franklin added, "I feel the same way my wife does. We've read a number of books about raising kids, but even without the books, we know that Stevie was born more difficult to raise. We've spent hours thinking and talking about how to deal with him. We know we have to maintain authority as his parents. We know that some things are nonnegotiable. But we've found that if we select our battlegrounds carefully, if we give him some choice in certain matters, if we speak to him calmly, he's more reasonable and more cooperative when we ask him to do certain things. It's still a struggle at times, but things are going more smoothly, and there are fewer outbursts."

Upon hearing Tom's observations, Bill replied, "I'm glad how you've handled Stevie has worked, but it would never work for Jim. He only understands one thing: that when we spank him, we mean business and he'd better listen to us."

Applying the Purpose of Discipline

The Ewings and Franklins both believed they were effective disciplinarians, but their approaches contrasted sharply. Each set of parents believed that the manner in which they disciplined their children fostered the development of self-discipline and in doing so helped their son develop a resilient mindset. How can this be? If we incorrectly assume that there is only one true path, then one set of parents must have been using the wrong approach.

Reflect for a moment on your feelings about discipline. Which approach feels most comfortable to you? Which approach do you think would work best for your child or children?

As parents consider an array of disciplinary practices, they often ask us, "What are the best ways of disciplining children?" We prefer to reframe this question by first reminding parents of the meaning of the word *discipline*. Discipline derives from the word *disciple* and is best understood as a teaching process. To recognize discipline as a form of education, children should not associate it with intimidation, humiliation, or embarrassment.

Discipline is best understood as a teaching process.

Placing discipline in the context of an educational process, parents can ponder the main goals of discipline. Many goals are possible, but we believe that discipline has two major functions. The first is to ensure that children have a consistent, safe, and secure environment in which they can learn reasonable rules, limits, and consequences as well as develop an understanding of why these are important. The second function, equally important but not as readily emphasized, is to nurture self-discipline or self-control.

Applying discipline to teach self-discipline is often a challenging task. As with other human qualities or traits, children come to the world with different predispositions and capacities. Some children easily develop self-discipline, while others struggle. Some children are responsive to discipline, able to shift their behavior quickly after a single negative experience or disciplinary intervention, while others struggle. Still, in either case, we want children to incorporate rather than dismiss or resent what we are trying to teach them.

Given these two key functions of discipline, parents may wonder: "What skills must I possess to be an effective disciplinarian?" "What skills should I try to teach my children in order to nurture self-discipline?" In response to the first question, which we will cover in greater detail in the next chapter, we believe that disciplinary practices are most constructive when parents display empathy, good communication skills, the ability to change when their parenting activities are negative, an appreciation of each child's unique temperament, and realistic goals for their children.

However, we have found that many well-meaning parents do not demonstrate these qualities, so they fail to nurture self-discipline in their children. When parents are reactive, crisis-oriented, overly punitive, harsh, belittling, arbitrary, or inconsistent, the positive goals of discipline are likely to suffer. Ironically, when parents resort to screaming or hitting (as in the case of the Ewings spanking their son), they are actually displaying the very behaviors they wish to stop in their children, serving instead as models of poor self-discipline.

The development of self-discipline is also compromised when the parents have very different disciplinary styles or when parents hesitate to set limits for fear that their children will be angry with them. (Some children take advantage of this fear by reacting to consequences with the claim "You don't love me!") Finally, children will have difficulty developing self-discipline when parents impose unrealistic expectations for behavior; these children instead become increasingly frustrated and angry.

Developing Self-Discipline: Focus on Mindsets and Solutions

The question "What skills and attitudes are we trying to reinforce in children when we discipline them?" can also be posed in the following way: "What do we want to be the end result of our disciplinary techniques?" We believe the answer may be found within a concept we proposed in *Raising Resilient Children*: a resilient mindset. As noted earlier, a resilient mindset consists of assumptions and attitudes about ourselves that support the development of behaviors and skills that make us more resilient. In turn, our behaviors and skills influence our set of assumptions, so a dynamic process is constantly operating.

Children who possess a resilient mindset are hopeful and have high self-worth. They feel special and appreciated. They have learned to set realistic goals and expectations for themselves. They demonstrate self-discipline and have developed the ability to solve problems and make decisions. They are likely to view mistakes, hardships, and obstacles as challenges to confront rather than as stressors to avoid. They rely on productive coping strategies that foster growth rather than a feeling of defeat. Although these children are aware of their weaknesses and vulnerabilities, they also recognize their strong points and talents. Their self-concept is filled with images of strength and competence. They have developed effective interpersonal skills with peers and adults alike. They are able to seek out help and nurturance comfortably and appropriately from adults who can provide the support they need. Finally, they can define the aspects of their lives they have control over, and they focus their energy and attention on these, rather than on factors over which they have little, if any, influence.

It is difficult to imagine children being hopeful, optimistic, and prepared to handle challenges and hardship if they lack self-discipline, if they act before they think, if they fail to consider the potential outcomes of their behavior. Self-discipline likewise plays a role in what Daniel Goleman calls *emotional intelligence.* In his book *Emotional Intelligence,* Goleman identifies self-discipline as a significant component of emotional intelligence, a form of intelligence deemed essential for success in all aspects of our personal and professional lives, including our interpersonal relations.

Viewing self-discipline as a driving force for individuals with resilient mindsets and lifestyles makes it easier to identify the skills and attitudes we are trying to reinforce in children when we discipline them. As parents, we want our disciplinary techniques to nurture a resilient mindset, including self-discipline. We want our children to develop attitudes about themselves and others that are in keeping with a more optimistic outlook and lifestyle.

More specifically, we need to identify the qualities defining self-discipline and consider the mindset possessed by resilient, self-disciplined children compared with youngsters who lack resilience. As we have stated and will emphasize throughout this book, to be resilient, a child must display self-discipline.

> *Parents need to appreciate that helping their children develop positive attitudes, self-discipline, and a resilient mindset requires time; we can't do it with a quick fix.*

Parents need to appreciate that helping their children develop positive attitudes, self-discipline, and a resilient mindset requires time; we can't do it with a quick fix. This effort is most likely to

Children's Positive and Negative Attitudes

In the following list, positive attitudes are paired with their negative opposites. These are presented as statements by a child; a child or adolescent might not use these exact words, but they capture the feeling the child is likely to experience. Each of these attitudes will be discussed in greater detail in the remaining chapters of this book.

1. Feeling in (out of) control
   Positive: I can define what I can control or influence in my life, and I focus my time and energy on those areas.
   Negative: I have little, if any, control over circumstances in my life.

2. Ability to solve problems
   Positive: I can think before I act and solve problems in a thoughtful way.
   Negative: My solutions to problems rarely work. I just don't know how to approach a task.

3. Credit for successes
   Positive: My success is based on my own efforts and resources.
   Negative: I often think any success I have is luck, just a fluke, and I'm not sure I can succeed again.

4. Responsibility for failures
   Positive: When I make a mistake or fail at a task, I try to figure out what I can do differently next time to succeed.
   Negative: When I make a mistake, I question how smart I am or if I'll ever learn how to do things.

5. Self-worth
   Positive: I feel a sense of self-worth in particular areas of my life.
   Negative: I feel I have let myself and others down.

6. Response to setbacks
   Positive: Although some things in life may not seem fair, when they aren't, I must ask what I can do to improve the situation.
   Negative: I believe life is unfair and I have been dealt a lousy hand.

7. Relationships with others
   Positive: I believe most adults are helpful and compassionate and aren't annoyed or angry with me. I also think I can contribute to the well-being of others.
   Negative: I think people are always angry about things I say or do. I feel I get little, if any, support from others.

8. Optimism/pessimism
   Positive: Even when things aren't going well, I can think more optimistically and consider solutions to problems.
   Negative: I'm pessimistic about my life improving. I often feel hopeless about the future.

succeed when rooted in a strength-based approach—an approach that focuses on reinforcing a child's existing strengths and not simply on fixing problems. That type of approach appreciates that self-discipline is best nurtured when parents and the entire community are dedicated to raising resilient children.

In this book, we will expand our model for helping children develop a resilient mindset and apply it to the area of discipline and self-discipline. We will provide many examples of how understanding a resilient mindset can help parents be more effective as disciplinarians and build their child's self-discipline. Let's examine how this understanding helped Bill and Samantha Ewing change their son Jim's behavior.

The Ewing Family: "What Other Approach Can We Use?"

In our parenting workshop, we reviewed the Ewings' ongoing attempts to lessen Jim's problem behaviors. We discussed their assumptions that were contributing to an approach that seemed more focused on punishing than on teaching. They defended their use of spanking by asserting it was "the only language Jim understands."

Given the seeming ineffectiveness of spanking Jim, we introduced the possibility that they might want to change their style of discipline. When we did, Bill Ewing countered, "Are you saying it's our fault that Jim acts the way he does? If we back off and change, it will amount to giving in to him, and he'll never get better. If anything, he'll know that he can do whatever he wants without any consequence."

We have frequently heard this argument. We responded by agreeing with Bill's goal of wanting Jim to be more responsible and respectful, emphasizing that we were questioning only the *means* by which he attempted to achieve this goal. We have found that parents are more likely to consider new practices, especially those involving discipline, if we first genuinely validate the goals they express.

Thus, we told Bill that we agreed with his desire for Jim to meet his responsibilities and behave with respect. But we pointed out that Bill had complained that Jim had been showing a lack of respect for years and that spanking seemed to help only temporarily. We suggested that Bill and Samantha might need a new way to discipline him so he would really change. In our experience, if parents use a certain form of discipline and it doesn't work, the next logical step is to look at what they can do differently, rather than continuing to expect a sudden change in the child.

Fortunately, the Ewings recognized that we supported their wish for Jim to be more responsible and respectful. Bill asked, "What other approach can we use? I think we've exhausted every possible option. The calmer approach that Tom and Jennifer use with their son Stevie doesn't seem to work with Jim."

We suggested that the Ewings consider using discipline designed to develop a resilient mindset.

Samantha wondered, "What's that?"

We reviewed the attributes of a resilient mindset, focusing especially on increasing Jim's sense of ownership and responsibility for his own behavior by involving him in problem-solving activities. We suggested to the parents that they use an approach similar to that advanced by our colleague Myrna Shure. Dr. Shure has developed a successful program titled "I Can Problem Solve" in which children are engaged in arriving at solutions to difficult situations. More specifically, we recommended that the Ewings sit down with Jim during a quiet time and say to him, "We think we may be nagging you too much. What do you think?"

Bill immediately said, "I know Jim will say yes that we do nag him too much. But what he calls nagging we see as our job as his parents to make certain he meets his responsibilities."

We agreed with Bill's prediction and guessed that their son would also fail to see his role in all of this. We coached Bill that once Jim agreed his parents nag him too much, they could say they don't want to do it and want to figure out with him what will help.

Samantha said, "He'll probably say that what will help is for us to stop reminding him to do some things and stop spanking him when he's disrespectful."

We again agreed, advising the Ewings that if Jim said that, they could take ownership for their behavior by promising they would try not to yell or spank—and add that they wanted Jim to think about what *he* could do differently to improve the situation.

Bill answered with a sentiment we have heard from other parents when we've suggested this line of conversation: "Jim will probably say he doesn't know what will improve the situation. Or he might say that if we didn't nag him, he'd follow through and wouldn't speak disrespectfully to us. But we know that even if he says this, he really won't follow through."

We observed that even if he hasn't followed through in the past, our experience is that if children come up with ideas for remembering to do things or for being reminded if they forget, they are more likely to be cooperative, since the ideas came from them. This method increases their feeling of ownership, improves their problem-solving skills, and will help them become more resilient and cooperative.

Also, we advised that if Jim said he didn't know what he could do differently, Bill and Samantha should avoid putting him on the spot. Instead, they could simply say, "We wouldn't expect you to know at this moment, but think about it for a day or two."

We added that our goal is for children to become more respectful and cooperative, not for them to be compliant, obedient, resentful, or angry. We want them to develop self-discipline, which basically implies that they take ownership for their own behavior.

We cautioned the Ewings that changing the way they spoke with Jim or reacted to him would not lead to an overnight change. The problem had been going on for years and would take time and patience to correct. We said this because some parents who have gone out of their way to modify their own behavior become angry and resort to harsh punishments when they feel their children are not changing as quickly as they would like. However, we predicted that if Bill and Samantha would become less punitive and harsh, they would eventually see an improvement in Jim's behavior.

To define more clearly and support the changes the Ewings planned to make with Jim, we engaged in some role-playing activities. We asked the Ewings to consider various scenarios with Jim, what they thought his response would be to their changes in behavior, and how they would respond in kind. Although they had difficulty modifying their established scripts (patterns of responding), they recognized that the approach they had been using was leading to an angry and strained relationship with Jim. We encouraged the Ewings to link their disciplinary practices with these two questions: Is what we're doing reinforcing self-discipline and a resilient mindset in Jim? Is it leading to a more positive relationship with him?

The Ewings consulted with us for several months. Jim could prove challenging, so they occasionally questioned whether this more "reasonable" approach would be effective, but they stuck with it. One reason they persevered was that they recognized the extent to which their previous script had been negative and self-defeating. They found that a strength-based perspective of discipline, supported by the concept of a resilient mindset, offered an effective alternative to their earlier style of disciplining Jim.

The Ewings also discovered another important benefit of linking discipline to resilience: it greatly improved their relationship with their son. As we have emphasized in our previous books, discipline is most effective when carried out within a caring relationship. Such a relationship is the foundation upon which a resilient mindset, characterized by qualities such as self-discipline, compassion, respect, and responsibility, flourishes.

Nurturing Your Child's Capacity for Self-Discipline

In the chapters that follow, we will describe the ways in which meaningful connections to children can be used to nurture their capacity for self-discipline and resilience. When such connections exist, parents and other caregivers become disciplinarians in the true meaning of the term—as teachers who help children learn to reflect on the consequences of their actions, assume responsibility for their behavior, and consider the rights and feelings of others. The true power of resilience lies in children's ability to harness resilient qualities in their everyday lives. Efficient self-discipline is the fuel to make the resilience engine run.

2

The Mindset for Effective Discipline

In the first chapter, the Ewings and the Franklins held much different opinions about what kind of discipline is most effective. Their views, rooted in their assumptions about why children act the way they do, prompted them to use different disciplinary techniques. Let's look at two more examples showing other common responses parents have to their children's behavior. Then we'll identify basic categories of disciplinary styles and examine the mindset that we believe is most in accord with effective discipline and the teaching of self-discipline.

The Burns Family: "Wild Horses Have to Be Broken"

Louise Burns came to see us on the recommendation of her children's pediatrician. She was a single parent, the divorced mother of Jeffrey, age ten, and Amy, age thirteen. The divorce had been finalized five years earlier. The children's father, Mel, who had remarried and had one preschool child with his new wife, lived more than a thousand miles away. Although Mel spoke with Jeffrey and Amy at least once a week on the phone, the children's visits to their father were typically limited to a week during the school year and a month during the summer.

Louise was especially concerned about Jeffrey's "defiance" and "anger." She described him as having "a short fuse, often lying about what he had done or not done, and always trying to avoid responsibility." She said, "Even before Mel and I broke up, Jeffrey was a handful. Amy can have her moments, but when I tell her to do something, she does it. It's difficult to be a single parent. Most days I'm exhausted when I come home from work. The last thing I want to do is get into battles with my kids. Jeffrey threatens me that he wants to live with his father. He says his father isn't on his back all the time. Jeffrey doesn't realize that it's like a vacation when they visit Mel. Anyway, even if Mel would want Jeffrey to move in, which I don't think he does, I know his wife would be against it, especially with a toddler of her own."

We empathized with Louise's struggles and agreed that it's difficult being a single parent, working full-time, and trying to manage responsibilities at home. We asked her to tell us more about Jeffrey and Amy's behavior, including how she had handled tough situations. What had and hadn't worked?

"I'm not as concerned about Amy," she explained. "As I mentioned, she listens to me. She's an easier kid to raise. Not Jeffrey. He's ready to argue about everything; that's why I really have to be tough with him. If I'm not tough with him now, imagine what his behavior will be like in a couple of years when he becomes a teenager." Louise uttered this observation with a mixture of frustration, anger, and fear.

We asked her what worked best with Jeffrey.

She immediately replied, "He has to know who's in charge and that he can't do what he wants to do all of the time. If it were up to him, he would be a little dictator. He might think I'm on his back all of the time, but that's because of the way he behaves."

In our clinical work, we often find it helpful to ask parents whether their child reminds them of anyone. Often they mention another family member. Their association prompts discussion of the ways in which their response to their child is based, in part, on their feelings and thoughts about this family member, and that discussion leads to a more realistic portrait of their child. So we asked Louise if she thought Jeffrey reminded her of anyone.

Her answer was not typical, but it certainly helped to explain her punitive discipline style. She said, "Interesting you should ask a question like that. This may sound a little crazy. My first thought is that Jeffrey doesn't remind me of another person. When I think of Jeffrey, I think of a wild horse, and wild horses have to be broken."

As she shared her image of a horse needing to be broken, we couldn't help thinking of the statement she had made moments earlier: "He might think I'm on his back all of the time." We asked her what she meant by "broken."

Louise responded, "Well, maybe *tamed* would be a better word, but people do use the word *broken* when talking about wild horses."

We encouraged her to elaborate, so she continued. "I think kids are basically born wild—some more so than others. They want instant gratification and often just think about themselves. I think they have to learn they can't just do what they want or go their own way. They have to learn who's in charge."

The comparison of Jeffrey to wild horses was striking. Knowing that mindset helped us understand his mother's punitive style with him. Although it might seem obvious that a person's mindset affects the person's behavior, many people don't reflect upon their mindset, or if they do, many accept it as truth, rather than as assumptions that can and should be challenged. In the case of Louise Burns, we didn't believe that her mindset and disciplinary practices *caused* Jeffrey's problem behavior, but we suspected that they intensified the behavior and led to battles that might have been avoided with a different set of parental assumptions.

We will return to our intervention with Louise Burns later in this chapter. Let's now turn to another parental mindset we frequently see.

The West Family: "Don't You Slam That Door!"

Brian and Mary West sought our help because their ten-year-old daughter, Jessica, was experiencing ongoing headaches and stomachaches. A medical exam did not reveal any physical reasons for these symptoms.

Mary West described Jessica as "basically a good kid" who "had several close friends and did well in school." The Wests told us they were puzzled by Jessica's headaches and stomachaches, which first appeared three years ago but were becoming more intense.

We commented that sometimes headaches or stomachaches in a child are a sign of pressure or stress. We asked the parents whether they could think of anything that might be stressful to Jessica.

Brian responded, "No. I grew up in a home where there was a lot of screaming, so I know firsthand what that can do to a kid. My parents would yell at each other or yell at me and my brothers all the time."

Since Brian immediately associated the present issue with the emotional atmosphere of the home in which he grew up, we thought it would be helpful to understand the impact it had had on him. So we asked him how he had handled that kind of home environment and how it had affected him.

Brian replied, "All I wanted to do was get out of the house or lock myself in my room. It's tough to deal with that kind of anger all the time. When our son, Adam, was born, I told myself that things would be much different in our home—that we would not yell at each other or get angry with each other."

Mary looked at her husband and hesitantly said, "But sometimes I think we may have gone overboard."

We asked Mary what she meant, but Brian replied. "Mary thinks I'm too harsh with the kids—that I jump in too quickly to tell them to be quiet or not to argue. I think if you don't step in, things can get out of hand very quickly. Also, I don't yell at them when I step in."

Mary interjected, "But I wonder if we're too strict with them." As she said this, it was obvious that discipline was a source of tension in their household.

Brian countered, "I don't see how wanting to have a quiet house is being too strict."

We pointed out that it's common for parents to disagree about discipline. We asked Mary for an example of what she meant when she said they might be "too strict."

She said, "I can think of one situation that came up earlier this week. Jessica wanted to go with her friend to the mall. Brian and I told Jessica we thought she was too young to be spending time at the mall. Jessica said we never let her do anything that other kids are allowed to do. Before we could say anything, she ran up to her room and slammed her door. I know she felt frustrated and angry. I would have let it go, but Brian ran up, opened her door, and told her, 'Don't you slam that door. Don't be disrespectful.' He then grounded her for the weekend."

Brian objected to Mary's version of events. "I sound like the bad guy in this. I told her it was unacceptable to slam her door, and I said so in a low voice. I don't want things to get out of control."

We asked Brian what he meant by "things getting out of control."

"It's what I said before. I know from firsthand experience what it feels like when people get angry with each other."

Mary said, "I don't want things out of control either." She then voiced an intriguing question followed by an interesting comment: "How is Jessica supposed to show any anger? We all get angry. So she shut the door hard. Why punish her for that? I remember reading an article a few months ago about headaches and stomachaches. It said that sometimes they could be caused by people holding in their feelings all the time rather than expressing them."

Brian exclaimed, "So you just want Jessica going around screaming and yelling?"

Mary answered, "No, I'm not suggesting that at all, but I'm wondering if we allow her to express any negative feelings. Brian, I think one of the problems is that you see the smallest expression of anger as leading to a loss of control, and I don't see it that way at all. If anything, I wish Jessica would be more open with her feelings."

"I'm just trying to have a peaceful home."

In a supportive way, Mary said, "I know you are. I also want a peaceful home. I just think we have to look at some of what we're doing with the kids and see if we can let them express some feelings and still have a peaceful home."

As we listened to their exchange, we could see that the Wests had a caring, loving marriage. They were able to listen to each other respectfully, so we felt hopeful about being able to help them. This initial exchange between the Wests led to several fruitful sessions in which we began to include Jessica and Adam.

To someone outside the West family, it might seem obvious that because of Brian West's desire for a quiet household, he was forbidding and punishing even appropriate expressions of anger. You may wonder why Brian couldn't see this. However, it's common for people to be unaware that their behavior is sometimes directed by certain assumptions viewed as truths rather than assumptions. In this case, Brian truly did not appreciate the extent to which his mindset about anger, which had been forged in his childhood experiences, was hurting his daughter.

Through our interventions with the West family, including family therapy meetings, Brian learned that the expression of anger need not lead to a loss of control or an emotionally charged home. As Brian and Mary began allowing Jessica to express anger (in a respectful way) and stopped punishing her for doing so, her headaches and stomachaches disappeared. Mindsets are powerful determinants of our behavior.

Parenting Styles

As we have witnessed with the Ewing, Franklin, Burns, and West families, each of us brings to our role as parents a set of expectations and assumptions about ourselves and our children. These assumptions are based, in part, on our experiences with our own parents and other adults, as well as on the temperament and behavior of our children. As we have emphasized, our mindset will influence our actions, including the ways in which we discipline our children.

Psychologists and other child development specialists have examined how different parenting and disciplinary styles affect children. Diana Baumrind distinguished three major styles: authoritative, authoritarian, and permissive. As you read the description of each style, consider which category best describes your style. Which style do you think has been most associated with emotional well-being in adulthood? We'll answer that question after we've provided the descriptions.

Authoritative Parenting

Parents with an *authoritative* style demonstrate warmth and involvement with their children. They offer emotional support but are also firm in establishing guidelines, limits, and expectations. They listen actively to their children and encourage them to make their own decisions. When appropriate, they involve their children in the process of creating rules and consequences, so their children learn to understand and appreciate the rationale for rules. They focus on positive feedback, such as encouragement and praise, rather than on punishment. Authoritative parents recognize that discipline is most effective when it takes place in the context of a loving relationship. Also, the love shown is unconditional, not based on the child performing or behaving in a particular manner.

Authoritarian Parenting

Although the words *authoritative* and *authoritarian* sound similar, the parenting styles that are associated with each are vastly different. Authoritarian parents frequently are neither warm nor nurturing. They do not easily take their children's feelings into consideration, and they tend to be more rigid, imposing rules without discussing the rationale with their children. They are quick to say, "You do it because I told you to do it," or, "You do it because I'm your mother (or father)." They resort to authority, and whether they realize it or not, they basically seek compliance and obedience. Authoritarian parents may certainly show love, but more often than not, expressions of love are conditional, predicated on a child behaving in ways that parents deem appropriate. Authoritarian parents are likely to use corporal punishment rather than a problem-solving approach when they feel their children are not complying with their demands or have transgressed in some fashion.

Permissive Parenting

Parents whose style is *permissive* do not establish realistic goals, expectations, and limits for their children. Baumrind identified two kinds of permissive parents: *permissive-indulgent* and *disengaged*. Permissive-indulgent parents may demonstrate love and warmth, but they appear guided by the philosophy that children will learn on their own. These parents have difficulty setting rules and limits. The child begins to rule the roost. If parents eventually try to establish limits and say no, the child will often resist, having become accustomed to being in charge. In that situation, it is not unusual for the parents to become exhausted and eventually defer to their child's demands.

Disengaged parents do not indulge their children but rather fail to provide structure and emotional nourishment. They are often neglectful. The attachment between parent and child is tenuous at best. The positive connections that serve as the foundation for emotional development and well-being are absent.

Not only are authoritative parents more effective disciplinarians than parents using the other parenting styles, but they also are more likely to nurture a resilient, hopeful mindset in their children.

Which Style Works Best?

In various studies, researchers have identified families using each of these parenting styles and measured the outcomes (how the children turned out). In *How to Handle a Hard-to-Handle Kid*, psychologist C. Drew Edwards summarizes this outcome research. Edwards writes that the best news was for children whose parents used an authoritative approach:

> Children of authoritative parents tend to have healthy self-esteem, positive peer relationships, self-confidence, independence, and school success. They also seem to have fewer emotional difficulties than people who are raised with other styles of parenting. These children cope well with stress, strive toward goals, and balance self-control with curiosity and interest in a variety of situations. (pp. 56–57)

In our view, not only are authoritative parents more effective disciplinarians than parents using the other parenting styles, but they also are more likely to nurture a resilient, hopeful mindset in their children.

The outcome for children raised by authoritarian parents is in marked contrast to that of children growing up in households of authoritative parents. Edwards summarizes the downside:

> Research has shown that children of authoritarian parents may become inhibited, fearful, withdrawn, and at increased risk for depression. They also may have a difficult time making decisions for themselves, since they're used to being told what to do. Authoritarian parents don't tolerate much disagreement, so their children tend to struggle with independence. (p. 57)

While some children of authoritarian parents seem well behaved and present themselves as "good" children, others begin to resist the demands of their parents, and a negative, angry parent-child interaction cycle dominates.

Finally, the news is not good for children raised by either type of permissive parents. Children raised by permissive-indulgent parents become what Edwards calls classic "spoiled" children:

> They tend to be noncompliant with other adults. They are demanding, low in self-reliance, and lack self-control. They don't set goals or enjoy responsible activities. They may be pleasant and well behaved as long as things are going their way, but become frustrated when their desires aren't met. (p. 59)

The disengaged style is associated with what Edwards calls "the most negative effect upon children." Edwards details the problems: "These children are at high risk for emotional and behavioral problems, academic difficulties, low self-esteem, and alcohol or substance abuse." This sad outcome for children of disengaged, neglectful parents is not surprising, considering that the children haven't experienced unconditional love and acceptance.

The Right Mindset for Effective Discipline

Each of the parenting styles defined by Baumrind is associated with a different set of assumptions about the parents' role and the child's development. As we noted earlier, parents often do not reflect upon these assumptions or mindsets, but mindsets are powerful forces in determining our parenting and disciplinary practices and our relationship with our children. As parents get better at recognizing the assumptions that direct their behavior, they become able to modify practices that aren't working. In the process, they experience more positive interactions with their children.

Not surprisingly, given our focus on resilience, the characteristics of the authoritative parent are most in accord with what we view as the mindset of effective parents, who nurture resilience in their children and prepare them to meet the many challenges that they will face. These parents discipline by using techniques that reinforce self-discipline and resilience.

The following beliefs are typical of those in the mindset of parents who are effective disciplinarians. As you read the description of these beliefs, consider the extent to which your beliefs match this description of the mindset for effective discipline.

Discipline Is a Teaching Process

As we emphasized in Chapter 1, discipline is about teaching. Teaching should be free of humiliation and intimidation; it should not rely on punishments that overshadow positive feedback. If we view children as wild horses to be broken, as Louise Burns thought of Jeffrey, we are more likely to punish and intimidate, especially if our child does not respond promptly or consistently to our requests and demands.

If we think of discipline as a teaching process aimed at reinforcing self-discipline, then our actions can be guided by this question: "Are my children learning self-discipline, responsibil-

―――――――― ◎ ――――――――

If we think of discipline as a teaching process aimed at reinforcing self-discipline, then our actions can be guided by this question: "Are my children learning self-discipline, responsibility, and accountability from me, or is my message getting lost amid feelings of resentment and anger?"

―――――――― ◎ ――――――――

ity, and accountability from me, or is my message getting lost amid feelings of resentment and anger?" Having interviewed numerous children and adolescents in our clinical practice, we have been struck by how many cannot identify the reasons why their parents disciplined them, although they can recall the negative tone that pervaded their relationship with their parents. Similarly, as adults look back upon their childhoods, they are less likely to recall the message their parents were attempting to convey than the tone in which it was conveyed. In situations dominated by anger and humiliation, resentment rather than self-discipline was reinforced.

Effective Discipline Requires a Positive Relationship

Our patients and workshop participants frequently ask us what discipline techniques or strategies are most likely to stimulate self-discipline. Our answer is simple: a positive relationship with the child. Too often parents and other caregivers are so hungry to learn a cookbook of disciplinary approaches that they neglect to consider that children are more likely to listen and respond to requests, limits, and consequences when they trust the adult who is setting the rules and consequences.

Effective parents recognize that the quality of the parent-child relationship is an important part of a positive disciplinary approach. Children and adolescents are more likely to listen to adults they perceive as fair, empathic, and respectful than to adults who seem arbitrary, inconsistent, and angry. There is much truth in the saying "Children don't care what you know until they know you care." That saying applies to parent-child as well as teacher-student relationships.

At the end of one of our workshops, a couple came up to share a personal story with us, to reinforce our statement that a positive relationship is the foundation for

Children and adolescents are more likely to listen to adults they perceive as fair, empathic, and respectful than to adults who seem arbitrary, inconsistent, and angry.

effective discipline. They had two sons, ages seven and ten. The father commented that his memories of his own father, who was now deceased, were ambivalent at best.

He said, "My father didn't spank me, he didn't even raise his voice that much, but he was always very critical of me. He would put me down, ridicule things I was interested in, and was punitive. While he didn't yell or scream, he seemed angry most of the time. As I got older, his favorite ways of showing who was in charge were to ground me and take away privileges like watching TV. I really don't think I was what one might call a 'bad kid,' but I felt my father saw me that way. I felt he never really cared about me."

As he finished that sentence, tears filled his eyes, but he continued. "It's just like you said in your talk. The more limits he set, the more I tried to break them, often behind his back. Looking back, I guess my attitude was, 'You don't respect me; why should I respect you?' It didn't matter what the issue was; I wasn't going to listen."

His wife interjected, "When our older son was born, my husband and I talked a lot about the kind of relationship he had with his father and how he wanted a much different relationship with our son. I'm really proud of what a loving husband he is. Both of our sons know how much my husband loves them. He spends time with them, hugs them, and always finds time to compliment them. I know they're still pretty young and a lot can happen, especially when they become teens, but they really respect and listen to him."

Her husband said, "They do the same for my wife." From his comment, it was apparent that this husband and wife were supportive of each other and worked closely together to raise their sons.

The wife concluded, "It's like you said. Discipline is most effective in the context of a good relationship. [We were impressed that she remembered the exact words we had used.] They really listen to what we say, and they seem to understand that there are consequences to their actions. Their relationship with my husband is much different from his relationship with his father."

Although our interaction with this couple was brief, we could tell that this man was able to be a father to his children in a way that was very different from what he had received from his father. In changing the generational mindset and script, he became a disciplinarian in the true sense of the word: as a teacher of important values.

Empathy Is a Vital Part of Discipline

In all of our writings, we have highlighted empathy as a vital skill in developing satisfying, positive relationships. Empathy has been popularly defined as seeing the world through the eyes of others, appreciating their feelings and thoughts, understanding their perspective.

The Burns Family: Learning Empathy

In our work with Louise Burns, described earlier in this chapter, we returned to her observation that her son Jeffrey "might think I'm on his back all of the time, but that's because of the way he behaves." We did so in order to promote empathy and a more positive mindset.

Do You Have Empathy Toward Your Child?

We're so impressed by the importance of empathy in parenting that we regularly pose the following questions for parents to reflect upon:

- How do I hope my children would describe me?
- How would they actually describe me?
- How close are these descriptions? If they are far apart, how can I change so that the words I hope my children would use to describe me will match the words they would actually use?
- Would I want anyone to speak with me the way I am speaking with my children?
- In anything I say to or do with my children, what do I hope to accomplish? Most importantly, am I speaking or acting in a way that will make my children most willing to hear me and learn from me?

These questions are important to consider in our role as disciplinarians. We won't go so far as to expect children to thank us for setting limits and consequences, but we do hope they'll learn from us. If we come across as angry, arbitrary, harsh, and inflexible, our disciplinary practices will be compromised. Instead of self-discipline, our children may learn anger and resentment.

We asked Louise how else Jeffrey might describe her. After thinking for a few seconds, she said, "Lately, I think he would say I nag him all the time and scream at him. But he has to understand that if he did what was expected, I wouldn't be reminding him to do things all the time or screaming at him." (We often hear this type of reasoning that parents would be less negative if their kids did what the parents asked them to do without constant reminders.)

We asked our follow-up question: How would Louise like Jeffrey to describe her?

She responded, "I haven't really thought about that, but I guess I'd like him to say that I care about him, that I'm trying to do the best job possible as a single parent, that I'm fair. He feels I'm not fair and that I treat Amy better than I treat him. What he doesn't realize is that she listens to me and doesn't talk back to me. It's easier to be nicer to her. If he changed, if he got a better attitude, it would be easier to treat him better."

We agreed that Louise's role would be a lot easier if Jeffrey's behavior improved. However, we pointed out that what she had been doing with Jeffrey hadn't led to the results she wanted to see. Assuring Louise that we supported her goals of wanting him to be more cooperative and less defiant, we commented that we had different ideas for how to go about reaching those goals. We suggested that a different approach to discipline might lead to the results Louise hoped to see. As we explained our views to Louise, we attempted to convey empathy and an appreciation of the challenges of being a single parent. We also wanted to support particular goals she had for Jeffrey's behavior while introducing the idea that there might be more constructive ways of disciplining Jeffrey and reaching these goals.

She asked, "What do you mean by a different approach?"

We began by reminding Louise that she believed her son thought of her as "always being on his back," while she wanted him to see her as caring and fair. We asked Louise to consider whether, if she kept doing what she had been doing, Jeffrey was likely to change his view.

"No, but the fact is that I have been fair, and he has to learn that I have. He needs to change, not me."

We agreed that Jeffrey needed to change but restated our point that if Louise were to keep disciplining him in the same way, he would not change and would not see her as fair. We explained that we were not suggesting Louise should give in, but rather find a different way to discipline Jeffrey, a way that would help him be more cooperative and see her in the way she would like to be seen.

"I think I've tried just about everything." (This is another comment we have heard on many occasions from tired, frustrated parents.)

We agreed that Louise had probably tried a lot of different things, adding that there might be other things she hadn't tried that would work.

Louise smiled and said, "What do I have to lose? Things aren't working now."

With this invitation to continue, we introduced the issue of Louise's mindset and her casting Jeffrey in the same image as a wild horse. We felt this was a necessary step if she were to become a more effective disciplinarian. We also recognized that we had to convey our message in a way that avoided creating a feeling that we were being judgmental, so she would not become defensive and resist working with us. In essence, we had to demonstrate the same empathy toward Louise that we were asking her to show Jeffrey.

To accomplish this task, we used a strategy we have found successful in our clinical work: to voice our concerns about being perceived as accusatory or judgmental before offering our observations. We asked Louise to alert us if we began to sound critical. We assured Louise that our intention was not to criticize her but to see whether her way of thinking about Jeffrey was an obstacle to discovering a new, more effective approach to discipline. Specifically, we asked her to reflect on her belief that disciplining Jeffrey was like breaking a wild horse. Although a person skilled in breaking wild horses might say the process involves sensitivity and caring, as it probably does, we observed that taming or breaking a child seems to have a different meaning, one that is harsher and more punitive.

Louise listened carefully and said, "It's interesting you say that. I really don't see Amy in the same way. Jeffrey has always seemed wilder and more unpredictable than Amy." As soon as she uttered the word *wilder*, she smiled and noted, "There I go again. But you know he was much more rambunctious than Amy."

We accepted her observation, commenting that all children are different from birth, even coming from the same set of parents. We agreed that what works for one child may not work for another.

"What is it I can do differently with him?"

We advised that the more Louise could move away from being punitive and seeing him as a child who needs to be tamed and the more she could involve Jeffrey in helping to solve the problem, the less likely he would be to see her as always being on his back and the more likely he would be to begin cooperating.

"That would be a welcome relief. Where do I start?"

We suggested a problem-solving approach similar to the one we reported using with the Ewings in Chapter 1. Specifically, we counseled her to tell Jeffrey that she is tired of nagging and then to say, "I would really like us to figure out how you, Amy, and I can help each other without reminders or arguments. I would like to figure out how we can talk to each other without things turning into an argument."

At first Louise was skeptical about this approach, feeling she had already tried to be reasonable and it hadn't worked. We said that might be true, but it was worth another try, especially since what she was currently doing was not working. We emphasized that if Louise considered the questions we had posed about empathy, her discussion with Jeffrey might be more likely to succeed. We also encouraged Louise not to become discouraged if she did not see an immediate positive outcome. Changing negative scripts can take time.

The Primary Goals of Discipline

Ideally, the end result of discipline is not to produce compliant, obedient children. Such children may follow rules but often do so out of fear without appreciating the rationale for these rules. If youngsters do not understand the purpose of rules and consequences and if they believe rules are imposed upon them, they have more difficulty incorporating these rules as guideposts for their daily lives. Thus, many children who seem compliant actually misbehave behind the backs of their parents or at some point cast aside their "good persona" and act out their frustrations.

If, as we have advocated, a major goal of discipline is to promote self-discipline, parents should keep in mind that self-discipline involves a person accepting ownership and responsibility for the rules that govern his or her life. Self-discipline therefore is associated with one of the basic components of a resilient mindset: a sense of personal control. As we note in our book *The Power of Resilience*, personal control involves recognizing that we humans are the authors of our own lives, that we must not seek our happiness by waiting for someone else to change. Instead, when facing a problem, we must ask, "What can I do differently to change the situation?"

When children are young, parents understandably establish almost all of the rules and consequences that direct their children's lives. However, effective disciplinarians appreciate that as their children develop cognitively and emotionally, they must transfer a greater portion of responsibility and control to their children. Parents and other caregivers want children to incorporate values that will guide their behavior even when adults are not present. They want them to appreciate that different behaviors lead to different consequences and that they have a choice in deciding how to behave. As Edwards notes in *How to Handle a Hard-to-Handle Kid*, authoritative parents were more likely to raise children with "self-confidence and independence"—key ingredients of personal control—than authoritarian parents, whose children were likely to "have a difficult time making decisions for themselves, since they're used to being told what to do."

So that their children will gain a sense of personal control and self-discipline, parents must learn to apply disciplinary techniques that challenge their children to learn and use problem-solving and decision-making skills. Learning to think before acting and to consider different options for solving problems develops the very essence of self-discipline.

The Burns Family: "Our Mindsets Are Powerful Creatures"

Let's return to Louise Burns and see how she focused on the goal of self-discipline. Encouraged by our suggestions, she told her son, Jeffrey, that she knew he felt she was on his back all of the time and she wanted to change the way she reacted to him.

He said with some sarcasm, "Well, that would be great."

Rather than responding to the sarcasm, Louise said she thought it would be helpful if, as a start, the two of them and Jeffrey's sister, Amy, sat down to discuss what each of their responsibilities should be in the home and how they could meet these responsibilities without constant reminders.

Jeffrey was somewhat taken aback by this new approach and responded, "What if you and Amy gang up on me and tell me I have to do more than the two of you do?"

His mother asked, "Do you feel we gang up on you?"

"Sometimes I do."

With impressive skill and empathy, Louise responded, "What you just brought up is very important. Things will only work if all three of us feel we're being fair with each other. If any of us feels we're being treated unfairly, we won't be able to have a happier home. When we discuss responsibilities, we should let each other know if we think they are fair, and if one of us doesn't, we have to figure out how to correct the situation." Louise expected that Jeffrey might quickly say things were not fair, but by anticipating this possibility and emphasizing that they could find ways to correct the situation if it arose, she was establishing a problem-solving attitude.

Initially, Louise had spoken with us about the possibility of holding the discussion of responsibility in the context of family therapy sessions with us. Although we agreed with the arrangement, Louise discovered that on her own she could apply the parenting and discipline skills she learned in her meetings with us. She had expected Amy to cooperate, which she did, but was pleasantly surprised that Jeffrey also was receptive to her suggestions. He eagerly participated in defining expectations for each of them, deciding to alternate particular household chores that were "boring" and designing charts to be placed in each of their rooms and the kitchen to remind the family members of their duties.

During our final session, Louise thanked us for our suggestions and support. She noted that while Jeffrey still sometimes forgot to fulfill a responsibility and occasionally complained that things were not fair, these situations occurred less and less often. Also, when they did occur, she felt more comfortable responding in a way that did not seem to her son to be "nagging and yelling."

She said, "Since some of the ideas of how to remind each other were Jeffrey's ideas, he couldn't really accuse me of nagging when I was simply following his suggestions. Perhaps that's one of the reasons he has been more cooperative. As you once mentioned, he was involved in solving the problem rather than intensifying it." She continued, "But do you know what I constantly think about? It's the way I used to see Jeffrey as a wild horse to be broken. I felt it was my job to show him who was the boss. I realize now that I got what I expected."

Then, paraphrasing what she had heard on many occasions during our sessions, she added, "Our mindsets are powerful creatures." She laughed and explained, "By creatures, I don't mean wild horses."

To highlight Louise's contribution to the positive changes in her family, we observed with a smile that whatever the "creatures" were that lurk in mindsets, she had a good handle on all of them. We reminded Louise that not only had she changed her own mindset, but she had also helped to change Jeffrey's mindset toward her.

Discipline Techniques

So far we've talked about different parenting styles and how they relate to the mindset behind effective discipline. We've offered several case examples. But what else can parents do to put these ideas into practice on a day-to-day basis? The following techniques are consistent with discipline aimed at developing self-discipline in our children.

Use Natural and Logical Consequences

If disciplinary techniques are arbitrary (based on how we feel at the moment or changeable from one moment to the next) or very punitive, they are unlikely to nurture self-discipline and a resilient mindset. Instead, children must learn that their behavior results in consequences that are neither harsh nor arbitrary but are based on discussions that parents have had with them or, especially with very young children, actions parents have taken. Some of the most effective controls are natural and logical consequences, which are appropriate when the situation doesn't threaten the child's safety or the safety of others.

Natural consequences are those that result from a child's actions; parents don't have to enforce them because they follow naturally from the child's behavior. These consequences can teach children that their actions or choices are within their control and lead to specific consequences. For instance, at one of our workshops, a mother described a situation in which her nine-year-old daughter went out to play on a chilly day. This mother was soon involved in an argument with her daughter about wearing gloves. Finally, she stepped back and told herself that this really was not an issue of safety, because if her daughter's hands got cold, she would either place them in the pockets of her jacket or come into the house to get gloves. About thirty minutes after being outside, the girl came in for her gloves, saving face by telling her mother the temperature had dipped a lot since she went out, a statement that the mother wisely accepted. This girl learned more about the consequences of her choices than she could have from all of the lecturing her mother could have done.

While *logical consequences* sometimes overlap with natural consequences, they typically involve some action taken by parents in response to their child's behavior. This action is directly related to the behavior and does not involve harsh treatments, such as spanking. An example of logical consequences was offered by a father at one of our workshops. He had repeatedly reminded his nine-year-old son to put his bicycle in the garage at the end of the day. He told his son that if it rained, the bike could be damaged, or if it were left outside overnight, someone could even take it. He finally tired of reminding his son and informed him that it would be the boy's responsibility to remember. His son left the bike outside, where it became damaged during a rainstorm.

The damage of the bike could be seen as a natural consequence of this boy's behavior. Then, when the son became upset and asked his father to have the bike repaired, the father's response represented a logical consequence. He did not resort to saying, "I told you so." Instead, when his son said the bike was "ruined," the father replied that they could take it to the bike store to see if it could be repaired but that it would be the boy's responsibility to pay for the repairs. If the bike were beyond fixing, the son would be responsible for purchasing a new bike out of his savings. This kind of response is effective if presented in a neutral tone; the child learns from the consequence itself, not from the parent lecturing about the consequence.

Natural and logical consequences should fit the "crime." Also, as much as possible, our children should know of the rules and consequences in advance. For example, if a seventeen-year-old plans to go out on a Saturday night and has a midnight curfew, the parents should make sure that this teenager is clear about what the consequences are if the curfew is broken. In one household, breaking curfew meant that the boy would be grounded the following Saturday night. The boy came in at 12:30 A.M. and explained that he was late because he had to drive several friends home from a party. His father calmly responded, "Next time you have friends to drive home, you have to leave the party earlier so that you can be back by midnight. But this was your choice. You know the consequence we agreed on; next week you cannot go out on Saturday night."

The adolescent countered that he had just been trying to help his friends. The father calmly said, "I'm glad you wanted to help your friends by driving them home, but you'll have to figure out a way of doing so in the future without breaking your curfew."

The father added at our workshop, "I was almost ready to give in, but I realized that my son had not met his responsibility and for me to excuse his being late would communicate that I did not take our agreement seriously. Of course, if some extenuating circumstances had come up, such as the car having mechanical problems, I would have been more tolerant, but in this case, what happened was within my son's control. By the way, I think the approach worked, since it was the last time he broke his curfew."

These examples illustrate the ways in which discipline can reinforce self-discipline and a resilient mindset. They involve four actions by parents:

1. Deciding with your children rules, expectations, and consequences
2. Identifying and stating behaviors that require modification
3. Considering possible solutions for problem behaviors
4. Highlighting for your children that they have choices in what solutions to use but that each choice leads to different consequences

This process strengthens a feeling of accountability and ownership as well as a sense of control over one's life.

Focus on Prevention, Not Intervention

Effective discipline applies the old saying "An ounce of prevention is worth a pound of cure." Parents who are effective disciplinarians recognize that they get better results from a proactive rather than a reactive approach. A proactive approach fits in with the problem-solving, resilience model of discipline that we are advocating. It encourages parents to be empathic, to try to understand what is eliciting their child's problematic behavior, and then to ask themselves, "Are there ways of modifying the situation in order to deter my child from behaving in that way?" It also prompts parents to consider ways in which they can involve their child in considering different options for solving the problem.

When we suggest that parents try to understand why their children are acting the way they do, we don't mean parents need to become armchair psychologists, analyzing every word and action of their children. Rather, it is helpful to step back from time to time and ask what is triggering the behavior, rather than giving an immediate punishment. We have encountered many well-meaning parents who punish their children because of misguided assumptions about their behavior.

The Ashlund Family: Bedtime Tantrums

A case in point is a family we described in our book *Raising Resilient Children*. John and Cathy Ashlund sought our help because their four-year-old son, Robert, had difficult bedtime behavior. When it was time for bed, Robert would run through the house with his parents pursuing him. When they caught him, he would scream and yell and wouldn't calm down. They noted that this behavior had occurred for at least six months. Before then, Robert had not exhibited bedtime problems.

To evaluate the parents' mindset about Robert's behavior, we asked them how they understood what was transpiring. It immediately became clear that they interpreted Robert's actions as opposition and a need for attention. Since the Ashlunds felt that Robert received a great deal of their attention during the day, they responded angrily when he resisted going to bed. Their perception that his behavior was an expression of opposition to them often prompted them to respond to his screaming with loud, angry words. Several times, out of frustration, they resorted to spanking. Although they reported being upset when they used corporal punishment, they also said that the spanking typically "worked." Robert would remain in bed after being spanked, often crying himself to sleep.

The mindset of the Ashlunds resembled that of Louise Burns, who understood Jeffrey's behavior as oppositional, as a wild horse needing to be tamed. Since Robert's behavior persisted night after night despite their actions, we questioned whether spanking really "worked"; after all, it hadn't achieved long-lasting results. The parents' view of the problem as an indication of opposition and hunger for what they considered to be unwarranted attention appeared to increase their anger and diminish their capacity for empathy. A vicious cycle had been set in motion. The Ashlunds, displaying less and less empathy, viewed Robert's behavior in only one way, keeping them in a punitive mode of response. Their yelling and spanking heightened Robert's tantrums.

We scheduled an interview with Robert and were impressed with his insight into the problem. During our session, we asked whether he ever had "scary dreams." Robert looked surprised, responding, "How did you know?"

We explained that many kids his age have nightmares and that we wondered about his. A sense of relief was evident on his face as he was given the opportunity to describe his bad dreams, which involved monsters pursuing him and his family. We then suggested that Robert draw a picture of one of these dreams so that we could show it to his parents. As Robert began drawing, we asked him more questions about his dreams. Robert revealed that he was afraid to go to sleep because then he would have bad dreams.

Although Robert's parents saw his bedtime behavior as oppositional and manipulative, allowing this precocious child to express his feelings showed us that the onset of his bedtime problems was rooted in his attempt to avoid the anxiety associated with nightmares. Robert's parents, after seeing his drawing and hearing our accounts of his session, were willing to consider this alternative explanation. This shift in their thinking immediately led them to be more empathic and less punitive as they kept in mind the near-desperate feelings Robert had been experiencing each evening.

In keeping with our belief that children, even those as young as Robert, are capable of coming up with solutions, we asked him what he thought would help. We have found that the insights of children often provide information that can be used to prevent problems. Robert didn't disappoint us. He offered two suggestions. He asked for a night-light, which his parents had previously refused, feeling that it would keep him from falling asleep. His second suggestion could be highlighted in any book about child rearing. He requested that a photo of his parents be placed by his bed, explaining that if he felt afraid, he could look at their picture. John and Cathy Ashlund readily agreed to these recommendations, voicing regret that they had prevented Robert from having a night-light. They also decided to read him an extra story at bedtime and to leave the door to his room open.

When the Ashlunds adopted this preventive approach, housed in empathy and problem solving, Robert discontinued his tantrums and resistance of going to bed. The household atmosphere, especially at bedtime, improved markedly.

The Centro Family: "Is There a Chance You Could Die?"

In another situation involving prevention as a powerful form of discipline, Tony and Celeste Centro consulted us about their ten-year-old daughter, Cynthia. They noted that she was becoming increasingly "sassy" toward them. She often refused to help out with household responsibilities and uttered put-downs about them.

Celeste said, "Up until a year ago, she was cooperative. Maybe it's the adolescent hormones kicking in early. She's not very pleasant to be with."

We asked if anything had happened in the family during the past year. Interestingly, Tony said he had been diagnosed with what he termed "a mild case of skin cancer." He added that he was fine now, and it was no big deal. We asked about Cynthia's reaction to his cancer. This obviously loving father said, "We just told her that I would be OK. And I was. We told her there was no need to worry about it. She seemed to accept this."

In our interview with Cynthia, we received a very different version of her father's "mild case of skin cancer." She immediately spoke about another child in her class whose father had died of cancer, adding, "I'm not sure things are OK, since my parents seem to be hiding something. If I ask a question, they just say things are OK, and then they don't seem to want to talk about it. They treat me like a baby."

As we listened to Cynthia, we wondered whether her "sassy" behavior masked a great deal of anxiety. We decided to schedule a family meeting with Tony and Celeste, Cynthia, and her eight-year-old brother, Sam.

With Cynthia's permission, we began the meeting by saying that Cynthia had questions about her father's skin cancer. Cynthia voiced the concerns she had shared with us. The parents told their children that they had mistakenly believed that talking too much about Tony's cancer would cause the children to be more rather than less worried. They said they now realized that their hesitancy to speak directly about Tony's cancer was only adding to Cynthia and Sam's anxiety.

This openness permitted Cynthia to ask, "But do you think there's a chance the cancer will come back and you could die from it?"

Her father responded, "From everything the doctor told me, I'm fine, and they said they would check regularly to make sure that things were going OK."

Cynthia wondered, "Are you sure that's how the doctor feels?"

Tony said yes, and we suggested that if the doctor were willing, it might be helpful for Cynthia and Sam to join their father at the next meeting he had with his doctor. The physician agreed. The parents called to say that after the meeting, Cynthia "appeared noticeably happier and more relaxed." In a follow-up phone call, they reported an end to Cynthia's "sassiness and lack of cooperation."

Find the Triggers

There should be consequences when children misbehave, but as the cases of Robert and Cynthia indicate, sometimes the best way to handle misbehavior is to focus on what is triggering

—————— ◎ ——————

Sometimes the best way to handle misbehavior is to focus on what is triggering the behavior.

—————— ◎ ——————

the behavior. Then, rather than imposing stricter and harsher consequences, the parents may be able to minimize the conditions that are the catalyst for the negative behavior.

Prevention also involves having realistic expectations for your children and not placing them in situations that are likely to result in misbehavior. If you have an active preschool child, you can almost predict that the child will have difficulty remaining seated at a fancy restaurant for a meal that takes two hours to finish. So why take the child in the first place?

At one of our workshops, a mother described her four-year-old daughter as a "terror" when they went shopping. Even in the supermarket, her daughter would run down the aisles, grabbing food. This mother continued, "When I place her in the shopping cart, she screams that she wants to get out. She's a very fidgety child, and I know she hates to be confined in the shopping cart, but I can't let her run around. On a few occasions, I've actually stopped my shopping, taken her out of the store, and returned home. I've warned her in advance not to scream or shout or grab things, but the moment we start walking down the aisle, she either forgets the warnings or just doesn't care. I must admit that at the end of these episodes, I'm not very patient and find myself yelling at her."

As we heard this mother's laments and recognized that she had tried several strategies, including preparing her daughter in advance, we asked a question that took the mother aback. We simply inquired whether the mother thought her daughter was able at that age to handle going shopping with her.

The mother responded, "What do you mean?"

Noting that children are very different from one another, we pointed out that some four-year-olds have no problem handling visits to stores, but other four-year-olds do. Recalling that the mother had described her daughter as fidgety, we observed that some children need to run around, and some are more impulsive than others and grab things. Presumably, at some point, these children will be able to demonstrate more control, but right now they're not able to do so.

The mother asked, "Are you suggesting I not take my daughter shopping with me?"

We acknowledged that this was our suggestion, especially if the mother could shop while someone watched her daughter at home.

The mother said, "It is possible, but how can my daughter learn to act OK when she goes shopping with me if I don't take her shopping? In your talk, you said we should help kids to develop self-discipline. How do we help them if we don't bring them into certain situations?"

Acknowledging that the mother had a good question, we explained that we weren't suggesting the mother never take her daughter shopping. Rather, we wanted her to consider whether, at that time, the daughter was capable of going shopping with her. We pointed out that the mother had told us that when she took her daughter to the store, she ended up not being able to shop, and she had a screaming daughter—and even screamed herself.

"So what should I do?"

We advised her to think of this strategy as a process. Given that the mother's goal was for her daughter to be able to act more appropriately when they went shopping, the process would involve keeping that goal and developing a plan of action to prevent the outbursts that had been taking place. For example, since the mother could make arrangements for someone to watch her daughter while she shopped, she would do that for the next few months. Then the first time the mother took her daughter shopping, they would go to a small store, perhaps to buy just one or two things.

The mother interrupted, "Why a small store to buy one or two things?"

We pointed out that such an errand would keep the trip brief so that if the daughter began to act up, they could leave quickly without leaving behind a cart full of food. Also, it might be easier for the daughter to handle a short shopping period than a long one. We emphasized that the main goal was for the daughter to develop self-control when she accompanied the mother to stores, but we also saw an additional goal: preventing the mother from getting frustrated and angry and yelling at her daughter. We reminded the mother that her daughter might need more time to learn to handle these trips than other kids her age.

The mother said, "What do I have to lose? I become anxious the moment I have to go shopping with her."

Do you wonder why this mother had not thought about this solution before we made our suggestion? Remember that people's mindsets are not always open to reflection and change. This mother rightfully set as a goal that her daughter should develop self-discipline, but unfortunately, her approach was not in keeping with her daughter's temperament or developmental level. As this mother was to learn, if she adopted a prevention model that took into consideration her daughter's capabilities, she could still maintain her major goal but with a different timetable for achieving this goal.

Offer Positive Feedback and Encouragement

In our clinical practice and workshops, it is revealing that most of the questions parents ask us about discipline pertain to punishment. Listening to questions such as "What should I do when my older son hits his younger brother?" or "What should I do when my daughter talks back to me?" or "What's the best punishment to get my daughter to stop lying to me?" would lead one to believe that discipline and punishment are synonymous.

Actually, however, punishment and negative consequences for behavior are just one form of discipline—and typically not the most effective form.

Effective disciplinarians tend to have the mindset that positive feedback and encouragement are the most influential components of discipline, especially for help-ing children develop resilience and self-discipline. We advise parents to "catch your child doing things right and let them know." Although it might sound easy to provide children with positive comments when they are meet-

> *Positive feedback and encouragement are the most influential components of discipline, especially for helping children develop resilience and self-discipline.*

ing realistic expectations and acting appropriately, many parents fail to do it. Instead, they spend more time communicating to children what they are doing wrong than expressing appreciation for what they are doing right.

The Berkshire Family: "Daniel Is Exhausting"

Lisa and Walt Berkshire had one child, nine-year-old Daniel. They were frustrated by Daniel's behavior, describing him as "a whiner, always putting his own needs above anyone else's, inter-rupting us when we are speaking to someone on the phone, and feeling we should get him whatever he wants."

Walt observed, "Daniel is exhausting. He is a high-maintenance kid. I think one problem is that we end up giving in to him. He outlasts us. He won't take no for an answer."

Lisa shared her husband's frustrations by noting, "I hate to admit this as his mother, but I don't look forward to spending time with Daniel." Tears accompanied these words.

While we will spend more time with the Berkshires in later chapters, one thing we learned in our work with them applies here: They weren't giving Daniel positive feedback. During one of our sessions, we acknowledged that Daniel was a challenging boy but asked Walt and Lisa to try to tell us about some occasions when they enjoyed being with him, when he hadn't been "a whiner" or demanding. (This is a question we ask most parents.)

This question was a way for us to try a form of intervention called solution-focused therapy, which includes a technique called the *exception rule*. That rule invites people to consider exceptions to the usual behavior displayed by themselves or others. A focus on exceptions can be helpful in our work with parents, especially those who use words such as *always* and *all of the time* to describe the negative behavior of their children. If parents can recall instances in which their children have displayed positive behavior, we can try to figure out with them not only why the positive behaviors may have appeared, but also how the parents responded to these appropriate behaviors.

The Berkshires, after some reflection, could think of examples in which Daniel behaved well, times when he did not whine or interrupt them. We asked Walt and Lisa what they said on those occasions when Daniel didn't whine or interrupt them.

Lisa looked puzzled. "What should we have said? He was acting the way he should be acting."

Reinforce What You Want to See

Again, what may seem obvious was not. If we want positive behaviors to continue, we must reward them. Often we forget that simple comments—such as "Thanks for speaking in a regular voice, since it's easier for us to hear what you have to say when you don't whine" or "We appreciate that you waited until we were off the phone to ask us something"—can dramatically change a child's negative behavior. As we have described in other writings, some parents fall into the trap of running a "praise deficit." They believe that when children do something right, it is expected and nothing really has to be said, but when children engage in negative behaviors, they must be lectured and punished. As a result, the amount of praise these parents give their children is far less than the amount of criticism they offer.

We all thrive on positive feedback. Well-timed expressions of encouragement and love are valuable to a child's self-esteem and dignity. As we emphasized earlier in this chapter, discipline is most effective when housed within a positive relationship. When children feel loved and appreciated and when they receive encouragement and support for things they are doing right, they are less likely to engage in negative behaviors. Some youngsters, especially those with a so-called difficult temperament, may require more positive feedback than others, but as many parents have observed, devoting that extra time is the best form of discipline they have tried.

What's Next?

Adopting the principles or mindset we have outlined in this chapter equips parents to discipline in ways that will promote a resilient mindset and self-discipline in their children. The more of these principles you can adopt, the more effective your discipline will become. As we noted in Chapter 1, we have organized the remaining chapters of this book to show you how to foster in your child the mindset of resilient, self-disciplined youngsters, in contrast to children who lack self-discipline and are not very hopeful or optimistic. As children develop that mindset, they not only become more self-disciplined but also display the other characteristics of resiliency, which will help them become happy and successful.

3

Helping Your Child
Take Control

Those familiar with our writings about resilience are aware of the importance we place on developing a sense of personal control. A major task of parenting is to help children assume increasing responsibility for their lives. We want them to appreciate that they are the authors of their lives. If they aren't content with a situation, they must ask, "What can I do differently to improve this situation?" If they wait for others to change first, they will be waiting for a very long and unhappy time.

Yet we have observed, in our clinical practice and consultations, that many people of all ages believe their happiness is rooted in others changing first. We frequently hear observations such as these:

- "I'd be happy if my husband showed more affection."
- "I'd be a better teacher if I didn't have unmotivated students."
- "My existence would be so much better if my parents weren't on my back all of the time. They treat me like I'm five years old."

- ▧ "My boss is overly critical. I wish he'd retire."
- ▧ "I think I was born with a dark cloud over my head, and I can't get it to move."

Except for the last weather-related interpretation, there is some truth to each of these beliefs. Most husbands and wives would be happier if their spouses were affectionate. Teaching is less challenging and tiresome when students are motivated and eager to learn. Some youths would like parents off their backs. Employees who are unhappy with their supervisors would be more cheerful if their supervisors departed.

However, when people wait for these events to occur, they often grow weary, frustrated, and angry. They will actually be less stressed if they consider the "givens" of the situation and the steps they can take (the factors over which they have control) to change the existing scenario. Learning to recognize what is within one's control and what is not is a first step toward achieving a sense of personal control. This represents a critical lesson for all children.

Learning to recognize what is within one's control and what is not is a first step toward achieving a sense of personal control.

In *A Whack on the Side of the Head*, Roger von Oech offers a powerful example of looking within oneself for change rather than assigning responsibility or blame to others:

> Several years ago I did a seminar with the direct sales force of a large pharmaceutical company. Prior to the session, I had the opportunity to talk to the people in the bottom 25% of sales performance. I asked them, "Why aren't you more successful?" They answered with such comments as:
>
> "Our products cost too much."
>
> "I've got a crummy territory."

"I don't get along with my manager."

"The moon is in Sagittarius." [Some people certainly offer interesting reasons for their lack of success.] (p. 163)

Von Oech concluded, "What was their problem? They weren't taking responsibility for their own performance. They spent their time creating excuses rather than thinking of innovative sales solutions."

Von Oech contrasted this defeatist perspective with the mind-set of successful salespeople. He noted that the latter group said, for example, "If I get turned down by a physician or nurse, I think of a second way to get the business, a third way, and sometimes a fifth way." In essence, the successful group did not wait passively, hoping that factors outside their control would miraculously change first. They appreciated that effective change resided within themselves and their behavior.

As we emphasized in *The Power of Resilience*, research supports the importance of personal control as a major force in emotional and physical well-being. An article in the *Boston Globe* on July 25, 1997, reported a study published in the British journal *Lancet*. The ongoing research, conducted by Michael Marmot of University College in London, found that senior executives were less likely to die of heart attacks than were their clerks and secretaries. Even taking into consideration such variables as smoking and poor nutrition, the researchers found that "the lower the job category and the less the control," the more likely people were to suffer from heart disease.

What can workers do about this? We can't all be senior executives, but we can find factors to control. Marmot's group suggested, "Greater attention to the design of work environments may be one important way to reduce inequalities in health." Others concur that it is easier to give people more control and choice at work than to change their social status. As reported in the same *Boston Globe* article, Leonard Syme and Jennifer Balfour, commenting on the Marmot study, write, "Although it may be difficult to intervene on social class inequalities in health, there are more opportunities to intervene on control. It may also be possible to change environmental forces in the workplace or the community so that more flexibility and control are available."

Similar findings were reported by Laura Kubzansky, a researcher at the Harvard School of Public Health, in a November 27, 2001, *Boston Globe* article by Patricia Wen. Kubzansky, taking into account such risk factors for heart disease as smoking, high cholesterol, blood pressure, drinking, and family history, found that men in their sixties were less likely to develop coronary heart disease if they had an optimistic outlook on life. Kubzansky noted, "This shows again there's a link between how people look at the world and what happens to them physically. This also shows that optimism can be protective." A major component of optimism, as reported in the Kubzansky study, was the belief that the future will be more pleasant because we can control to a great extent some important events in our lives.

These two studies and others highlight that a sense of personal control plays a major role in emotional and physical well-being, including hopefulness and the ability to deal with stress and pressure. Thus, this feeling of control is a major feature of a resilient mindset.

How Discipline Affects Your Child's Sense of Control

It is difficult to imagine the emergence of personal control in a person who lacks self-discipline. As Stephen Covey notes in his bestselling book *The Seven Habits of Highly Effective People*, we all have "circles of concern," but effective people focus on their "circles of influence." The ability to focus on and act upon the circles where we have influence involves several of the main features of self-discipline, including being empathic, thinking before acting, and considering different options to handle problems.

When individuals believe they lack personal control and feel impotent to effect change in their lives, they often resort to self-defeating coping strategies to manage their frustration and sense of helplessness. Some may withdraw in resignation, passively waiting for things to improve without any effort on their part. Others may determine they are being told what to do and then respond by adopting an angry, inflexible stance, protesting loudly through words and actions that say, "I'll show you who's in charge!" They may act impulsively as they desperately seek to demonstrate that they hold the upper hand.

When you discipline your children, consider whether your actions nurture personal control or contribute to a victim mentality. Parents are responsible for setting rules and consequences, but if personal control is to flourish, children must feel actively involved in the disciplinary process and not perceive themselves as passive recipients of rules and regulations. The extent of involvement will be based upon the child's level of cognitive ability. It's important to help youngsters understand the rationale for rules and lessen the feeling that

When you discipline your children, consider whether your actions nurture personal control or contribute to a victim mentality.

rules are arbitrarily imposed. Bill and Samantha Ewing (introduced in Chapter 1) and Louise Burns (in Chapter 2) became more effective disciplinarians once they subscribed to this view of discipline and shifted from an authoritarian to an authoritative style of parenting.

Ways to Nurture Personal Control

Several guidelines will help you apply disciplinary practices that enhance a feeling of personal control while lessening your child's feeling of being a victim. Let's consider these guidelines one at a time.

Foster a Shift from Parental Control to Self-Control

During the first few years of a child's life, parents realize that they have to establish rules and guidelines for their child based on little, if any, input from the child. Children are not born with self-discipline. They lack the cognitive skills to think before they act. Many of the rules that parents set for their young children involve issues of safety and security and are not open for debate. For example, we wouldn't permit three-year-olds to cross the street alone or to play with matches, even if they wanted to do so. As children develop their thinking skills so that they learn to reflect upon their actions and the consequences of these actions, parents should slowly delegate more responsibility to the children. When children handle these new responsibilities effectively, their behavior shows that they are developing self-discipline and personal control.

At one of our workshops, a father asked, "Isn't it obvious that a main goal for our kids is for them to develop self-discipline and that the best way for them to develop self-discipline is to make certain that they become more responsible for their behavior? If we always tell them what to do, isn't it much more difficult for them to develop self-discipline? Don't most parents recognize that fact?"

We acknowledged that this idea might seem obvious, but even well-meaning parents may fail to encourage self-discipline and personal control. We've worked with parents who are overly controlling and rob their children of opportunities to make decisions. In contrast, some parents believe children will learn on their own and need little input from them. Still other parents are not as involved as they should be with their children's lives; they offer little guidance or direction.

We explained to the father at the workshop that our parenting roles are influenced by the experiences we had with our own parents. The extent to which we were given opportunities as children to make choices, the degree to which our parents were supportive, and the kinds of discipline our parents used all play a part in determining the ways in which we discipline our children. We all carry some "excess baggage" from our childhood, and we may not even be aware of how it contributes to actions that have a negative impact on our children.

The father who asked the question listened intently and said, "It's so interesting how we all have our blind spots, even when it comes to our own kids."

He was right. The parenting of Joanne and Alex Lister illustrates the struggles and burdens that are part of our own excess baggage.

The Lister Family: "Our Parenting Has Backfired"

Joanne and Alex Lister had one child, Marie, age thirteen. Joanne contacted us at the recommendation of the school counselor. During the initial phone call, she told us that Marie, who was in the seventh grade in middle school, was in danger of failing several classes, not only because of low grades on tests but also for neglecting to turn in many homework assignments. In addition, when Marie's teachers and parents tried to discuss their concerns with her, she spoke to them rudely. She was quick to argue that they had no right to tell her what to do and should mind their own business.

In setting up an appointment, we discussed the possibility of Marie attending the first meeting with her parents. Joanne said that would be fine, but she wasn't certain Marie would agree to participate. The next day, Joanne called again and said, "Marie refuses to come to the appointment. She says she doesn't have any problems, that if anyone has problems, it's me and my husband. I don't feel we can force her to come in. We can't drag her in."

We concurred that, given Marie's age, they couldn't just pick her up and drag her in. We suggested trying one other approach that sometimes works with adolescents: telling Marie that if she came to the appointment, she could provide her perspective and also offer suggestions for the ways in which her parents could change.

Joanne said that might work. But it didn't. Marie refused to attend the session. Following our recommendation, however, Joanne and Alex came in so that we could gather information, consider actions they might take to help the situation, and perhaps figure out a strategy for encouraging Marie's participation in individual or family therapy meetings.

At our first meeting, the Listers recounted their struggles with Marie, noting her failing grades, lack of respect for adults, and defiance about following any rules. As we gathered the family's history, we asked how long that behavior had existed.

Alex responded, "A quick answer is that it has been going on for the past couple of years, but actually there have been many signs for a long time."

We asked him to explain how long and tell us what signs he had observed. He replied, "I can think of examples from the time Marie was four or five. She had tantrums and informed us that she could do what she wanted. I remember that one time when she was about six, she told us she didn't want anyone to boss her around. Can you imagine a six-year-old saying something like that?" He turned to his wife and asked, "Joanne, what do you think?"

She answered, "Alex is right. I remember when Marie said she didn't want anyone to boss her around. I was trying to remember what the incident was when she said it, but I can't. Not that it matters; almost everything she does is with the attitude 'You can't tell me what to do.' However, as Alex said, while her defiance has been around for a while, it has gotten worse during the past year or two. Certainly her schoolwork and grades have suffered, especially since she entered middle school last year. In elementary school, she did her homework, and there were no behavior problems, at least in school. Her fifth-grade teacher actually wrote on Marie's report card that she was 'cooperative' and 'helpful.' We were glad they saw her that way at school, since we wouldn't have used the words *cooperative* or *helpful* to describe her at home. In middle school her teachers are seeing some of the same behaviors we see at home. Maybe the adolescent hormones really began to kick in when she began middle school."

Before we could pose more questions, Alex offered an interesting comment: "It has really been frustrating. You do your best to raise a child to feel loved, to be responsible and thoughtful, to feel comfortable trying new things, and what you get is a child who thinks only about herself, is inconsiderate, and the new things she tries are questionable, such as the group of kids she has started to hang out with. The kind of person we envisioned Marie would be when she was born is not the kind of person she has turned out to be, at least so far." With an air of frustration and sadness, he added, "Our parenting has backfired."

We asked Alex to explain what he meant by "backfired."

"Joanne and I grew up in similar homes. We often heard, 'You do it because I'm your mother or I'm your father.' Our parents were very strict about everything: who our friends were, where we could go, unreasonable curfews. We heard much criticism and little praise. We were both what you might call 'good kids,' but on the one or two occasions where we didn't follow what our parents dictated, their punishments seemed severe. I remember once forgetting to take the garbage out when I was a teenager, and I was grounded for two weekends." The word *dictate* vividly captured Mr. Lister's perception of his childhood.

Joanne added, "Alex and I often laugh when we hear that opposites attract. In our case, 'similars' attracted each other. Our backgrounds, values, and interests are pretty similar. We wanted children, but given the importance of our careers to each of us, we decided we would have only one child. When I became pregnant with Marie, we were excited and spoke endlessly about how we weren't going to be the same kind of parents that our parents were to us. We could spend hours telling you about the ambivalent relations we had and continue to have with our parents, but we're here to discuss Marie."

We responded that it probably would be helpful to hear about their feelings toward their parents, especially since they had discussed, during Joanne's pregnancy, how they intended to be different from their parents. We asked the couple to tell us more about how they planned to be different.

Joanne said, "One major way was in terms of discipline. We felt that you could guide kids without being punitive, but as I look back, I think we were too permissive. We've read about the different temperaments kids have, and as I think about Marie, I would say that she was born with a more stubborn temperament. Alex and I have done a lot of talking recently about Marie, and we realize that in our effort not to come across as punitive or to squash her spirit, we often failed to set limits or follow through on consequences. We often caved in."

The Listers offered several examples of "caving in" to Marie's demands, including buying her something that they initially had told her they would not purchase or permitting her to stay up beyond her bedtime. In addition, in response to her tantrums, they gave her what she wanted, and there were few, if any, consequences for her behavior.

Although Marie might have been born with a more "stubborn temperament," that wouldn't necessarily prevent her parents from teaching her to respect realistic limits and consequences and to act in a more civil manner. These episodes of caving in had served as a foundation for Marie's behavior as a young adolescent. In their quest to avoid being overly punitive, the Listers had maintained a permissive, laissez-faire style of discipline that had robbed Marie of opportunities to develop self-discipline.

When Children Don't Get What They Want

Although Marie lacked self-discipline, some people might guess that she possessed a strong sense of personal control, since she was able to get what she wanted. True, Marie might have felt that she was in control, since her demands were being met. However, her personal control was illusory. Personal control is not the same as having one's demands being gratified, especially when a person acts like a dictator demanding one thing after another. At various times in the future, Marie will interact with people, including her teachers, who don't cater to her demands and who expect her to meet her responsibilities and behave with respect. For those interactions, she will need personal control, which is best understood within a context of cooperation, not bullying or intimidation. Parents nurture personal control in children when they help the children learn limits for their behavior.

We have worked with many youngsters whose parents gave in to their demands. Interestingly, behind a facade of satisfaction that they were receiving what they demanded, these children experienced other, less positive feelings. Some felt anxious, recognizing at some level that, although they got what they wanted, no adults were setting limits and guidelines to protect them. Others interpreted their parents' unwillingness to discipline them and hold them accountable for their actions as a sign that their parents did not love them. While they may have balked at their parents' limits, they would have felt more reassured of their parents' concern if their parents had not caved in.

The Hart Family: "At Least I Would Have Known She Cared"

This desire to feel loved by a parent was vividly captured in our work with fourteen-year-old Katie. Katie's parents had been divorced for several years, and she had little contact with her father, who lived several thousand miles away. Katie's mother, Andi Hart, had been receiving counseling from one of our colleagues, who referred Katie to us after Katie became pregnant and had an abortion. The information we received in the referral was that Andi found it difficult to establish limits and consequences for her daughter. Apparently, Andi frequently threatened consequences, especially when Katie stayed out to whatever time she wished. However, Katie responded to her mother's warnings with ridicule, shouting, "I don't have to listen to you!" or "You can't make me do anything I don't want to do!" Andi was at a loss over how to handle her daughter and felt intimidated by her. She told her therapist she feared that if she were "too tough," Katie might run away from home.

After Katie's abortion, a judge mandated that she see a therapist. Although Katie complied with the judge's directive, she did not enter therapy with enthusiasm. She immediately demonstrated her feelings by telling us how "stupid" seeing a therapist was. She announced, "I don't have to tell you anything." We agreed that what she said or did not say was her decision. She countered any comment or question we raised with challenging questions of her own: "Did you use pot when you were a teenager?" "When was the first time you had sex?" "Did you ever break the law?" "Were your parents divorced?"

It would be easy to interpret Katie's provocative questions simply as an attempt to deflect attention from herself or put us on the defensive (her questioning could be unrelenting). However, the nature of her questions invited another interpretation—that she was desperately assessing whether we could understand her experiences and whether she could trust us. We believed she was asking, "Can you understand what I'm going through? Can you remember what it was like when you were a teenager? If I'm willing to open up in therapy, will you be understanding or judgmental and accusatory?"

We walked the fine line that many therapists must traverse when working with adolescents. We validated Katie's questions by letting her know that she could ask any questions in therapy. However, we also set limits by conveying that there were some questions we could answer without hesitation, but we might not be able to answer others. We told her we would try to be as open as we could, since we were asking her to do the same, and that whether we responded would be guided by our understanding of why she was asking the question and whether or not we thought our answering would be helpful to her.

Since we anticipated that Katie would accuse us of not being open or helpful, we encouraged her to let us know if she ever felt we weren't being helpful. She did so on many occasions.

Katie's barrage of questions continued. In addition, one of her favorite observations was, "You always play the shrink game."

We asked her what she meant.

"You try to analyze everything I say and do, but you don't answer any of the questions I ask you."

We tried to maintain a consistent, empathic stance, answering or not answering questions based upon whether we felt our answers would help her gain a better understanding of her actions. Unlike her mother, we were consistent in our approach and didn't give in or become annoyed. Because her behavior was so provocative, remaining empathic was difficult. We sometimes felt as if she were a prosecuting attorney, determined to discover a transgression we had committed in our past for which we would be sent away for life.

Although we were making only slow progress in therapy, Katie's defensiveness and anger showed signs of abating. In one revealing session, following Katie's demand to hear about our own adolescent experiences, we told Katie our thoughts about her questioning. Assuring her that we weren't trying to play the "shrink game," we said that when she asked us questions about how we were as a teenager, we sometimes thought she might be wondering whether we could understand what she was going through. (The reason we mentioned the possibility that she might think of our comment as part of the shrink game was that we have found that this direct approach conveys empathy and lessens defensiveness.)

Katie's response was fascinating. While not wishing to let her guard down, she gave us clear indications that she was permitting us into her world. Almost playfully, she replied, "I'm getting used to shrink games. What else can shrinks do but play shrink games? You get years of training to play shrink games."

With some humor, we acknowledged that it does take years of training, and it's not always easy. She smiled, and we asked her directly whether she wondered if we could understand what she was going through.

Instead of resorting to one of her seemingly programmed responses—such as "I couldn't care less whether you understand me or not" or "It doesn't matter to me"—Katie allowed herself to lower her guard. She said, "Sometimes I do wonder if you can remember what it was like when you were a teenager or understand what I'm going through."

We asked whether speaking with us about her experiences would be easier if she felt we could appreciate what she was going through.

Katie said, "Definitely. I don't want lectures about what I've done."

We asked her to tell us what she wanted.

Katie was somewhat startled by this question. Rather than a provocative comeback, she simply uttered, "I'm not sure."

We responded that people often are uncertain what they want in therapy.

We added that the answer was something we could try to figure out with her.

This was a watershed moment in therapy. Katie began to speak about her parents' divorce, her anger at her mother (she perceived her mother as having "kicked her father out"), her sexual relationship with an adolescent boy, and her pregnancy and abortion.

In a later session, reflecting upon her mother's style of discipline, Katie noted, "If my mother set a curfew and followed through on it, I probably would have fought her tooth and nail."

She then paused and, with tears flowing freely from her eyes for the first time in our sessions, added, "But at least I would have known she cared about me."

Katie's insights and lack of defensiveness paved the way for joint sessions with her mother. After several months, her mother established realistic expectations, rules, and consequences. Andi learned an important lesson that all parents should keep in mind: setting realistic limits and following through on consequences conveys caring and love, and it reinforces self-discipline and personal control in our children.

Cultivate Problem-Solving and Decision-Making Skills

A critical component of a strength-based approach is to cultivate your child's problem-solving and decision-making skills. If a primary goal of discipline is to reinforce self-control and personal control, parents must also consider the ways in which their disciplinary practices strengthen problem-solving abilities. It is difficult to imagine self-control emerging in a person who lacks problem-solving skills.

Parents who simply demand that their children do what the parents want them to do, instead of helping them learn to think about what to do, fall into the trap of being authoritarian. As we saw in Chapter 2, children of authoritarian parents may do as directed, but they may not understand how to approach or handle similar situations in the future. They may also end up rebelling at these parental dictates.

Teaching problem-solving skills is so important that we have devoted the entire next chapter to elaborating upon this theme. In this chapter, we will simply emphasize that we have already illustrated the effectiveness of problem solving as a disciplinary technique in our description of the Ashlund, Ewing, and Burns families. As another example, let's return to the Berkshires, a family we introduced in the previous chapter.

The Berkshires: "Our Child Is a Whiner"

Lisa and Walt Berkshire described their nine-year-old son, Daniel, as a "high-maintenance kid" and as a "whiner, always putting his own needs above anyone else's." In Chapter 2, we referred to the Berkshires as an example of parents who had become so annoyed with their son that they neglected to praise or reinforce him when he was cooperative. In this chapter, we want to highlight the interventions we suggested to the Berkshires so they would develop Daniel's ability to reflect on his behavior and consider more appropriate responses to meet his needs.

The Berkshires lamented that Daniel was "exhausting" and said they would "end up giving in to him." Like the Lister family, the Berkshire household contained a child who was controlling but at the expense of developing self-control. In our interventions with the Berkshires, we discussed the concepts of self-discipline and personal control and the parents' responsibility for establishing authority. As an example, we asked them to tell us about Daniel's whining.

Lisa said, "You can spend five minutes in our house, and you would hear five minutes of whining." She smiled and asked, half joking but perhaps half not, "Do you think there's a whining gene?"

Smiling back, we said that whether or not such a gene existed, there were things she and Walt could do to lessen the whining.

Walt asked, "Like what?"

We promised to share some thoughts but said we first wanted to get a sense of how Lisa and Walt typically responded to Daniel's whining. We explained that this information might give us some ideas about what to do.

Walt said, "As we mentioned, we usually give in to him. He has amazing perseverance. He can really outlast us. His whining drives us crazy, and after a while, we'll do anything to stop him."

We asked how long they typically let him whine.

Walt said, "For a long time, maybe a half hour or an hour. But he's persistent. It just doesn't let up. As I said, we finally give in, and he stops whining."

We verified that the only way they had found to stop the whining was to give Daniel what he wanted.

Lisa sheepishly said, "I guess that *is* our only response. But as we're talking about it, I feel like such a wimp, letting a child rule the house."

Given the playful quality the Berkshires had displayed, we smiled and asked them whether they could think of a time when they didn't give in, when they were not what Lisa had called *wimps.* Along with that question, we asked whether either of them could think of a term that is opposite of *wimp.*

Walt mused, "I never thought of the opposite of *wimp.* That's an interesting question."

We commented that it can be helpful to have a term to describe what we would like ourselves or our child to be. Having a name for it is like having a goal to reach.

Lisa said, "You know what word comes to mind? *Moxie.*"

Walt responded, "Yeah, I like that word."

We agreed that *moxie* sounded like a good word and asked the Berkshires what the word meant to them.

Lisa answered, "The first word that comes to mind is *determination.*" Her husband concurred.

We believe that when we use particular words and metaphors, they become integral parts of our mindsets, which direct our behavior. So we pursued this line of thinking by suggesting that we get out the dictionary in our office and look up the dictionary definition of *moxie.* The Berkshires, who were enjoying this playful excursion, readily agreed. The first definition listed was "a trademark for a soft drink."

Lisa laughed. "That's not what I had in mind."

She was pleased when we read further and exclaimed that her word choice was right on target. We read the next two definitions: "determination" and "courage."

Lisa responded, "That's much better."

Equipped with a word to contrast with *wimp*, we returned to our earlier question. We again asked the Berkshires to think of a time they showed determination and did not act like wimps. (Once again, we were looking for the "exception to the rule," as we described in Chapter 2.)

At least a half minute went by with no response. Finally Walt broke the silence and said, "I'm certain there were times, but lately all I can think about is how much we give in to Daniel. The other night we even told Daniel that he could whine and cry all he wanted, but he could not have a third helping of ice cream—that he already had had enough sweets for the day."

We asked what had happened next.

"He whined and whined and said we didn't love him. We should have ignored his whining, but we did what we almost always do: we gave him the ice cream, and he stopped whining."

Shifting gears, we commented that Daniel was in control, and given the benefits he received from this behavior, it would be hard for him to let go of this role. Thus, we advised (noting that some people would disagree with our suggestion) that the best way to begin changing Daniel's behavior would be to have him feel a sense of control, although the parents would actually be orchestrating the situation.

Lisa wondered, "What do you mean?"

We explained that we have found that unless a situation represents an immediate danger in which parents have to act swiftly to protect a child, parents can be firm and at the same time give their children a feeling of ownership. They could do this by engaging the children in a discussion about their behavior and by encouraging them to consider alternative ways of acting. In this way, parents can teach their children that while they can't have everything they want, there is a lot they can get—but not by whining or being demanding. We added that this approach is related to the importance of helping children develop self-discipline and personal control. If parents who have given in to their kids suddenly lay down the law in an inflexible way, it may actually rob kids of developing personal control.

Walt interrupted, "But maybe that's what Daniel needs. Just tell him what to do and don't budge an inch. He has to learn who's in charge."

We agreed that Walt and Lisa should be firm, but we pointed out that if they went from one extreme to the other, Daniel might not learn how to solve problems, even if he began to comply with their requests. He might appear more cooperative in front of them and might whine less. Although on the surface that might seem like progress, the progress might not last long. For long-lasting progress, Walt and Lisa would have to help Daniel develop the tools to manage his feelings when he doesn't get what he wants. He would be more likely to maintain progress if he felt he played a role in the changes taking place. The goal, we explained, would be for Daniel to feel some control, but control that would lead to self-control. We emphasized that allowing children to feel some control doesn't mean giving in to them. If possible, we want children to incorporate what we're trying to teach them, so that even when we're not with them, they will think about what we taught them. We want them to feel like active participants in learning to manage their behavior.

In our interventions with many parents, we have learned that they truly aren't sure what to say or do when modifying their typical responses with their children, even if these responses have proven counterproductive. They are trapped in a negative "script" (a pattern of words and actions that are used repeatedly without satisfactory results). They are unable to author a new, more constructive course of action. Even when they see a need to change, they may not know what to do. To counteract this sense of being stuck, we use a therapeutic technique, called *behavior rehearsal*, in which we review with parents actual words and actions they might use with their children to change the scenario in their homes. In addition, we help them anticipate how their children will respond to a new parental script. By rehearsing their behavior, parents prepare themselves not to resort to former, negative ways of behaving. In addition, behavior rehearsal can go more smoothly if we start by reviewing a specific example from the past. So we asked the Berkshires to select an actual incident in which they had given in to Daniel's whining.

In an exasperated tone, Walt said, "There are many. I can give you an example from the other night. It's something that happens a lot. We all have chores to do. We even alternate them from month to month, since they aren't the most exciting activities. One of Daniel's chores this month was to put the dishes in the dishwasher. After we finished dinner, Daniel left the kitchen. We called him back to put the dishes in the washer. He said he had a lot of homework and had to get it done. We said he could begin his homework right after he put the dishes away."

Lisa, also with a look of exasperation, interrupted. "I reminded Daniel that he had watched ninety minutes of TV before dinner and told him he should have started his homework then. He yelled back that school is tough and he needs some time to rest. He has an answer for everything. He started to whine that we put too much pressure on him. I'm not certain where that came from; if anything, we think he has it pretty easy in terms of responsibilities."

There was a pause. We asked what happened next.

Lisa said, "What happens too often. We got so tired of his whining that we said, 'OK, we'll put the dishes in the washer tonight, but you have to do it tomorrow.'"

We asked what happened the next day.

Walt responded, "The same battle."

We asked the Berkshires what they thought Daniel had learned from their response to his whining.

Lisa said, "I never really thought about it in that way."

We asked her to explain her comment.

"When you asked, 'What is he learning?' I never thought about what he's learning. The first thing that pops up in my mind is that he's learning to avoid his responsibilities."

We commented that her guess was a good one. We asked whether she and Walt had any other ideas.

Walt jumped in. "This is right out of an introductory psychology book or parenting book. He learned that whining pays off."

Lisa said, "But he can be so exhausting. He seems to have more energy than us and outlasts us."

We agreed that Daniel had a lot of energy but added that he would have a difficult time developing self-discipline and responsibility if this approach to parenting continued. We pointed out that a change would be in his best interest, as well as Lisa's and Walt's. We told them we were ready to suggest some other possibilities for them to consider.

Until they faced the fact that "whining pays off" and that their failure to hold their son responsible for his actions was robbing him of opportunities to become more self-disciplined and responsible, the Berkshires were caught in a common negative script. Parents in this situation often fail to perceive the obvious, and if they do, they are at a loss about what to do.

We will continue our intervention with the Berkshires in the next chapter. For now, consider what new script you would suggest to the Berkshires so they could respond more effectively to Daniel. As you reflect on this question, keep in mind that the discipline approach should encourage the growth of self-discipline and personal control, especially since Daniel had a pronounced need to be in charge. He would have to feel he had a choice, but not a choice to avoid his responsibilities. In addition, think about how Daniel might react to the Berkshires' new script. As the parents anticipate Daniel's response to their new script, how should they plan to reply to him?

Use Prevention to Nurture Personal Control

In Chapter 2, we discussed how using a preventive approach lessens the emergence of discipline problems. A preventive approach gives parents opportunities to reinforce their children's sense of personal control and ownership for their behavior. Depending on their child's age and ability, sometimes parents must devise a prevention plan without their child's input. For example, in the previous chapter, the mother of a four-year-old daughter who had meltdowns when they went shopping decided to prevent problems by leaving the daughter at home. That was a necessary first step. Eventually, however, the goal is for parents to provide experiences that allow their children to be involved in the prevention plan so the children can develop self-discipline.

> *The goal is for parents to provide experiences that allow their children to be involved in the prevention plan so the children can develop self-discipline.*

As we will see even more clearly in Chapter 4, we often can invite even young children to participate in preventing problems and, in the process, bolster self-discipline. That's how, in the previous chapter, we worked with the Ashlunds to help their son Robert, the four-year-old boy who had difficulty going to bed. When asked, Robert offered impressive ideas for what he needed to ease his nighttime anxiety—namely, to have a night-light and a photo of his parents by his bed.

Mollie and Her Son: "How Can We Help Each Other Remember?"

At one of our workshops, a mother named Mollie offered a similar example of what she did with her six-year-old son. The example is noteworthy because of its effectiveness and simplicity. Mollie described her son as having been diagnosed with attention-deficit/hyperactivity disorder (ADHD). She said, "I found myself nagging him every day to do things like brush his teeth, wash his hands, and put the towel back on the rack instead of on the floor. At one point, he told me that I was always on his back. I'm not even certain where he learned that phrase, but that's how he described what I was doing."

Mollie continued, "I would tell him that if he did what he was supposed to do, I wouldn't have to remind him. I also resorted to punishment, taking things like TV time away from him for not doing what he was expected to do. That really didn't help, since he still didn't do many of the things. Finally, a couple of things dawned on me. One, even though the tasks seemed simple enough, maybe he really had trouble remembering what he should do. Two, my son and I were having very little fun together, since what he called my nagging was taking over our entire relationship."

Another mother in the room exclaimed, "That sounds a lot like my son. What did you do?"

Mollie answered, "This may sound silly, but I sat down with my son and said that I really didn't want to keep reminding him to do things. He said if I didn't want to keep reminding him to do things, I would stop. I then asked him a question I hadn't thought of asking before, and it turned out great. I said that I might forget to do some things, just like he might forget to do some things. How could we help each other remember?"

The second mother jumped in to say, "I think my son would just answer, 'I don't know.'"

We interrupted to observe that many children might say "I don't know" when asked how to prevent a problem. We advised that unless the situation is an emergency, the parents should avoid getting into a struggle with them. Instead, they should simply say, "That's OK. Many kids might not know what to do, but we can take time to think about it." After sharing this advice, we returned our attention to Mollie's story.

Mollie continued, "I was fortunate. Amazingly, my son said, 'Let's make a list. We do that in school.' He told me that they also have pictures next to the words on the list to remind them what the words mean. We made a list of things he should do and I should do. I was careful to keep the number of things he needed to do to a reasonable amount, so that it didn't seem overwhelming. He decided to place the list in the hallway between his bedroom and the bathroom. We put a check mark next to an item when it was completed."

She added, "There's something else I realized a few minutes ago. He seemed genuinely happy when he checked something off. It wasn't for a reward, since we didn't give rewards; he didn't even ask for any. I may be wrong, but I think the check mark was a concrete way for him to see that he had accomplished something, not by my reminding him, but by him reminding himself. It's like what you were talking about: reinforcing a sense of ownership."

Mollie hesitated for a couple of seconds and asked, "Does that sound crazy? Am I reading too much into a check mark?"

We assured her that she was not, adding that her conclusions made a lot of sense. She had invited her son to come up with a solution to a behavior problem, and not only was his idea successful, but he felt a sense of pride for such a positive outcome.

Mollie's example vividly illustrates the ways in which different forms of discipline, including methods of preventive discipline, can advance personal control and lead to self-discipline.

Be Consistent

If you attend any parenting workshop or read any book about parenting (including ours), when the discussion turns to discipline, the parenting expert is likely to use the word *consistency*. The emphasis on consistency is justified. Without consistency, discipline is unlikely to result in self-discipline or personal control. Rather, inconsistency breeds confusion and poorly defined expectations and consequences.

Consistency over Time

As most parents appreciate, discipline is most effective when governed by clear and realistic expectations and when consequences follow consistently. But achieving this kind of practice is frequently a challenge. For example, your mood or stress level on a particular day can make consistency difficult. No parent can be consistent all of the time, but if the dominant pattern is consistency associated with reasonable rules and consequences, children will become increasingly caring and responsible.

Consistency does not mean that parents should be rigid or inflexible. Rather, when you make changes, base them on careful consideration and, assuming your children are old enough, help them understand the reasons for the changes. For example, a couple at one of our workshops said they were strict about the time at which their six-year-old son and eight-year-old daughter should go to bed. Since both parents worked, they felt (appropriately) that it was important to have a routine in which they spent time with their children but also had some time for themselves.

However, after hearing about a shooting in a school, the two children became clingy. For several days, the parents spent extra time talking with them about how upsetting the shooting was and reassuring them that although shootings in schools do occur, they are rare. The parents also were more tolerant when either of the children called for them from bed and asked for a glass of water, recognizing that the real agenda was the child's need to be comforted. During this time of anxiety, the children went to bed a little later than usual, since the situation justified a temporary modification of the rules. The parents emphasized at the workshop that it was a "temporary" adjustment and, after a couple of weeks, the old routine and expectations were restored. To use the concepts we have been elaborating in this chapter, the parents' actions allowed the children to feel more in control, since the parents skillfully managed the issues of worry, safety, and security.

Consistency Between Parents

Along with consistency over time, another significant form of consistency is necessary: consistency between the parents. Of course, parents cannot and should not become clones of each other, but they should try to arrive at common goals and disciplinary practices. Doing this often involves negotiation and compromise. We recommend the effort even when parents are divorced.

Choose Your Words with Care

Children who possess self-discipline and a sense of personal control believe they are responsible for their own behavior. They are less apt to make excuses for their actions, and they increasingly focus on what they can do differently to change undesirable situations. Obviously, this kind of mindset is not formed overnight, but rather is based on countless interactions with parents and other adults. To help children develop this mindset, parents should give their children feedback that emphasizes ownership and personal control.

The Leopold Family: "You'll Never Learn"

Mona and Lawrence Leopold consulted with us about their three children: Liz, age twelve; Madison, age ten; and Manny, age eight. Their initial complaint was that all three children were "rude." We could write a volume about our work with the Leopolds, but for the purposes of this section, we will focus on the ways in which the words we use either reinforce or harm a sense of personal control.

When we first began to consult with the Leopolds, we were impressed with their inconsistency in setting limits on their children's behavior. When their children called them derogatory names, the parents either said nothing or became very angry, shouting at one of them or all three with such comments as, "You always act like brats," or "You never treat each other nicely," or "You'll never learn how to be kind." Words such as *always* and *never* used in this way are apt to trigger anger and do not help to develop self-control. Judgmental phrases such as *you'll never learn* convey a message that works against the development of self-discipline and personal control.

To help the Leopolds become more empathic and appreciate the impact of their words on their children, we made a point of adopting an empathic stance toward them, lest they experience our observations as being critical of their parenting skills. Thus, we acknowledged their frustration and their wish for their children to be more "considerate" and "cooperative" and less "rude." We also highlighted our agreement with their goals, but commented that the ways they were trying to reach those goals might actually be working against achieving them. We explained with an example, asking how they would feel if someone said to them, "You'll never learn to act in a kind way" or "You always act like brats."

We had barely asked the question when Lawrence said, "Maybe not great, but when I say things like that to the kids, it's how I feel. I really worry about whether they will ever learn to be nice."

We acknowledged that Lawrence was honestly expressing how he felt, but we asked him to consider what he thought his children learned when he said those words.

Lawrence looked at us, puzzled. "I'm not sure. They haven't changed. They keep doing the same things." Smiling, he added, "I guess what I'm saying to them isn't very effective."

We returned his smile as we observed that if parents keep doing the same thing repeatedly even if it doesn't work, it would be a big surprise if the children changed their behavior.

Mona said, "You're right. I think we're ready to learn new techniques."

Her comment prompted us to focus on their words and actions with their children. Many parents, especially when angry or disappointed, don't think about how their words affect their children. In some instances, these words work against a child cultivating a feeling of personal control. And as we have learned in recent investigations about peer bullying, the saying "Sticks and stones may break my bones, but words will never hurt me" is false. Certain words hurt not only at the time they are uttered but also for years to come.

We spent many sessions helping the Leopolds to establish realistic expectations for their children and to follow through with reasonable consequences. We also focused on the specific language they used in their communications with their children, moving away from negative, accusatory words to words that reinforce positive behavior and self-discipline. After this shift in disciplinary practices, their children began displaying more responsible, respectful behavior.

Tell Children What They're Doing Right

Refraining from the use of hurtful language is not the only advice we offer parents. Most importantly, we emphasize that not only should we provide positive feedback, but when reinforcing our children's behavior, we should use words that specifically reinforce self-discipline, responsibility, and personal control. Thus, as we advised the Leopolds, when you catch your children doing something good, such as acting cooperatively, you should tell them what you see: "It's really nice to see you play together." In addition, you can promote a feeling of ownership if you add, "It's a good choice you made." Or, when your children clean up the family room without being told to do so, one of the messages might be, "You reminded yourself to do it—that's great." As simple as these comments may seem, their continued, deliberate use slowly fortifies a responsible attitude and a resilient mindset.

We make a similar suggestion to parents whose children take medications for ADHD or mood disorders. Medications may help a child focus more effectively, feel less stressed, and feel less depressed. However, if children

> *When you catch your children doing something good, such as acting cooperatively, you should tell them what you see. You can promote a feeling of ownership if you add, "It's a good choice you made."*

attribute their positive changes simply to a pill, this way of thinking may not reinforce an attitude of self-discipline and personal control. Thus, we recommend that parents say, "The pill helps you to focus or to feel calmer, but once you feel this way, then it's going to be your choice or decision how to act." This statement highlights for the children that they play a major role in determining their behaviors.

Concluding Thought

As the preceding examples illustrate, when you use disciplinary techniques guided by a resilience model, you help your children develop greater responsibility and ownership for their actions, enhance self-discipline, and strengthen a sense of personal control. In addition, to reinforce personal control, you must nurture problem-solving skills in your children, a theme we will address in the next chapter.

4

Teaching Your Child to Solve Problems

At our parenting workshops, we often ask, "Have you ever been confronted with a problem in which your first reaction was to feel overwhelmed, because you had no idea how to begin solving it?" Most parents will nod.

We continue by asking them to imagine what it would be like if they had that kind of reaction to almost every problem they faced—feeling at a loss over how to go about solving the problem. Parents agree that such a situation would truly be overwhelming.

As we mentioned in the previous chapter, developing self-control is difficult without some problem-solving skills. Therefore, if the parents' manner of discipline does not encourage or allow children to become skillful at solving problems, then discipline has failed to achieve one of its major goals. Discipline has to teach children to think for themselves, to reflect upon their actions and the consequences that flow from these actions.

In our previous books about resilience, we have emphasized that the ability to solve problems is linked to all features of a resilient mindset. Problem-solving ability enables youngsters to meet challenges by relying on actions within their control. They can weigh different options and display decision-making prowess as they modify negative scripts in their lives. Children skilled in addressing problems anticipate possible obstacles to choices that they make, viewing setbacks or mistakes as experiences from which to learn. As we have witnessed with the Ashlund, Burns, and Ewing families, when the discipline process focuses on problem solving, children are less likely to engage in power struggles, since they feel a sense of empowerment.

In contrast, when children struggle to solve problems, they often have trouble talking about and defining problems, considering options, planning, or managing the hard knocks that inevitably come to each of us. In many ways, these children are adrift, similar to a captain lost at sea without a compass, following one course or another but without any reasonable judgment to guide their actions. In such a situation, some children may become paralyzed, not knowing what to do, while others may act impulsively without considering the consequences of their behavior. One of the reasons that some clinicians describe certain children as "difficult" is that these youngsters have difficulty reflecting on what to do, demonstrating a lack of self-discipline.

When the discipline process focuses on problem solving, children are less likely to engage in power struggles, since they feel a sense of empowerment.

The Wilkins Family: "We Always Have to Tell Her What to Do"

Susan and Jack Wilkins were constantly angry with their twelve-year-old daughter, Melanie. In our first session with the Wilkinses, they quickly compared Melanie with her fourteen-year-old sister, Patty.

Susan said, "You wouldn't believe that our two daughters came from the same set of parents. Patty came into this world with a mellow, calm personality. I think she was responsible from day one. We almost never have to remind her to do anything. When she does something wrong, which is very rare, we just have to tell her once, and she remembers the next time."

Jack interrupted to offer an interesting observation with a trace of humor: "If Melanie acted like Patty or if Patty were our only child, we'd wonder why there were so many parenting books on the shelves of bookstores, especially books that focus on discipline."

Susan smiled and added, "But once Melanie was born, we understood why there are so many parenting books. To be honest, she was and continues to be a handful. She seemed more anxious than Patty right from birth. Patty always seems self-assured and knows how to handle things. Melanie doesn't. We always have to tell Melanie what to do. Yet when we tell her, she doesn't seem to listen. We've been getting into more and more battles with her lately. We're spending so much time with Melanie that we feel we're not giving Patty enough attention, although Patty seems pretty understanding of the situation. She really loves Melanie."

We asked what specific difficulties the Wilkinses were having with Melanie.

Susan responded, "Many. She often forgets to do things such as clean her room or make her bed. She can be demanding and talks rudely to us. A couple of days ago, when we were ready to sit down for dinner, she said there was some art material she needed for a project and insisted that we take her to the store at that moment. When we said we'd take her after dinner, she yelled that we didn't love her, that if Patty had needed art supplies, we would have taken her right away. After dinner we took her to the store to get the supplies. She was grumpy the entire time and didn't even say thank you."

Jack continued the story. "The next day, she asked me to help her with the art project. However, it soon became the kind of situation it always becomes. After thirty seconds, Melanie said she didn't know what to do and that I should help her. I said I'd help her, but what she meant is what she always seems to mean— namely, that we should do the project for her. When Patty asks for help, she's more than willing to take some of our suggestions and run with them. Not Melanie."

We asked the Wilkinses what they typically did when Melanie kept asking for their help.

Jack responded, "It's not a pretty scene. We often tell her that she's not even trying to do it and that if she would try, she'd discover she could do many of the things she was asking us to help her with. When we say this, Melanie tells us that we don't love her, that she really doesn't know how to do it, and that we should help her more than we do."

Susan added, "When Melanie says this, we repeat that we're there to help her but that she just wants us to do everything for her and she has to learn to do some things on her own. It's upsetting, because she starts to yell, and soon we're yelling at her. Melanie often accuses us of yelling at her. There's some truth to this, since she really frustrates us."

As we processed the Wilkinses' remarks, we were impressed with several points. Almost any observation they offered about Melanie was paired with more favorable comments about Patty. Those constant comparisons with her easygoing sister magnified Melanie's difficulties. The parents' disappointment with Melanie was apparent. In addition, their frustration with Melanie lessened their empathy and prompted frustrated comments that Melanie interpreted as accusations and yelling.

The parents did try to launch a problem-solving approach by encouraging Melanie to think about how best to meet challenges. But when Melanie claimed she didn't know how to do things, they reacted with anger, rather than considering how they might encourage their daughter to feel more confident about solving problems. Their disciplinary style, which was often influenced by frustration and disappointment, contained authoritarian qualities that implied Melanie was to blame for their anger.

We saw the Wilkinses as caring people who had difficulty responding to a more challenging child. If we were to promote an empathic, problem-solving approach in their parenting and disciplinary practices, we would have to demonstrate these same qualities in our interactions with them.

In the previous chapter, we asked you to think about what changes you would recommend to the Berkshires to improve their disciplinary tactics with their son, Daniel. We now ask the same question about the Wilkinses. What disciplinary strategies would you suggest they use with Melanie to strengthen her problem-solving skills and her ability to be more independent, confident, and secure? Also, what change in mindset would be necessary to accompany this shift in their discipline approach? We will describe our continued interventions with the Berkshires at the end of this chapter and with the Wilkinses in Chapter 6.

Ways to Reinforce Problem-Solving and Decision-Making Skills

The framework that directs our problem-solving approach, which we have described in other writings such as *Raising Resilient Children*, is based on ideas from our friend and colleague Myrna Shure. Dr. Shure was instrumental in developing a program called I Can Problem Solve (ICPS), which is outlined in her books *Raising a Thinking Child, Raising a Thinking Preteen*, and *Thinking Parent, Thinking Child*. Her work offers evidence that even preschool children can learn skills to enhance their ability to solve problems. While we have added some of our own ideas to Dr. Shure's approach, the framework has been significantly influenced by her work.

Several principles serve as a foundation for our approach to developing problem-solving skills. An understanding of these principles is important when we discipline children, especially if we keep in mind that effective disciplinary practices not only make use of problem solving, but also promote these skills for children to apply in the future. Let's consider those principles one at a time.

Serve as a Model of Problem Solving

There is ample evidence that our children carefully observe our behaviors, including the ways in which we cope with different situations. If your children frequently witness angry outbursts when you mete out discipline or deal with challenging events, they won't have a chance to learn problem-solving skills from your example. For this reason, we ask parents to think about how their children would answer the following questions:

> *If your children frequently witness angry outbursts when you mete out discipline or deal with challenging events, they won't have a chance to learn problem-solving skills from your example.*

- ■ "How do your parents solve problems and make decisions when they face difficult situations?"
- ■ "Do you think there is a better way for them to solve problems and make decisions? If so, what would you suggest?"
- ■ "How do your parents teach you and involve you in decision making?"
- ■ "Does the way they usually discipline you help you to be a better problem solver?"

In some families, effective problem solving is a natural part of the repertoire, while other families typically arrive at arbitrary decisions with little, if any, input from the children. Some parents—often without fully appreciating the meaning of their actions—resort to forms of discipline that actually model the behaviors they intend to eliminate in their children. It is ironic to observe a parent slapping a child while screaming, "This will teach you not to hit your younger sister again." Unfortunately, in such a scenario, the child's problem-solving skills are not strengthened.

The Upton Family: "I Think They're Too Old to Spank Now"

Dorothy and Jules Upton consulted us about their two sons, thirteen-year-old Carl and eleven-year-old Frank. Jules began by explaining, "I never thought we'd need professional help with our kids, but they just don't listen to us. They fight all the time. They constantly scream at each other. They can't pass each other without saying something mean. It has been this way for several years, but it's getting worse. Nothing we do seems to work."

We asked the Uptons to tell us what they typically did when the boys fought.

Jules answered, "A lot. I think they're too old to spank now, but we used to spank them. I thought that worked. They seemed better right after we spanked them, but it didn't seem to last. Maybe we should have spanked them more often. I also told them that if they kept fighting, we'd take time away from their playing computer games or watching TV. That seemed to work for a little while, but soon losing computer or TV time didn't seem to matter."

This father's disciplinary techniques were typical of an authoritarian style. Jules did not observe an improvement in his sons' behavior, but he kept plunging ahead with his punitive style, expecting that at some point his sons would learn to do what he was telling them to do.

Although Jules frequently used the word *we* to describe the discipline that was used, we observed his wife's silence. As her husband was speaking, Dorothy nodded on a couple of occasions but offered no comments of her own. We wondered about the reason for her seeming lack of involvement. To bring her into the discussion, we mentioned that mothers and fathers sometimes have different experiences with their children. We asked Dorothy what she would like to add to her husband's comments.

"Nothing really," she replied. "Jules tends to handle the discipline in the home, so he probably has a better picture of what is going on." As Dorothy said this, she glanced at her husband. The tension between them was obvious.

Speaking directly to Dorothy, we said that even though her husband might be more involved with disciplining the boys, we wished she would share her views about the discipline that was taking place.

Interestingly, before his wife could respond, Jules jumped in and said, "I feel Dottie is too lenient with them. I don't think we'd be having the problems we're having with the boys if she would be able to set limits. I think my approach would be more effective if Dottie hadn't spoiled them."

Dorothy angrily told us, "My husband always blames me for anything the boys do wrong. Maybe I should be more forceful with the boys at times, but I could never do what he does or has done."

We asked what she was referring to.

"As he mentioned before, he used to spank them a lot. Now he yells and criticizes them all of the time. He says that's the only way they listen to him. I think they act like they listen to him because they fear him. And even though they may fear him, they don't really listen to him. I think things are going to get worse as they get older."

Jules, obviously angry, countered, "They would listen if Dottie supported me more. And what's wrong with your kids fearing you if it helps them to respect you?"

Dorothy retorted, "How can I support you doing things I don't agree with? And I don't think they respect you." She added a perceptive comment: "If they respected you or me, I don't think they'd be acting the way they do."

A couple of weeks after that first session, we conducted a family meeting with Jules, Dorothy, and their two sons. We thought a family meeting would help us learn the perspectives of Carl and

Frank and give us a chance to observe the family interaction and begin developing a problem-solving approach.

At the meeting, Jules angrily described his frustration over his sons' constant fighting with each other. He observed, "I have two brothers and a sister, and I know that siblings can argue, but with Carl and Frank, it's getting out of hand. They push and shove each other and say really nasty things. Also, when they're not fighting with each other, they don't show much respect to Dottie and me. I've been trying to teach them to be more civil for years, but they can't get what I'm trying to teach them through their heads. They've got to learn respect."

Carl and Frank glared at their father but said nothing. Dorothy looked down and began to cry. Before we could say anything, Carl confronted his father with an insightful observation: "You keep talking about Frank and me being nice to each other, about respecting you, but it's a one-way street with you."

We asked Carl to explain what he meant by a one-way street.

In a remarkably calm voice, he answered, "He talks about our showing respect, but he doesn't practice what he preaches. He always puts us down, and when we were younger, he would spank us for the littlest thing. We always heard, 'You do what I tell you! I'm your father!' And he doesn't talk that way only to us. You should hear how he talks to Mom. I don't know why she takes it."

Not surprisingly, Jules shot back, "Don't you talk that way to me! I wouldn't have to yell or spank you if you and your brother acted right. You don't listen unless I yell."

Carl got up to leave the office, commenting bitterly, "What good is it saying anything?"

We prevailed upon him to stay. We pointed out how angry and frustrated everyone was and said that while they might not agree with each other's view of the situation, it was important to begin to understand how each family member saw the others. We also emphasized that any anger in our office was not to be carried outside the office. We were especially concerned about Jules becoming more punitive because of what Carl had said.

We had more family meetings as well as parent sessions. Slowly Dorothy could acknowledge her anger toward her husband for the way in which he treated her. At one point in a meeting attended by just the parents, she said, "I'm not trying to blame Jules, since I know I've played a role in all of the anger and unhappiness in the family, but I keep thinking of what Carl said about how Jules asks for respect but doesn't display any. I have to admit that when Jules puts me down, I feel scared. I wish I would have had the courage to tell him that I won't tolerate his speaking to me that way anymore. I wish when he screamed or hit the kids, I would have had the courage to tell him privately that he shouldn't continue doing that. Not only do they see Jules acting with such disrespect and anger, but I can't help but think that our sons see me act with a lack of self-respect."

It was very difficult for Jules to hear this. He was entrenched in his viewpoint. He said his wife and sons used our sessions to "dump on him." Although we tried to be empathic and to cast the struggles they were having as a "family problem," not just as his problem, he became increasingly disenchanted with therapy and began to miss sessions. Eventually, primarily at Dorothy's initiative, the two of them separated. Although that decision was painful, Dorothy said with some pride, "I finally found my voice."

There is much we could say about the Upton family. However, one of the most unforgettable moments was when Carl contrasted what his father preached with what he actually did. Because of his authoritarian demeanor, Jules did not give his sons a chance to learn how to solve problems. His approach was in striking contrast to that displayed by the Ewings in Chapter 1. The Ewings helped their difficult son, Jim, learn how to solve problems and assume ownership for his actions; they nurtured a resilient mindset in their son. In contrast, Jules Upton triggered anger and resentment in his sons.

Offer Choices at an Early Age

We have already emphasized that when we discipline our children, a goal is to strengthen their self-discipline and personal control so that we don't have to keep doing the job for them. To achieve this goal, parents must ensure that children learn the skills involved in solving problems and making decisions. We recommend that, as a way of building these skills at an early age, parents give their children simple choices. Most parents do this as part of their typical parenting practices. Here are a few examples:

- ■ "Do you want pizza or a burger for dinner?"
- ■ "Do you want to wear your blue dress or your green dress?"
- ■ "Do you want me to remind you ten minutes or fifteen minutes before bedtime to get ready for bed?"
- ■ "Do you want to clean up by yourself, or would you like me to help you?"

We suggest that at the end of each question, parents add the comment "It's your choice." We emphasize the word *choice* as a way of expressing to children that we trust their ability to make a decision. Such simple steps begin to establish and reinforce problem-solving skills. These choices also nurture self-discipline, especially when they include consequences:

- ■ "It's your choice. If you don't put the toys away, they won't be available for you to play with tomorrow."
- ■ "If you continue to kick your sister under the table, you'll have to leave the table. It's your choice."

Parents often ask how they should react if children don't like either of the choices offered. In our experience, this rarely occurs with young children, but if it does, parents can say, "Well, those are the only two choices. Think about them, and let me know what will be best for you." In some situations, parents might ask their child to think of an alternative choice, and if the child's selection is reasonable, the parents can agree to it.

Use a Process for Solving Problems

The ability to solve problems and make decisions involves a process with interrelated components. As we shall see, these components can be used successfully when disciplining children. The most important features of this sequence are highlighted here.

State the Problem and Agree That It Is a Problem

For children and adults alike, the effort to make a change seems worthwhile only if we see a problem and care about it. If a problem is not clearly defined, and if children don't agree with their parents that it is a problem, then requests to arrive at a solution will fall on deaf ears. Imagine for a moment someone saying to you, "You're watching too much TV, and you need to cut back," or, "You lose your temper all the time, and you have to demonstrate more self-control." If you believe you watch a reasonable amount of television and do a pretty good job of controlling your temper, you probably wouldn't react to those criticisms by saying, "Thank you for reminding me that I have a problem. I'll work on correcting it." More likely, you would believe that the person who made those statements is a nag who is bugging you about nonexistent problems. In that case, your attitude would hardly be cooperative.

So what should you do if you see a problem but your child denies that a problem exists? Parents should not simply accept the child's version of reality. Instead, be empathic and ask the kinds of questions we outlined in Chapter 2 to evaluate how you are expressing the problem:

▪ Would I want anyone to speak with me the way I am speaking with my children?
▪ In anything I say or do with my children, what do I hope to accomplish?
▪ Am I communicating in a way that would make my children most receptive to listening to me and learning from me? For example, do I first validate what my child is saying ("I can see you think we are not being fair") before attempting to change my child's behavior? We must remember that validation does not imply agreement, but rather that you are searching to understand your child's perspective.

The Heath Family: "Stop Bugging Me." Janine and Mike Heath spoke with us about their eleven-year-old daughter, Marissa. They said Marissa's favorite phrase was "Stop bugging me," which she would elaborate on by complaining, "It's not my problem! None of my friends' parents bug them like you bug me." According to the Heaths, Marissa would utter this well-rehearsed speech on numerous occasions, most often in response to their reminding her to fulfill what they considered were reasonable requests such as cleaning her room, putting the dishes in the dishwasher after dinner, taking the dog (which she had wanted) out for a walk, and putting away her clean clothes.

Janine said, "Everything is a battle. She seems to have never heard the word *cooperation*. We remind her, and she keeps saying it's not her problem."

We asked how they generally responded to that declaration.

Janine replied, "At first we tried to be calm and reasonable. We told her that these are responsibilities she has, just as we have responsibilities. That didn't seem to work. We told her we'd make a list for her to remember. She said OK but then didn't look at the list. In the last year or two, she responds to us as if we were the Gestapo and keeps telling us that it's not a problem whether her room is spotless or her clothes are put away. She even said we could use paper plates so they wouldn't have to be put in the dishwasher. Sometimes we're not sure if she's joking or serious."

We commented that, from their description, none of their efforts seemed to have succeeded.

Mike answered, "Not by the results. If anything, Marissa seems to have become less cooperative, and we've become more punitive. We've taken away privileges such as TV time, but that seems to have had little effect. We've yelled at her, but that hasn't worked."

We asked them to consider why Marissa hadn't learned what they had tried to teach her. We were hoping to obtain a sense of the Heaths' mindset, especially their understanding of their daughter's behavior.

Janine said, "Mike and I aren't sure. I know that sometimes we haven't been consistent. We know it's wrong, but it's sometimes easier just to clear the dishes ourselves or clean up her room."

Mike jumped in. "And sometimes we think Marissa is just a self-centered girl and will do what she wants to do. We're not sure why she's like that, but she never seems to help out."

We asked whether Marissa had been more helpful in the past.

Janine said, "I don't think so. It has always been a battle to get her to do what we expect her to do. It might have been a little easier when she was younger, but that's because she responded more to our threats of punishment."

We asked the Heaths to think of a time when Marissa surprised them and actually cleaned her room or cleared the dirty dishes without their reminding her to do so. We were looking for any exception to the rule as a possible starting point for changing Marissa's problem behavior.

Mike answered, "That's an interesting question. Right off the top of my head, I can't think of any. Well, maybe if there was a reward she really wanted, like going to a movie the next day. But it has been hard to figure out what rewards would work."

He turned to his wife and asked what she thought. Janine agreed with her husband. "It's hard to figure out what will work with Marissa, since so few things actually work. Once in a while, we hit on a reward that's so important to her that she may actually do what we ask."

Admitting that our question might seem strange, we asked the Heaths whether it might be possible that Marissa really didn't see what she was doing or not doing as a problem.

Janine exclaimed, "I can't believe she doesn't see it as a problem. We've reminded her many, many times."

Conceding that our original question might not have been specific enough, we asked whether Marissa saw her actions and inactions as her problem or her parents'.

Mike said, "Well, according to her comments, Marissa sees it as our problem. She's always saying none of her friends have parents who nag their kids the way we nag her."

We suggested that we might need to start with her perspective and work from there. Mike, looking incredulous, asked, "Are you saying we should agree with Marissa that she's fine and has overbearing parents, and that we should just give in to her?"

We quickly assured Mike that is not what we meant. But before we could explain further, he jumped in and said, "We think that when Marissa accuses us of bugging her and tells us it's our problem and not hers, she's just using it as an excuse so she doesn't have to meet her responsibilities."

We agreed that he was probably right. Even so, we suggested, the Heaths might have more success in helping her to be more responsible if they assumed she really did believe they were bugging her unfairly—even if she was using that reasoning as an excuse to avoid her responsibilities.

With a puzzled look, Janine asked, "But if she knows she's using it as an excuse, shouldn't we continue to confront her? We feel we haven't been as consistent as we should be. We don't want her to think she can do whatever she wants."

We acknowledged that more consistency would certainly be helpful, because being inconsistent sends a message that children don't always have to listen to their parents. We explained that we were making an additional suggestion: that Janine and Mike discuss with Marissa the impact her behavior was having on the atmosphere that existed in their home and on her relationship with them.

Janine interrupted. "We've often told her that the way she behaves is causing a lot of tension in our home and that if she would just follow our requests, everyone would get along much better."

Empathizing with Janine, we acknowledged that she and her husband had worked hard to help Marissa be more responsible. But we pointed out that she still kept hearing their message as evidence they were being unfair to her and persecuting her. We emphasized that we were merely trying to figure out a way of approaching Marissa so that she would begin to take more ownership for her behavior and stop blaming her parents.

With a smile, Janine said, "I would love to see that."

We explained that she and Mike would have to realize that the way they had been reminding their daughter to do things wasn't working. We guessed that part of the reason was that Marissa viewed them as unreasonable and the problem as her parents', not her own.

Mike asked, "Well, what should we do?"

We described an approach we have recommended to many parents, including Louise Burns in Chapter 2. We suggested that the Heaths tell Marissa that they feel they haven't conveyed to her the importance of her cooperation in the family and that their constant reminders just seem to be making matters worse.

Once again Janine jumped in, complaining, "That almost seems to be apologizing to Marissa."

We agreed that it could seem that way but assured Janine that there would be more to say to Marissa.

"Like what?"

We explained that a main goal would be for Marissa to see that her behavior was a problem. However, if she continued to hear her parents' message as an accusation, she would immediately feel that they were being arbitrary and unfair. We advised Janine and Mike to find a calm moment and use it to give Marissa the message we had just suggested: how important it was for the three of them to cooperate, as well as the parents' desire to stop nagging. Then they could ask her to identify two or three things she could do differently to help the situation, as well as two or three things her parents could do differently.

Mike chuckled. "I can guess what she'll say. She'll tell us to stop being on her back and punishing her."

We told him it would be good if she said that.

"Good?"

We explained that if she said that, he could tell her that he and her mother didn't want to be on her back or punish her. Mike could also acknowledge that Marissa saw things in the house as being her parents' problem, but that he and Janine felt it to be the whole family's problem to solve.

Keeping in mind the Heaths' early comments, we predicted that Marissa might tell them that the best way to solve the problem would be for them to stop bugging her. We advised Mike and Janine not to worry if she said that. Instead, they should try to remain calm and tell her that their goal was similar to hers—namely, not having to constantly remind her to do things. Then they could add that, just as the two of them were willing to change their approach, they expected her to meet certain responsibilities.

With an air of exasperation, Mike said, "I think we have told her things like that already."

We acknowledged that they very well might have done so, at least to some extent. We explained that we were suggesting changes in their wording, tone of voice, and the timing of what they would say, so that they weren't bringing up the subject during the heat of battle. Although the dialogue we recommended might seem similar to what the Heaths had tried already, our suggestion shifted the emphasis to a problem-solving approach designed to help Marissa appreciate her contribution to the problem and what can be done to resolve the problem.

Janine smiled again and said, "I'm not certain what will happen if we try to do what you're suggesting, but I'm beginning to understand the differences between what Mike and I have done in the past and what you're recommending we do in the future."

At our next session, the Heaths reported what had occurred when they took our advice and sat down with Marissa. They said that the moment they began to speak, Marissa yelled, "Oh, no, not another lecture! I don't want to hear another lecture!"

Rather than taking the bait, the Heaths changed their usual script and calmly responded, "We agree with you. And we don't want to give another lecture. We feel we've been lecturing too much."

Mike reported, "Marissa rolled her eyes when we said that. She seemed to be waiting for another lecture, but it never came. We told her that we felt it would be helpful for all of us to understand the things we were responsible for and what we might do to lessen the tension in our home. At first Marissa didn't seem to be paying attention, but we described a few responsibilities that each of us had. She actually began to listen, especially when we emphasized that one of our goals was to cut out the nagging."

During the next few weeks, the Heaths persisted in this kind of dialogue with Marissa. They avoided angry confrontations but remained consistent in their expectations. They also invited Marissa to think about what expectations she had for them as parents. They said they wanted to get a sense of what changes she felt they could make to improve life in their home. They validated her concerns, but they were careful not to imply that they would agree with all of her suggestions.

We will continue to describe our intervention with the Heaths in the next phase of the problem-solving sequence.

Consider Possible Solutions and Their Likely Outcomes

The process of defining and agreeing about the problem leads naturally to the next step: arriving at possible solutions. You can engage children in this task by speculating about various options. As much as possible, parents should encourage their children to generate the solutions and should try not to dismiss any suggestion unless it goes counter to a nonnegotiable rule.

For instance, if you are discussing how late your ten-year-old child should be permitted to stay up on a school night and the child says 1:00 A.M., you have every right to say, "We know you want to stay up that late, but if you did, we wouldn't be able to get up for school the next day, so we feel that either 9:30 or 9:45 would be the latest. It's your choice." This statement creates limits but still provides your child with some choice. In our experience, when parents build in some leeway, children are much more willing to compromise.

As much as possible, parents should encourage their children to generate the solutions and should try not to dismiss any suggestion unless it goes counter to a nonnegotiable rule.

The Heaths used this strategy with Marissa. After several weeks of discussions that included the parents articulating their expectations, Marissa began to abandon her patented response that things would be better if they simply stopped "bugging" her. She appeared less defensive, most likely in response to her parents' change of strategy. Her parents, rather than becoming angry or giving in to her demands or casting the blame back on her, emphasized that they believed each member of the family had responsibilities to fulfill in their home.

Marissa voiced several options to improve the situation, one of which was intriguing. When the Heaths told us about it, we joked that Marissa must have read a book about parenting and motivation. According to Mike and Janine, Marissa had suggested that the three of them make a list of responsibilities they expected of each other and that every month they alternate these responsibilities. The Heaths preferred this option to another proposed by Marissa, which was that each week she could select a "day off" during which she was absolved from her responsibilities. Actually, this suggestion also included an intriguing element—namely, that each parent would also have a day off and they would all take turns covering for each other. It was a promising option, but the parents felt there was less likelihood of misunderstanding with the first suggestion. However, they were impressed that Marissa was involved in this problem-solving process.

We want to emphasize a point that has been demonstrated by Myrna Shure's problem-solving program: when given the opportunity, even children in the preschool years can arrive at realistic solutions to existing problems. Robert Ashlund, the four-year-old we met in Chapter 2, is an example. He was misbehaving before bedtime, prompting his parents to spank him. Robert was able to share with us the "scary dreams" he was having and that he was afraid to go to sleep and face these dreams. When asked if he had any ideas what might help, he came up with the remarkable suggestions of having a night-light in his room and a photo of his parents by his bedside. These solutions were very effective.

Finally, it is important to recognize that when children are asked for possible solutions to problems, their first response might be "I don't know." In fact, this response may mean they really don't know, or they might be hesitant to offer a solution, uncertain why parents have suddenly asked for their suggestions. Whatever the reason behind "I don't know," an appropriate response from the parents would be "That's OK. I wouldn't expect you to know right away. It's something for you to think about, since I'd really like your thoughts about what steps we can take to help solve the problem." Such a comment reinforces respect for a child's opinion and provides the foundation for the development of effective problem-solving skills.

Find a Way to Remind Each Other to Follow Through

Even when families arrive at solutions and everyone agrees to participate, lapses may occur. Family members may forget what they agreed on or may offer excuses for why they didn't follow through. One of the best remedies to avoid nagging when a family member neglects to do something is to establish a strategy for reminding each other to follow through on the agreed-upon plan.

In our clinical practice and parenting workshops, we advise that once a family has decided on a plan to manage a problem, one of the parents should say, "This sounds great, but since we're human and may forget what we agreed on, how can we remind each other so that we're not nagging each other?" Many parents have attested that asking children how they would like to be reminded helps minimize the impression that parents are breathing down their backs, since the children helped to develop the plan. This strategy works most effectively if parents inform their children how they would like to be reminded should they forget to do something.

Asking children how they would like to be reminded helps minimize the impression that parents are breathing down their backs, since the children helped to develop the plan.

The Heaths applied this strategy with Marissa. After agreeing with her suggestion of alternating responsibilities, they introduced the question of how best to remind each other should they forget to meet a responsibility. Marissa at first contended, "I won't forget."

The parents wisely responded that they didn't expect Marissa to forget, but that it would be best to build in a "safety net" just in case they or Marissa inadvertently did forget. They suggested that if *they* forgot, Marissa could simply remind them in a soft voice.

Marissa's suggestion was that a list of responsibilities be posted in her room and on the refrigerator. She said if she forgot, they could simply say the word *list*. Once this word was uttered, she would check the list to see what she had neglected to do.

We continue to be impressed with the strategies children suggest when encouraged to do so.

Although the Heaths had tried what they perceived to be similar interventions in the past, their new strategies contained important ingredients that were absent from their earlier parenting practices. Not only were they more consistent and less angry, but they actively involved Marissa in the process of solving existing problems. They had initially worried that this involvement might backfire. They worried Marissa might take advantage of their inviting her input and offer even more excuses for not helping out. In fact, the opposite occurred. Marissa felt increasingly empowered, becoming more responsible and accountable for her behavior. The Heaths' change in strategy helped them nurture self-discipline in their daughter.

Plan What to Do if the Solution Doesn't Work

As important as ensuring follow-through is to anticipate and plan for possible roadblocks to the success of a strategy. When we have raised this possibility, some people have wondered, "Why bring up possible obstacles? Can't that be interpreted as a self-fulfilling prophecy of failure?" Our response is that when potential trouble spots are defined, families are better prepared to avoid them, deal with them if necessary, or switch to a backup intervention.

We learned the benefit of foreseeing possible obstacles to success from our interactions with many families. We discovered that ideas with all the markings of brilliant strategies in our office were not as brilliant in actual practice. In addition, we found that when parents and children tried strategies they had helped to design and these strategies proved ineffective, the family often felt more defeated and incompetent and were less disposed to try other interventions. However, families gained a sense of hope and perseverance if they considered likely roadblocks in advance, knowing that if one approach did not work, others might.

The Berkshire Family: Solving the Whining Problem

In Chapter 3 we described several interviews we had with Lisa and Walt Berkshire about their nine-year-old son, Daniel. The Berkshires described Daniel as a "whiner" and often gave in to his demands so that he would stop whining. They saw themselves as "wimps" but wanted to see themselves as having "moxie" or determination. Lisa observed, "Daniel can be so exhausting. He seems to have more energy than us and outlasts us." However, they began to recognize that their disciplinary style was contributing to Daniel's belief that whining pays off. In addition, by not holding their son responsible for his actions, they were robbing him of opportunities to become more self-disciplined and responsible.

Our interventions with the Berkshires were similar to those we used with the Heaths. We advised the Berkshires that consistency was essential for helping Daniel stop whining and develop more effective ways of coping when his demands were not met. We also noted that, although some people would disagree with what we were going to suggest, we believed the best way to begin changing Daniel's behavior would be to have him feel a sense of control in situations actually orchestrated by the parents. We explained that parents can be firm and at the same time give their children a feeling of ownership.

We reviewed our problem-solving approach with the Berk-shires. Like other parents, the Berkshires were convinced that Daniel would contend that the problem was theirs, not his. We agreed that most likely he would blame them.

Lisa said, "The problem-solving approach you suggested seems to make sense, but I'm not sure where to begin."

We advised Lisa and Walt to keep in mind their wish to show moxie and be consistent, as well as their goal to help Daniel become more responsible for his behavior. We reminded them that they wanted Daniel to develop self-discipline and not resort to whining. Also, we recalled, they wanted him to feel a sense of ownership rather than a sense of entitlement.

As we suggest with most families, we advised the Berkshires to find a quiet time in which to point out to Daniel that there had been a lot of arguments in the family. At that time, they could add that they feel they sometimes have gotten angrier than they would like to get and that they plan to change their behav-ior. They could add that sometimes they feel he can whine and whine. That would be the opportunity to ask Daniel whether he saw the whining and anger as a problem.

Walt said, "What if he says that the only problem is our get-ting angry at him? We do get angry, but only after his constant whining."

We acknowledged the possibility that Daniel would blame his parents for all of the problems. Then we suggested looking at each possible response from Daniel, beginning with the possibil-ity of a more positive response, as unlikely as that might be. We advised that if Daniel agreed that he also contributes to the ten-sion and arguments in the home, Walt and Lisa could respond by saying, "Together, we can try to figure out what to do to have fewer arguments." However, if Daniel declared that the prob-lem was his parents', because they would not give him what he wanted and they would yell at him, Walt and Lisa should avoid getting into an argument. They should avoid giving Daniel a list of all the things he had done wrong. Instead, they might say, "We know you think everything would be fine at home if only we changed and gave you everything you wanted, but we believe we all have a responsibility to solve the problem. We're tired of yelling and being angry with each other."

Lisa asked, "And what then?"

We counseled that she and Walt would have to be very specific in mentioning a couple of things they wanted to see change in his behavior and should ask Daniel what he would like to see change in theirs. Then they would ask Daniel what solutions he had for helping with the problem. They shouldn't worry if Daniel couldn't come up with any answers right away. Rather, the goal at this stage would be to begin a process that would last a while. We reminded the Berkshires to keep in mind the goal of helping Daniel develop greater self-discipline.

At our next session, the Berkshires came in looking somewhat defeated. They reported that their attempts to engage Daniel in the dialogue we had suggested were unsuccessful. Walt said, "Daniel kept telling us that all his friends' parents gave them the things he was asking for and he couldn't understand why he couldn't have them. He blamed us."

We asked what happened when Daniel blamed them for the problems.

Lisa hesitantly responded, "Even though we thought we were prepared for any resistance on his part, and even though you had warned us that our approach might not work at first, all of my feelings about being an inadequate mother and his being a brat came up. I guess I lost it and told him he was making our lives miserable. You can imagine that nothing good came from that statement."

Walt said, "I just sat there feeling frustrated. Daniel started to cry and said we didn't love him. I said we did, but we were angry about his behavior. I don't think he got the distinction."

We told the Berkshires that we wished our suggestions in the office would always succeed when they were put into practice in the "real world." We admitted that we probably should have spent more time during the previous session on anticipating what to say or do if Daniel weren't cooperative. We then assured the Berkshires that, even as frustrated and disappointed as they were feeling, it wasn't too late to try again.

Lisa sighed, "What do we have to lose?"

We encouraged the Berkshires to look at what might have been a more helpful response when Daniel blamed them for all the problems in their home. We suggested that sometimes it's best to respond in an unpredictable way if we want children to change their usual responses.

"What do you mean?" asked Lisa.

We pointed out that when she and Walt responded with frustration and anger, it was probably what Daniel had been expecting. We suggested that the next time, they might say, "We're glad you could tell us how you feel. We see things differently than you do, but it helps us to know how you feel." Basically, this response would validate Daniel's comments. We assured the Berkshires that validating would not mean they necessarily agreed with their son's opinion, only that they were trying to understand it.

Walt asked, "And what would follow next?"

We suggested that the Berkshires might tell Daniel that they knew there were things his mother and father could do differently, but they also felt there were some things he could do differently so that all three of them could get along better. We counseled the Berkshires not to worry if Daniel disagreed and said the only people who had to change were his parents. If that happened, they should just say there were changes they would make, but it was important for Daniel to help out as well.

Lisa commented, "I hope Walt and I don't seem like little kids when we ask you for specific things we should say and do, but sometimes we're at a real loss for what to say and do. And we screw things up."

We reassured the Berkshires that we didn't think they were acting like little kids at all. When learning to change our usual scripts, it's often helpful to have concrete suggestions about the contents of a new script. However, as we generally do with parents, we reminded the Berkshires that the new script we were suggesting was more of an outline to provide an idea of what to say. The actual words would vary based on the situation and the child's response.

We continued by advising that, whether or not Daniel took some responsibility for his behavior, Walt and Lisa could let him know that, in the future, if they told him he couldn't have something, they wouldn't change their mind. They could tell him that when they say he can't have something, it would be after they had carefully considered their decision. They should emphasize that it would be Daniel's choice of how to behave. He could continue to whine and have less time to do fun things with them, or he could stop whining, leaving more time for fun things. We emphasized that Walt and Lisa should use the word *choice*, so that Daniel would begin to recognize that he has different options and has some control of the situation.

Lisa said, "It sounds so easy when you say it that way."

Smiling, Walt added, "Maybe we can make a tape about the benefits of Daniel being more cooperative and play it for him while he's asleep. Perhaps he'll get the message subliminally."

We laughed and commented that if taping such a message would work, parenting would be far easier.

The Berkshires entered the following session in a much better mood. They reported that when they had initiated a discussion with Daniel about his whining and behavior, he resorted to blaming them. However, they remained calm and applied the new script we had reviewed during our previous sessions.

Lisa said, "Daniel actually looked bewildered. He was waiting for our typical response and wasn't sure what to say when we gave him a new response. He became more vocal in blaming us. I think he was testing our determination. For once we didn't take the bait, and he walked away. The following day we introduced the discussion again. Once again he blamed us. Once again we didn't take the bait. He walked away, but as he did, we told him that he had a choice: he could speak with us either later that day or the next day. We emphasized the word *choice*."

We praised their careful determination.

Lisa continued, "And much to our surprise, he returned in a few minutes. Even more to our surprise, we had a pretty nice discussion."

Walt added, "I think why we felt so good is that it was one of the first times I can remember that we felt we had a sense of direction and purpose. Even if Daniel hadn't been more cooperative, I still would have felt better."

We reinforced Walt's comment by telling him that we understood how he felt. We explained that people who tend to be optimistic and resilient have a sense of personal control. Resilient people focus on what they can influence and are willing to replace unsuccessful scripts with new scripts. We observed that this kind of focus seemed to be what Walt had experienced with Daniel. Similarly, one of the Berkshires' goals for Daniel was to help him realize that he has choices in life. We and his parents wanted Daniel to learn how to solve problems and make better decisions. We wanted him to develop self-discipline.

During the next few weeks, the Berkshires continued their discussions with Daniel, emphasizing the choices he had and helping him appreciate that he had more to gain from acting cooperatively than from whining. The parents maintained their consistency. They asked Daniel what would help him remember not to whine and to be more cooperative when he was asked to do things. At first he responded that he didn't know. Since the parents knew how much he enjoyed playing games on the computer, they offered a possible incentive. There was a limit of how much time he could spend each day playing these games. They said that if there was no whining during the day and if he had completed all of his homework, as a reward he could have a choice of either an additional ten or fifteen minutes of computer game time.

Walt laughed, noting, "Would it surprise you that Daniel asked if he could have an additional thirty minutes? We simply said it was his choice, but it would be either ten or fifteen minutes. He started to whine when we said this, but he was able to catch himself and selected fifteen minutes."

Lisa jumped in. "I just want to confirm what Walt said in an earlier meeting. Just as he did, I felt so much better because we finally had a sense of direction with Daniel. I know there are going to be bumps in the road and that he won't always cooperate, but I expect we'll be more consistent. And I agree with something you've mentioned several times in the past few weeks that's very important. Our new approach will help Daniel become more disciplined."

We continued to see the Berkshires during the following eighteen months, but as their experiences improved, we moved from meeting weekly to twice a month, and then to once a month. Although some difficult moments arose with Daniel, they were less frequent and less intense than in the past. The Berkshires had truly transformed their disciplinary techniques into an authoritative style.

Problem-Solving Skills: A Basis for Self-Discipline

When disciplinary strategies are rooted in and reinforce problem-solving skills, they are most likely to strengthen self-discipline in your children and give them a feeling of personal control over their lives. For those reasons, parents need to ensure that their manner of discipline strengthens their child's capacity to solve problems.

5

Showing Your Child That He or She Is Competent

As highlighted in previous chapters, if children are to develop self-discipline, they must become accountable for their actions. These actions include their accomplishments as well, and parents can help their children to assume, rather than minimize, credit for them.

The Taunton Family: "A Child Without Joy"

Luke and Meredith Taunton contacted us about their ten-year-old son, Jeremy, at the suggestion of Jeremy's school counselor. During our initial phone call with the Tauntons, they reported that Jeremy was struggling with his schoolwork, especially reading; was quickly provoked into angry outbursts; and bullied smaller children. We set up an appointment to see the parents, and they asked that we speak with Jeremy's counselor, who could provide a more complete picture of what was transpiring in school.

In a phone conversation, Jeremy's counselor said, "Jeremy seems angry a lot of the time, and he often looks very sad. Also, we've noticed that when Jeremy does well on an assignment or in sports and his teachers or coaches compliment him, he quickly minimizes or dismisses their compliments."

We asked the counselor to explain how Jeremy dismissed the compliments.

"Sometimes he says nothing, not even a 'thank-you,' and walks away. Sometimes he contends that he was lucky or that it was no big deal. A couple of times, he has angrily told the teacher not to say anything. When we've discussed Jeremy at our team meetings, we've wondered why he's so quick to reject our compliments."

We asked the counselor whether the team had come up with any explanations.

"A few, but to be honest, we're not sure. Some teachers believe Jeremy doesn't think he deserves positive feedback and thinks that we're not being honest with him when we do give it to him. Other team members think Jeremy might feel we're trying to set him up or manipulate him to do more and more work. Whatever the reason, it's frustrating when you try to compliment him or give him positive feedback and he rejects it."

We asked the counselor about Jeremy's outbursts.

"They seem to come up when he's having trouble with academic work, especially reading. He has actually run out of the room, screaming, 'This is stupid!' On occasion, he has thrown down his book."

We asked whether Jeremy's teacher had found an effective way of dealing with Jeremy's outbursts.

"To some extent. She has reminded him on several occasions that most kids need some help at some point, and rather than throw things or run out of the room, he should just ask her for assistance. Sometimes he has asked her for help, but at other times he has had outbursts. When he throws things or leaves the room, typically the principal or I have spoken softly to him and helped him calm down. He seems to respond, at least for a little while."

The counselor added, "Another problem is his bullying younger kids during recess. Most of his bullying is verbal, but he has on occasion pushed some kids down. When he has been physical, we've immediately contacted his parents. I know you've spoken briefly with his parents and have a meeting set up with them. I should let you know that one of our concerns is that we think they can be overly punitive with Jeremy. Jeremy has an eight-year-old sister, Lucille, who once mentioned to her teacher that her parents yell at Jeremy a lot and sometimes spank him when he's naughty. The teacher assumed Lucille told her this because the yelling and spanking upset her. When her teacher informed me about it, we discussed whether I should contact the parents. I thought we should, given the concerns we had about Jeremy, as well as Lucille's obvious distress. The teacher talked with Lucille, and at first she said she didn't want the teacher or me to call her parents. However, the teacher handled things well and explained to Lucille that we were just trying to help her parents figure out better ways to help Jeremy. So the teacher and I scheduled a meeting with the Tauntons."

We asked the counselor to share the parents' reaction to what Lucille had said.

"Basically they told us that Lucille is a sensitive girl. They didn't deny that sometimes they yell at or spank Jeremy, but the father claimed, 'Jeremy got what he deserved and had to learn how to behave.' When I offered to have a couple of follow-up meetings with them to discuss different ways of responding to Jeremy, they weren't interested."

We asked the counselor to speculate about why the parents were willing to follow through on his recommendation for them to call us.

"I'm not totally sure. During the meeting, the teacher and I really emphasized our ongoing concerns about Jeremy. I told them that sometimes parents prefer to see someone from outside the school rather than a school counselor and asked them their thoughts about that option. They seemed more at ease with seeing someone outside the school system. Also, they were more than willing for me to discuss our concerns with you. The father even said I could let you know what Lucille had told her teacher about the discipline they use with Jeremy."

We thanked the counselor for his observations and told him we would be back in touch after our session with Jeremy's parents.

When we met with Luke and Meredith Taunton, we told them that we had spoken with the school counselor. Meredith asked, "What did he say?"

We first summarized some of the counselor's concerns about Jeremy's behavior in school, including his outbursts, his bullying of younger kids, and his difficulty in accepting positive feedback. Before we could continue, Luke jumped in and asked, "Did he bring up our discipline style?"

We replied that he had.

"What did he say?"

Since the counselor had mentioned the Tauntons' permission to discuss what Lucille had told her teacher, we felt comfortable saying the counselor had told us about Lucille mentioning to her teacher that her parents yelled at Jeremy a lot and spanked him. We also shared the counselor's report that the Tauntons felt their daughter was overly sensitive and that they were giving Jeremy what he deserved.

Somewhat defensively, Meredith said, "Jeremy is a challenging boy. We feel we have to be very firm with him. Sometimes the only thing he seems to respond to is our raising our voice or hitting him on the rear end. To be honest, even though they didn't say it, we think the teacher and school counselor interpreted Lucille's comments to mean we were being harsh or even abusive to Jeremy. We'd be interested in your thoughts."

We explained that one of the things we often talk about with parents is the most effective way to discipline children. Adding that we planned to discuss the subject with Luke and Meredith, we explained that it would be easier for us to offer our thoughts after we had learned more about Jeremy and the Taunton family.

Luke responded, "That makes sense." Then the Tauntons began to tell us about Jeremy. They said that from a very young age, he had been difficult to "soothe or satisfy," often becoming frustrated. When Jeremy was a preschooler, their primary form of discipline was to put him on a chair for time-out. Unfortunately, time-out often didn't work, because he would leave his chair. Luke explained, "That's when we'd spank Jeremy on the rear end. When we spanked him, he'd cry, but then he'd stay on the chair until he calmed down."

Meredith added, "But it just didn't stick."

We asked her to explain.

She replied, "Our punishment didn't stick. He didn't seem to learn from it. He would repeat the same behaviors next time. I got frustrated and started to raise my voice a lot more with him and sometimes would spank him."

We reminded her that she had told us this approach didn't seem effective.

Luke said, "I think the spanking worked better than other things we tried."

We decided to shift from the topic of spanking and turned to their concern that Jeremy became frustrated easily. We asked what kinds of things would frustrate him.

Meredith said, "What stands out most for me is when things didn't seem to go as he wanted. I remember very clearly that, as a toddler, when Jeremy tried to build things with blocks, if the blocks fell, he'd get angry and start to throw them around the room. And, when we told him not to touch something like an electrical outlet, he'd also get angry and would often yell or throw things."

Luke chimed in, "I think the problems got worse once he began school, especially when he was learning to read. As we mentioned, he had and still has a hard time with reading. The school did an evaluation back in the first grade, and they found that he has some reading problems, and they've given him extra help with reading. I'm not sure if it has done much good. By the second grade, we began getting reports that he was throwing his book down and having outbursts."

After speaking for a few more minutes about Jeremy's struggles in school and his problematic behavior, we suggested that we switch gears for a while. We noted that we'd been hearing about some of Jeremy's problems, so we said we'd like to hear about what Jeremy enjoyed doing and what his parents thought he did rather well.

Luke's reply was an interesting observation: "I think it's important to separate what he does well from what brings him pleasure. You just hit on something that has been frustrating to Meredith and me for years. Jeremy is pretty good at several things. He's a good artist and also is good in sports, especially soccer and Little League. Yet he minimizes his success. His counselor probably told you that."

We acknowledged that.

Luke continued, "I know that some kids can be modest and have a little difficulty accepting compliments. Jeremy goes beyond that. It's not just that he doesn't accept compliments, but he doesn't seem to believe them. Or maybe he doesn't feel he deserves them. You'd think, with all of the problems he has, that he'd be thrilled to hear a compliment, that it would bring him joy. Not Jeremy." Luke then offered an unforgettable comment: "Jeremy is a child without joy."

We asked him to explain.

"That's how he seems to Meredith and me. He doesn't seem very happy about any of his accomplishments, even when we think he should be. Just the other day in a soccer game, he made a great move to get around a defender, and he scored a goal.

After the game, I told him what a great move he made and what a great goal he scored. Rather than say thank you or show any joy, do you know how he responded? He said, 'I was lucky. The defender wasn't very good, and he slipped as I started to go by him.' " After a pause, Luke continued, "I was really upset and maybe said some things I shouldn't have said, but I think Jeremy has to hear the truth."

We asked him to share what he had said to his son.

"I said, 'What are you talking about? The move you put on the kid was great, and if he slipped, it was because of how much you faked him out. You have a terrible attitude. Even when you score a goal, you can't just feel good and give yourself some credit. You'd better wake up and change, or you're going to feel miserable your entire life. If you keep the attitude you have right now, maybe you shouldn't even play. None of the other kids are going to like to play with you.' "

We asked Luke to describe Jeremy's reaction.

"He cursed at me and told me I didn't care about him. I told him I cared about him, but not his negative attitude. I told him he was making everyone in the family miserable, and I grounded him for the month. I told him it would give him time to think about his lousy attitude."

As Luke recounted what he had said to his son, his frustration and anger with Jeremy were obvious. Unfortunately, this father's reaction and disciplinary practices were actually contributing to, rather than alleviating, Jeremy's negative outlook on life. As we emphasized in Chapter 3, children with a resilient mindset experience a sense of control over their life. An ingredient of their feeling personal control is that they take realistic credit for their accomplishments. If children (or adults) constantly dismiss their achievements, if they interpret these achievements as resulting from luck or chance or a "defender not being very good and slipping," then they are less likely to feel confident about future success. They are less likely to be resilient. Punishing children for this attitude will not improve their perspective; instead, it might reinforce their feeling that they don't deserve their success.

Who Gets the Credit, and Who Gets the Blame?

To understand this type of mindset possessed by Jeremy and many others, therapists apply a theory that can give parents direction for reforming a child's self-defeating mindset and behaviors. A helpful way to learn about this theory is to think about two experiences you have had: one that resulted in success and another that ended in failure. For each experience, try to identify the factors that, in your opinion, contributed to each outcome. Then notice to what extent you believe you played a role in each outcome.

From the time we are very young children, we encounter numerous tasks and situations that result in either successes or setbacks. Often without realizing it, we give ourselves reasons for these different outcomes—for example, "I'm strong" or "The teacher was unfair." Researchers have discovered that the kinds of reasons we use are strongly linked to an individual's self-esteem and resilience. Their observations form the basis of *attribution theory*, originally proposed by psychologist Bernard Weiner and expanded upon by psychologist Martin Seligman and his colleagues in their study of optimism and pessimism.

Attribution theory places the spotlight on the factors to which we attribute our successes and failures—that is, who or what we give credit to when we succeed and who or what we blame when we fail. In this chapter, we will examine one side of attribution theory: the implications of how we give credit for successes in our lives. In the next chapter, we will consider what attribution theory teaches us about the ways people deal with mistakes.

As we have noted, children with resilient mindsets feel a sense of control over their lives and believe (within reason) that they are masters of their destiny. They share a belief that what transpires in their lives depends greatly on their own choices and decisions. They perceive that success is rooted in their efforts and ability. Research about attribution theory supports this dynamic.

For instance, when children with high self-esteem learn to ride a bicycle, obtain a solid grade in school, score a goal, or perform with distinction in a concert, they typically acknowledge the help

> *Children with resilient mindsets perceive that success is rooted in their efforts and ability.*

and input of adults but believe they are influential participants in determining positive outcomes. They assume realistic credit for their accomplishments.

The picture is markedly different for children burdened by low self-esteem and a lack of confidence. Youngsters such as Jeremy fail to experience success in situations that others would interpret as success. As a result of their temperament, negative feedback they have received, unrealistic expectations, or ineffective disciplinary practices, they are quick to minimize their achievements, attributing the outcome to luck or chance—that is, to factors outside their control. When this kind of mindset dominates children's thinking, they are more vulnerable to future self-doubt and less likely to deal with setbacks effectively. Instead, they resort to coping strategies that worsen their plight, such as avoiding or quitting a task.

Look for Islands of Competence

Attribution theory gives parents valuable guideposts for disciplining their children. Not only does it suggest specific strategies for dealing with negative behaviors, as we shall see in the next chapter, but it also reminds us to distinguish discipline from punishment. Remember, two of the most powerful forms of effective discipline are the use of positive feedback and encouragement and a focus on prevention, rather than reaction.

In this instance, parents should use a preventive approach by encouraging and reinforcing their children's strengths—what we call "islands of competence." The more that children are engaged in activities in which they use their strengths, the less time they have available for self-defeating or counterproductive behaviors, and the less interest they have in getting involved in such behaviors. Also, the specific words and comments parents use when reinforcing their children's islands of competence will shape the attributions for success that their children learn and take to heart.

> *The more that children are engaged in activities in which they use their strengths, the less time they have available for self-defeating or counterproductive behaviors, and the less interest they have in getting involved in such behaviors.*

Many parents have validated our belief that a focus on building up their child's strengths prevents the display of negative behavior. For example, several years ago, a mother told us about her son, who was struggling with learning problems and depression and having difficulty in school. She attended one of our presentations, and when she heard us talk about islands of competence, she recognized that she had been "punishing him for school failure" by taking away after-school activities that he enjoyed.

As her remarks remind us, parents' strategies to discipline and motivate children and adolescents can unintentionally punish suffering youngsters, rather than help them develop a sense of self-worth and dignity. Wisely, this mother not only stopped removing particular activities, but she encouraged her son to engage in after-school experiences that he found especially enjoyable and rewarding, such as skiing.

She wrote to us later to report that she had shifted her mindset and behavior from a punitive approach to encouragement of her son's involvement in one of his islands of competence (skiing), with a wonderful outcome: "This resulted in a five-year position on National Ski Patrol, which led to an interest in EMT and paramedic training. It further provided other ways for him to feel success. He is now a third-year student and has wonderful self-esteem! School is still very challenging, but the life skills he learned gave him experience to carry over into goals and to persevere. This is the experience and information I enjoy sharing with other parents and teachers."

Raising a Compassionate Man

A mother who heard one of our talks later wrote to tell us about her son. Her words reflect the importance of shifting from a negative to a positive perspective:

Dear Dr. Brooks,

It was my pleasure to hear you speak in Florida around 1997. At that time I was just beginning to cope with my son's learning disability. Not only did he struggle with ADHD, he was color blind and spoke as if he had a mouth full of marbles, trying to get everything out all at once. I sat in your audience as a participant from the school district I worked for at the time. You had me. You had me at "islands of competence." I left that seminar and went home with a different attitude, a fresh attitude about what my son would possibly achieve vs. what I was being told the likelihood of success for him would be—incidentally, that at most he would be at a fourth-grade level academically.

If what you are doing is not having a positive effect, why continue to do it? The definition of insanity is doing the same thing over and over and expecting different results. We must think outside the box. The first thing I changed was my outlook. I began focusing on my son's abilities rather than his disability. Rather than yielding to frustrations, I concurred with him and encouraged him to expect to be frustrated but to do the best he could. In time the ready-to-quit attitude was replaced by a deep, stern nose into the wind.

continued

I write to you now the mother of a man. He is beautiful, awesome, handsome, and talented. There is a compassionate side to his personality that I don't believe would be there had he not struggled and succeeded with his own unique learning differences. My son graduated from high school. He is also the recipient of the President's Academic Award for achieving As in his senior year. He is going to college too!

We believe that shifts such as this mother's promote not only self-dignity and self-esteem but also an enhanced sense of responsibility and ownership for one's life.

Noah: "I Like to Cook"

When we first evaluated Noah, he was a pleasant eight-year-old with significant learning disabilities. Despite his struggles in school, Noah was fortunate to possess a great smile and the ability to relate equally well to children and adults. His parents held postgraduate degrees and vowed to do everything possible to help their son succeed in school and someday graduate from college. Noah had two older siblings who excelled in school. Year after year, with a smile on his face, Noah spent countless hours after school and during the summer working to catch up and keep up with his classmates.

We met during his junior year in high school and asked him how things were going.

"Great," Noah responded, "but school is getting harder. I want to go to college like my brother and sister and parents, but I worry about failing."

We asked Noah if he had failed in the past.

"No, but in college you have to stand on your own two feet—no special classes or, for that matter, mothers to check up on you."

We described to Noah the types of support services available to college students with learning disabilities. He seemed relieved. During a later visit, we spoke with his college counselor about finding the right school for Noah. During his senior year in high school, Noah applied to and was accepted by a small, private liberal arts college.

That fall Noah went off to college with great optimism. His mother called us about two months into the term and asked if we could complete an updated assessment when Noah came home over the Christmas holidays. Despite academic support, Noah was struggling to keep up with the pace of instruction. On all other fronts, he had made a very good adjustment to school. His academic counselor hoped we could identify further strategies to help Noah. We agreed to test Noah but informed his mother that we would like to meet with Noah and his parents before the testing. They agreed.

Six weeks later, Noah and his mother came for that appointment. His father was out of town on business but conveyed his support of Noah via e-mail. In his message, he wondered if college was the right choice for Noah.

Noah greeted us with a handshake and a winning smile. He said, "I've probably taken more tests in my life than all the kids in my graduating class combined, but if you think there's a test that can help me be more successful in college, I'll take it."

We first asked Noah about his successes at college. He had made a good group of friends, participated in intramural sports, and enjoyed his classes. Despite his hard work, he was generally receiving Cs. He added, "I know you've told me over the years that I should focus on the effort, not the outcome, but college is expensive, and I feel like I'm letting my parents down when I earn a C."

We turned to Noah's mother and asked her to say whether she felt let down.

"Absolutely not," she answered, taking Noah's hand. "We just want you to be happy and enjoy whatever you do."

We took the initiative and asked Noah what he liked to do.

Noah paused for a moment and then replied, "I like to cook."

We remembered the chocolate cake Noah had baked for our office staff a number of years before. We asked him if he liked cooking enough to want to make a career in the culinary arts.

"I think so, but I feel like I would be letting my family down if I don't attend college."

As we expected, Noah's mother spoke. "If you want to be a chef, then that's what you should do. Your father and I love you and will support you."

A great weight seemed to be lifted from Noah's shoulders. Instead of starting testing, we spent the remainder of the hour exploring culinary arts programs at local colleges. Noah decided not to return to the liberal arts college, even though the decision meant he wouldn't see his new friends. He began taking classes the next semester at a local culinary arts program, applied for full-time admission, and was accepted. In this program he blossomed. We didn't hear from Noah again for several years, until we received a letter and newspaper clipping from his mother.

Noah's mother wrote, "You changed my son's life, our lives. Noah completed the culinary arts degree and went to work in San Francisco. He changed jobs a number of times, each time getting a promotion. Better yet, he loves what he does. Noah moved to St. Louis last year at the invitation of an investor to open his own restaurant. This year it was voted the best new restaurant in St. Louis. Thank you."

A few weeks later, we received a postcard from Noah. On the front was a picture of his restaurant.

Learn—and Appreciate—Your Child's Strengths

These vignettes capture the importance of identifying and reinforcing your children's islands of competence. Here's an exercise we typically suggest to parents: Make a list of at least three of your child's islands of competence. Next to each item on the list, write the ways in which you honor and reinforce these islands.

Unfortunately, we have worked with many parents who do not value the particular strengths of their child. That attitude often reinforces their child's negative behavior. For example, in one family, the parents favor athletic prowess but have a son who prefers artwork. In another, the parents value academics while their teenage daughter struggles with schoolwork but finds enjoyment and success in working at a pet store and caring for animals.

To help parents become aware of not valuing their child's strengths, we ask them to create a list of what they wish were their child's strengths. Then we have them compare their wish list with their list of what they view as their child's actual strengths. We ask, "How close is what you perceive to be your child's strengths to what you wish they were?"

In most instances, there is some discrepancy between the two lists. If the differences are small, parents can more easily make appropriate adjustments in their expectations. If the discrepancies are noteworthy, the child is acutely aware of the parents' disappointment when he or she doesn't meet expectations. Children also recognize when their parents view their successes as unimportant or irrelevant. In such a scenario, parent-child relationships suffer, and children are filled with anger and sadness. The conditions are set for children to behave in ways that invite parents to use increasingly punitive measures. Families then suffer from a negative cycle of anger and acting out followed by harsh discipline.

Throughout our writings, we have emphasized that parents must learn to accept their children for who they are, not what the parents had hoped they would be. We have worked with countless families in which the disciplinary

> *Parents must learn to accept their children for who they are, not what the parents had hoped they would be.*

issues displayed by children were rooted, in part, in the parents' inability to feel and communicate joy in their children's interests and accomplishments.

The Breem Family: Surprised by a "Singing Gene"

Lilly and Paul Breem are an example of parents who could adjust their expectations for their two sons and, in the process, demonstrated that discipline is most effective when housed within an accepting, loving relationship. Both of the Breems had grown up as star athletes and students. They expected their two sons to follow in their footsteps, demonstrating successes in the same areas. When we met the Breems, Lilly said with a laugh, "Our sons came from a great gene pool that seemed destined to produce great athletes and scholars. Maybe I should have checked Paul's genes before we decided to have children."

With a smile, Paul replied, "That's the line I usually use, but I say we should have checked Lilly's genetic line."

They explained that their fourteen-year-old, Phillip, displayed the same islands of competence as they did. His accomplishments matched their wishes for him. However, the story was different for Wade, their twelve-year-old. Wade's grades were average at best, and he demonstrated little interest or proficiency in sports, although he was willing to participate in youth leagues in the town where they lived. At first, Paul and Lilly were surprised and even disappointed, since Wade's journey was taking him down a different path from the one they had taken or that Phillip was currently traveling.

When parents' dreams for their children are not realized, many of those parents fall into using negative scripts. However, much to their credit, the Breems displayed the insight and courage to change their perspective. They considered Wade's interests, which turned out to be in the fields of singing and acting. They gathered information about classes that Wade might take to learn more about acting and improve his skills. They also encouraged him to take singing lessons, which he was happy to do.

Lilly joked, "We're not sure where Wade's singing genes came from, since everyone in my family and Paul's family is tone deaf."

This story of acceptance and focus on strengths went further. The Breems did not harp on Wade's less-than-exemplary grades, although they did set clear expectations for him to complete his homework and be prepared for school. They displayed delight in his singing skill and recorded several of his songs to send to each set of grandparents. They attended his plays, and just as they expressed to Phillip how proud they were of his achievements in sports and academics, they let Wade know how proud they were of his musical accomplishments. They acknowledged his many hours of practice and rehearsal. Through their words, they reinforced his feeling of ownership of his success.

Wade truly enjoyed and felt responsible for his success. This success might not have been in the areas that the Breems had originally anticipated, but they were able to recognize early in their sons' lives that each was different and each could achieve success and joy with parental support in his own areas of interest and expertise.

The White Family: An "Embarrassing" Love of Gardening

When parents fail to adjust their expectations and to honor their children's islands of competence, disciplinary problems are likely to result. Parents must learn that one of the best preventive disciplinary techniques is to appreciate, nourish, and harness their children's natural inclinations and strengths. When children are not noticed for their strengths, they will soon be noticed for their negative behaviors as their anger and resentment build up.

> *Parents must learn that one of the best preventive disciplinary techniques is to appreciate, nourish, and harness their children's natural inclinations and strengths.*

In our clinical practice, we encountered a graphic example of a lack of acceptance of a child's islands of competence when we met Paige and Mitchell White and their thirteen-year-old son, George. George had been referred to us because he had set a fire at school. Of course, setting fires is serious, but this misdeed was a very "controlled" act of fire setting. George had found an empty room at school, lit one piece of paper on fire, and carefully placed it in a wastebasket to burn itself out. He left the classroom door open, inviting discovery of his action. Given the details, the incident seemed to have the flavor of a cry for help, rather than an attempt to burn down the school.

Paige and Mitchell described George as shy and said he tended to be a loner, had few friends, and was barely passing his classes in school. George experienced difficulty with both fine and large motor skills, so he wasn't interested in engaging in sports. Reading and writing were a struggle for him. In contrast, George's sixteen-year-old sister, Linda, had an easy temperament, excellent interpersonal skills, and many friends. She was a star athlete and an A student.

When we met the Whites, it was evident that they not only felt angry with and disappointed in George but also had set into motion a "good child–bad child" dynamic similar to what we witnessed in the previous chapter with the Wilkinses and their two daughters, Melanie and Patty. For every negative description the Whites offered of George, they provided a positive, loving description of Linda. They constantly seemed to be pleading, "Why can't George be more like Linda?"

In one of our parent sessions, we asked the Whites to describe their own childhoods and adult lives. Not surprisingly, their life experiences and personality styles resonated with the script that Linda was manifesting in all aspects of her life.

Mitchell said, "I was on two teams in high school and still found the time for my studies. George does nothing extra and still can't seem to find enough time to complete his schoolwork."

Paige told a similar story, noting that she had been involved in many activities outside of school. "In college I was the class president one year. Although I had many additional responsibilities, I not only found time for school but also pledged a sorority and worked part-time. George was fired from his only part-time job after just a week because he was late every day."

"If George wanted to, he could turn his life around," Mitchell opined with obvious frustration.

It was evident the Whites had difficulty understanding the challenges that George faced, although the school psychologist had in the past reviewed his learning, motor, and social problems. When we discussed what the school psychologist had told them about George's learning and social problems, Paige and Mitchell could accurately recall many of the details of the discussion. However, their interpretation of his problems was that, even with these problems, he could succeed "if he wanted to."

Mitchell commented, "George is lazy and always has been. He never assumes responsibility. He blames everyone else for his shortcomings."

As we do in our sessions with parents, we wanted to move the discussion away from George's problems to what the parents viewed his strengths to be. We commented that we wanted to shift gears from discussing some of George's problems. Explaining that we find it helpful to hear about a child's strengths, we asked the parents what George did well.

The Whites shrugged, and we sensed discomfort as they glanced at each other. We varied our question by asking what George really enjoyed doing. We asked the Whites to identify what George would choose to do over any other activity.

In almost every instance, when we ask parents to tell us what they perceive as the strengths of their child, they can do so without hesitation. Although parents consult us about their child's difficulties, they are typically eager to discuss their child's strengths. A parent once remarked, "I'm glad you asked about my daughter's interests and strengths. It's so easy when you come for an appointment with a psychologist to just talk about her problems. Even though I know my daughter is having a hard time with school and friends and often says she's a loser, it's important for us not to forget that she has many wonderful qualities."

However, the Whites did not eagerly respond to our question about George's strengths. Instead, they again glanced at each other uncomfortably. Mitchell then said something unusual: "We're somewhat embarrassed to tell you. We just don't think it's the kind of activity that a thirteen-year-old boy should be spending much of his time doing."

We interpreted Mitchell's discomfort as an indication that he was referring to some type of antisocial behavior. Fortunately, this wasn't the case. Rather, his reluctance to describe his son's island of competence reflected the difficulty he and his wife were having in accepting George's temperament and interests. Mitchell finally said, "He likes to garden and take care of plants. That would be OK if he did well in school and was involved in other activities. How can a thirteen-year-old boy be so interested in plants?"

We responded that it was evident how upset they were. We added that we were pleased they could share with us their feelings about George's activities. However, we commented that George's interest in horticulture was not as unusual as they believed. We suggested there might even be ways they could join him in these activities so they could help him manage other areas of his life more successfully.

Rather than find fault with the Whites' reactions to their son, we tried to help them understand how their mindset was trapping them in a negative script that unintentionally was leading George to act out. They were blinded by their image of an "ideal" child, one that George could not come close to fulfilling. By the same token, it was easy for them to accept and take pride in Linda because her temperament and behavior matched their own.

In our sessions with the Whites, we helped them understand their unrealistic expectations for George, the source of these expectations, and the frustration and anger that these unmet hopes had bred. Their anger was expressed through the words they used when disciplining George, words that added to George's feelings of failure and his anger. We interpreted the act of setting the fire in school as both an expression of George's anger and a cry for recognition and help. We emphasized George's care to set the fire in a wastepaper basket so it wouldn't get out of hand.

The Whites' disappointment in George was deeply entrenched. Even though they could list his learning and social problems, they constantly returned to the belief that their son "could improve if he wanted to." At first they had difficulty appreciating that George desperately wanted to be accepted by them but knew that their acceptance and love were conditional, based upon his meeting expectations that he wasn't capable of meeting.

However, to their credit, the Whites continued their parent counseling sessions and slowly began to accept George's strengths. Mitchell made a point of asking George to show him how to take care of certain plants, one of which he took to his office. He let George know that the plant was "thriving" in the office, thanks to George's advice. Positive feedback like this and encouraging messages from his parents led to an improvement in Paige and Mitchell's relationship with George, and his anger subsided.

All youngsters are hungry for words of approval and acceptance from their parents. Such words are a powerful disciplinary force, more so than punishment and negative comments.

Give Credit for Successes

Parents have countless opportunities to shape their children's attributions about their accomplishments. Resilient children take credit for their success when that is realistic. A guiding principle is that parents should offer experiences and comments that show children they are active participants in their lives—especially that their successes greatly depend on their own efforts and talents.

Manny Spillane understood this. This father eagerly anticipated the first snowfall of the winter. When enough snow had
accumulated, he herded his three children outside to help build
the "family's snowman." It was a joy to observe the children work
with their father. He skillfully engaged them in creating the different parts of the snowman and asked them what they might use
as eyes or a nose. His enjoyment was apparent, especially when
he posted a sign in front of the snowman that read, "Our snowman welcomes you to the Spillanes'." When neighbors passed,
he would say matter-of-factly in front of his children, "Look
at the wonderful work my kids did." Manny's parental displays
of support and encouragement were not confined to the winter
and snowfalls. In spring, he would plant seeds with them, and as
the plants blossomed, he would compliment the children on the
lovely job they had done.

While some may question why we consider these seemingly small gestures of appreciation as forms of discipline, they
indeed qualify as disciplinary practices. We must move away
from definitions of discipline that are actually definitions of
punishment. Rather, discipline is a process of teaching, and
children learn best in an atmosphere in which their achievements and successes are noted. When parents communicate
to their children that the children have within themselves the
ability to find ways to succeed and solve problems, the children
are more likely to incorporate and apply this integral ingredient
of a resilient mindset.

As Manny Spillane demonstrated, parents have ample opportunities to convey these positive messages to their children. Of
course, we must avoid overly praising our children for every little
accomplishment, lest the praise become meaningless. Even so, we
can find many situations in which it is appropriate to say, "Nice
job," "You figured that out all by yourself," "You really stuck
with it and succeeded," or "I know I helped a little, but much of
the credit belongs to you." These and similar observations rein-

force a realistic ownership of one's success, which should always be a goal of discipline within a strength-based model.

The Tauntons: Learning to Praise

During our initial meeting with Luke and Meredith Taunton, we decided that it might be useful to hold several more sessions with the two of them before including Jeremy and perhaps Lucille. We wanted to assess the parents' ability to modify their mind-set and disciplinary style. We said we wanted to discuss possible strategies they might use to help Jeremy to manage his frustration and anger and to accept and appreciate his achievements.

In our second session, we acknowledged how frustrating Jeremy could be to his parents. We described the different temperaments with which children are born and noted that their description of Jeremy strongly suggested that he came into this world with what is called a "difficult" style.

In an empathic way, we observed that some children can be so challenging that they seem to invite a stricter discipline style. Other children, such as Lucille (according to her parents' description), just seem to know what is expected of them and follow through on our requests. They invite more positive feedback. Usually parents have a more relaxed relationship with these children and enjoy spending time with them.

Luke interrupted, "I agree, but even when we've tried to compliment Jeremy, he rejects what we have to say. After a while, Meredith and I feel, 'Why bother saying anything positive? It seems to make Jeremy angrier, which then makes us angrier, since he rejected our positive comments.' I hope I'm being clear."

We assured Luke that he was very clear. We encouraged Luke and Meredith to think of dealing with two main problems. One was how they could begin giving Jeremy positive feedback in a way that he would be less likely to reject, and the other was how they could begin to hold him accountable for his behavior in a way that might be more successful than it had been. We phrased our thoughts in a way that would reinforce the belief that our goal to help Jeremy be more responsible for his actions matched their goal while suggesting that a new approach was needed.

Meredith asked, "Do you think we've been too harsh with Jeremy? We think the people at school do, especially after what Lucille told them."

We expressed our understanding of the Tauntons' frustration but pointed out that what they had been doing hadn't been working. While they wanted a closer relationship with Jeremy, yelling and spanking drove a wedge between them and their son. Also, as the parents themselves had observed, Jeremy's behavior wasn't improving.

Luke retorted, "But after we yell or even hit his rear end, he does seem better."

We reminded him that the improvement was only temporary. Being yelled at or spanked might startle Jeremy, perhaps even scare him, but it didn't seem to have any long-term benefits. Also, it seemed to be upsetting their daughter, Lucille.

Luke asked, "What would you suggest instead?"

We proposed two main ideas. First was that the parents take a more systematic approach that emphasized Jeremy's strengths. We warned the Tauntons that this would take time. To begin with, Jeremy would have to learn that his outbursts and his rudeness toward his parents were not acceptable.

Before we could finish that point, Luke interrupted. "We've told him that hundreds of times. He just doesn't listen; that's why we end up yelling at him."

We acknowledged that the parents had told Jeremy hundreds of times that his rudeness and outbursts were unacceptable. Adding that we shared Luke and Meredith's goal to end these kinds of behavior, we explained that what was different was our idea for the best way to achieve that goal. (Identifying goals we have in common with parents is an important way to encourage the parents to collaborate with us in trying new strategies.)

Luke apologized for the interruption, and we expressed our understanding of his frustration.

Meredith said, "We are *very* frustrated." Tears filled her eyes as she lamented, "I can't speak for Luke, but I know I've felt like such a failure as a mother with Jeremy. The only thing that makes me feel better is when I think about how easy Lucille has been. Maybe I've done something right."

Luke replied, "I don't really feel like a failure with Jeremy. I think we've done what we can do, and he has to begin growing up."

We told the Tauntons that when children show some of the difficulties Jeremy had, parents may experience many different emotions, including discouragement (feeling like a failure), frustration, and anger. We explained that although it's important for parents to recognize these feelings, it also would be important for Luke and Meredith to figure out whether there were other ways of dealing with Jeremy. Our shared goals were for Jeremy to learn to be more responsible—and also more joyful. Based on what the parents had said, he seemed to be an unhappy boy.

Meredith confirmed our statement. We returned to sharing our recommendations. We repeated our opinion that it was important for Jeremy to realize that his rudeness and outbursts were not acceptable and would lead to certain consequences. However, we advised that the consequences be something other than the parents yelling, screaming, or spanking. We recommended that the parents instead discuss with Jeremy that they knew he got upset, but the way he showed he was upset was unacceptable. As a general principle, they could tell Jeremy that when he behaved in that way, he would lose something, whether a privilege or something he liked to do. We left it up to the parents to decide what the consequence should be. But we advised them to present these ideas with words emphasizing that his behavior would lead to the consequence, and the consequence would not be an arbitrary action on the parents' part.

Luke wondered, "How do we do that? Anytime we punish Jeremy, he quickly accuses us of being unfair, and he'll often throw in that we love Lucille more. We tell him we love him but it's easier to be with Lucille, since she doesn't have tantrums and isn't rude."

We replied that although it would take time to change Jeremy's view, it was important to try. We suggested they start by using certain words. Whenever the Tauntons told Jeremy that his outbursts and some of the things he said were unacceptable, they should inform him of what he would lose, emphasizing, "It's your choice. If you act this way, you will lose a certain privilege. You're really choosing whether you lose the privilege, since we think you can begin to learn better ways of handling your anger."

Meredith smiled and said, "I'm smiling because when you say it that way, it sounds so reasonable and logical, but I keep wondering if it will work with Jeremy."

Since she was smiling, we responded in a lighthearted way that we didn't expect Jeremy to say, "Thank you for your new approach; it will help me to see the light and change my behavior." Rather, we invited them to be suspicious if such an overly polite reaction occurred. We cautioned the Tauntons that when parents change their usual way of responding to their children, the children's behavior may actually become worse for a short time, because they are testing the parents' resolve. But we added that, in our experience, once children realize that the parents are determined not to give in, they slowly begin to change their behavior.

Before moving on to a discussion of possible consequences for Jeremy, we turned the topic to our second main strategy, aimed at helping Jeremy feel more comfortable accepting compliments and feel better about himself. We suggested to the Tauntons that this change would be easier for Jeremy if he felt his parents were less punitive and fairer toward him. Helping Jeremy appreciate his strengths would go hand in hand with the way Luke and Meredith handled his outbursts and his other negative behaviors.

Luke reminded us, "As we've said, Jeremy seems to have a knee-jerk reaction to our compliments. The school counselor said the same thing happens in school."

We replied that we have worked with many children whose responses to compliments are similar to Jeremy's. Sometimes it seems easier not to compliment them at all, since any positive feedback seems to invite a negative response. But if they deserve to be complimented and we hesitate to do so, our lack of response only reinforces a negative outlook. For that reason, we focus on finding a way that parents can compliment their child without prompting the son or daughter to immediately reject or minimize the compliment. We addressed Jeremy's case by expanding on that goal with this question: How can we say and do things so that Jeremy might begin to experience some joy and feeling of accomplishment? That question was based on our belief that joyful children are less likely to be angry and act negatively.

Meredith said, "If we could help change Jeremy's pessimistic view of himself, that would be wonderful. I know we've been comparing Jeremy with Lucille, and probably that's not fair, but it's such a pleasure to compliment Lucille and see the smile on her face."

We agreed that it feels great when our kids respond to our positive feedback with a smile or a "thank-you," and we reminded Meredith that this was one of our goals for Jeremy. While he might never be as enthusiastic in his response as other children, including his sister, we believed he could learn to be more content with his achievements.

Now that we had laid the foundation for offering specific strategies, we shared one of our favorite ideas: to prepare Jeremy in advance for the compliment. We discussed a couple of ways of doing this. First, the Tauntons could say to Jeremy that they had something they wanted to say to him, but that they wanted him to let them know if he disagreed. Then the parents would offer positive feedback about something Jeremy had done.

Luke objected, "But we know he will disagree."

We agreed that he probably would. But asking Jeremy in advance to say whether he disagreed with something they thought he might disagree with—strange as it might seem— actually would lessen the knee-jerk response and make him less defensive. This kind of question would allow Luke and Meredith to enter into a discussion with their son about the disagreement. In general, when children disagree, as they often do, we advise parents to say, "I'm glad you told me how you feel, but we have a different view of things. Let's talk about it." At that point, parents can offer another one of our favorite strategies.

Hearing that we had another strategy, Luke asked, "What's that?"

We replied that instead of getting angry with our kids and lecturing them that they don't appreciate us, we can say, "I feel a little stuck. I think you did a great job with that, and I want to let you know, but I find that the moment I try to give you positive feedback, you quickly disagree. I keep wondering if there is any way I can compliment you without you quickly disagreeing." We added a caution that if the Tauntons were to say something like that, they shouldn't expect Jeremy to give an answer. Most likely he would say, "I don't know. Stop bugging me." The important objective would be to introduce an important question and set the stage for a future constructive discussion. In doing this, parents should avoid invalidating feelings. For example, if parents tell a sad child that there is no reason for him or her to be sad, the child won't listen. We've never met anyone—child or adult— who liked to be told how he or she should feel or should respond to our positive feedback.

Luke said, "I just can't understand why Jeremy wouldn't be happy when someone praised him."

We agreed that his reaction was perplexing and expressed hope that the reasons might become clearer at some point. However, we added, even before he and Meredith figured out what those reasons might be, they could begin to change the way they usually interacted with him. We shared the comments of one of our teenage patients: "You can't force compliments down my throat."

Meredith exclaimed, "A teenager actually said that?"

We assured her that this was a genuine comment, adding that in this teenager's case, the parents had to use the strategies we had suggested the Tauntons apply with Jeremy to change his mindset.

Although Luke especially had reservations about the outcome of following our recommendations, he recognized that the approach he and his wife had followed for years was ineffective and contributed to the tension in the household. They both realized that changes had to be made and that before they could expect Jeremy to change, they had to examine what they could do differently. We discussed how their taking the initiative to modify their approach was not a sign of giving in (a concern voiced by Luke), but rather showed they had the courage to make changes in order to set the tone for Jeremy to take greater ownership and responsibility for his life.

We will continue our therapeutic journey with the Tauntons in Chapter 9. That process included individual sessions with Jeremy and Lucille, as well as family sessions. As will be evident, the interventions we suggested to help the parents set consequences for Jeremy's unacceptable behavior were done in a way that would permit Jeremy to learn from their discipline rather than resent it. Guidelines that made this possible included not punishing Jeremy for feeling sad or for having difficulty accepting positive feedback. Most importantly, on this last point, we wanted to help the Tauntons learn ways to communicate with Jeremy so that he didn't immediately dismiss compliments, but instead could begin to accept the acknowledgment of his achievements offered by his parents, teachers, and others. If this occurred, we felt sure, his negative behavior and depressive demeanor would slowly change.

The Joy of Building on Islands of Competence

When we are frustrated with our children's actions, we often become trapped in a negative disciplinary script that invites a punitive approach and maintains anger and frustration among family members. In contrast, if discipline is to promote increased responsibility, the words and actions of parents and other caregivers must heighten children's belief that their successes are based on their own resources and efforts. When children appreciate what they have accomplished and engage in activities that heighten a sense of joy (their islands of competence), they have less time for unacceptable behaviors that alienate them from others.

6

Teaching Your Child How to React to Mistakes

As we emphasized in the previous chapter, not all children experience success in the same way. Some, such as Jeremy Taunton, meet success and subsequent praise with discomfort and denial rather than excitement and joy. Similarly, the response to mistakes also varies from one child or parent to the next and is influenced by a parent's disciplinary style.

When we evaluate children, we typically ask parents how their child responds when he or she makes a mistake or when something doesn't go right. We have found that one of the most effective ways of evaluating self-esteem and the presence of a resilient mindset is to assess how children perceive and cope with setbacks that are a natural part of growing up. As you'll see, those who learn to deal with mistakes in different ways display different levels of self-discipline.

How Children Respond to Mistakes

Let's look at two eleven-year-old girls, Mia and Charlotte. Both failed a math test. Mia went to see her teacher and said, "I'm really having trouble with math, but I think I can learn some of the things that are confusing me. I just need some extra help." In sharp contrast, Charlotte told herself, "I could be a good math student, but my teacher doesn't know how to teach, and she makes up stupid tests. I don't know how they could let her teach."

Both girls played on a youth basketball team, where both missed making some baskets and foul shots during the course of a few games. Mia approached her coach and said, "I don't know what it is. I know I can shoot better than I have been. Maybe I'm not holding my hands the right way when I'm shooting. If you notice anything, please let me know, and I'll keep practicing." But Charlotte told her coach, "I think there's something wrong with the basketballs they've been using the last few weeks. Also, I've been getting fouled a lot, and the refs aren't calling it. I'd be one of the best scorers if the refs did a better job."

In response to Mia's struggles with math and basketball, her parents said, "We know you're having some difficulties right now, but we think things can improve with whatever help we or your coach or teacher can give you. Everyone has slumps at times, even professional athletes."

The reaction of Charlotte's parents was more negative. After one basketball game, which occurred on the same day she brought home a failing math test, her father yelled, "You always give up and make excuses. You don't even try." Charlotte retorted, "I do try. The teacher can't teach, and the refs stink." Her father replied, "There you go again—always blaming others. Maybe you have to face the fact that you're not good in math or in basketball!" Charlotte yelled back, "You always blame me! I hate you!" Her father responded, "Don't give me any more of your lip. You're grounded for the next month. You'd better learn how to speak with me!"

The comments offered by Mia's parents promoted a healthy attitude about mistakes and setbacks. While Charlotte's father was accurate about her inability to assume responsibility for her mistakes, the way in which he approached and disciplined her contributed to her becoming more defensive and angry and less capable of managing mistakes. Just as parental forms of discipline can significantly influence children's understanding of their success, disciplinary practices also have a major impact on the way youngsters interpret their mistakes and setbacks.

> *As parents, we influence the ways in which our children form their views about mistakes and can help children who are more negative by nature (given their inborn temperament) to adopt a more positive perspective.*

Some might contend that Mia's and Charlotte's parents responded in the ways that they did because the two girls had such differing outlooks and behaviors. For example, if you have a child with a positive attitude, it's easier to respond in a positive way to that child. Certainly, that belief is valid. But as parents, we influence the ways in which our children form their views about mistakes and can help children who are more negative by nature (given their inborn temperament) to adopt a more positive perspective about the presence of obstacles and mistakes.

Who Gets the Blame for Mistakes?

As we saw in Chapter 5, attribution theory helps us understand how people give credit for success; it also applies to the ways people assign blame for failures. Applying this theory to the contrasting mindsets of Mia and Charlotte, it is obvious that, especially if the task is realistically achievable, Mia attributes mistakes to factors that can be modified, such as applying more effort in a particular situation or using more productive strategies. Children such as Mia perceive parents and other adults (for example, teachers or coaches) as being available to help them rather than accuse or punish them. These children are comfortable seeking help when necessary. They possess one of the most important features of self-discipline and a resilient mindset: the belief that adversity can lead to growth, that difficult situations can be viewed as challenges rather than as stresses to avoid, and that there are solutions to problems.

While resilient and self-disciplined children persevere with difficult tasks, they have the insight and courage to recognize when a task may present demands that are beyond their current ability. However, at such times, rather than feeling dejected or defeated, these children remain optimistic and direct their energies toward other tasks that are within their capacity. They also appreciate that challenges appearing insurmountable at one time may not be so in the future. An air of hope and realism dominates their mindset and lives.

In contrast, children like Charlotte are unable to see the possible opportunities associated with mistakes. These children perceive mistakes as resulting from factors that cannot be easily changed, such as a lack of ability, low intelligence, outside interference, or "unfairness." Their mindset lacks an air of optimism. Instead, their perspective is dominated by what psychologist Martin Seligman refers to as *learned helplessness*—that is, the belief that "regardless of what I do, nothing good will come of it anyway." As feelings of helplessness and hopelessness pervade their lives, these children act to avoid what they perceive to be further humiliation. They are prone to blaming others, offering excuses, or assuming the role of the class clown or bully. They are often accused of not trying and of lacking motivation. Actually, they are highly motivated to avoid a situation that they believe will lead to failure even with their best efforts. Sadly, the very strategies they use to escape the possibility of mistakes actually worsen their plight, because they are driven further and further away from possible success. In addition, their actions often invite negative disciplinary reactions from frustrated parents.

The Rollins Family: "Born to Quit"
One of the most vivid examples of a child's negative view of mistakes is one we have described in our workshops. The plight of

ten-year-old Ron captures the often-desperate but self-defeating quest for relief that children seek when they believe they are destined for failure. Ron's parents, Jordan and Carrie Rollins, sought a consultation because of Ron's angry outbursts at school and his oppositional, sullen behavior at home. Each morning when Ron entered the school building, he hit the first child he encountered. There was no recognizable pattern to whom he hit; it was just the first student who crossed his path. He would be immediately sent to the principal's office, which led to several in-school suspensions. When we spoke with the principal, he told us he was at a loss about what else to do to change Ron's behavior. He had considered suspending Ron from school and trying to find an alternative placement in a class for children with behavioral problems.

In our meeting with the Rollinses, we learned that Ron had learning and attention problems and that school had always been a challenge for him—and was an even greater problem now that he was in the fifth grade and had longer and more frequent written assignments. School was not an environment in which Ron gathered strength. Instead, he perceived it as a place where his deficits were highlighted. The very act of entering the building was stressful, so he responded by trying to escape.

Jordan and Carrie Rollins reported that Ron had undergone treatments and surgeries for several medical problems during his first five years of life. Those procedures began with treatment for projectile vomiting when he was only four weeks old, followed by tubes being placed in his ears, and then by a hernia operation.

Although Ron's medical care was excellent, he frequently voiced concerns about his body, which he felt had had defects from birth.

The first few minutes of our initial session with Ron were among the most unforgettable, poignant moments we have ever spent with a child. Ron entered with an expression that was both angry and sad. We mentioned that we were there to help.

He responded angrily, "Why are you trying to help me?"

We replied by wondering why we *wouldn't* want to help.

Ron said with great intensity, "I was born to quit, and God made me that way!"

If we look at Ron's statement in light of attribution theory, we see how entrenched his views of mistakes were and how difficult it would be to modify his perception. In essence, Ron attributed his mistakes and quitting to the will of God. One of the most difficult tasks when disciplining a child for negative behavior is to do so in a way that keeps the child's self-dignity intact and nurtures his or her optimism and resilience, rather than magnifying any feelings of worthlessness and pessimism. When youngsters attribute their perceived failures to God or fate, the task assumes special challenges.

In our work with Ron, we helped him understand the basis of his aggression toward other children. In a very revealing session, Ron astutely observed, "I would rather hit a kid and be sent to the principal's office than have to be in the classroom where I feel stupid." We empathized with his burden but noted that there were other ways of dealing with his feelings of being stupid and incapable of learning.

As the Rollinses began to understand the roots of Ron's outbursts, they shifted from a punitive, authoritarian disciplinary style to one that was more in accord with an authoritative approach, which still held Ron accountable for his actions. They recognized that Ron interpreted his surgeries as a sign that he was "deformed" and that things were wrong with his body. They enlisted the help of Ron's pediatrician, who obtained x-rays of Ron's body that had been taken when he underwent surgery. The doctor reviewed with Ron the many operations he had undergone and showed him the x-rays. He assured Ron that his body was fine now and that he should be proud of all that he was able to do in spite of his earlier problems. This last statement especially served to reinforce a resilient mindset.

Similarly, we reviewed educational and intelligence testing that had been done, not only pointing out to Ron his areas of weakness, but also highlighting his many strengths. We emphasized that all children learn differently and that there were strategies that Ron's teachers could use to help him learn more effectively.

Ron continued to struggle with learning, but with the encouragement and input of his parents, pediatrician, and teachers, his confidence and self-esteem improved. He began to appreciate that mistakes were not an indictment of his skills or intelligence, but rather opportunities for learning. In a revealing story he wrote in therapy, an animal that thought it was born to quit (obviously a representation of himself) eventually realized that this was not so. By the end of his story, Ron had the animal's name changed from Quitter to Try. Most importantly, his aggressive outbursts ended. He began to demonstrate self-discipline because he began to appreciate the benefits of going to class rather than perceiving that he was better off in the principal's office.

Teaching Children to Learn from Mistakes

In the previous chapter, we recommended disciplinary actions and words that would help children appreciate their strengths or islands of competence and take realistic ownership of their accomplishments. Similarly, applying what we know about attributions can help you teach your children to be more comfortable with setbacks and obstacles. This is especially important, since as we have seen with Ron and other youngsters, many children and adolescents would rather act aggressively than appear stupid in the eyes of others. Unfortunately, when they act in this manner, they invite the wrath of adults, whose forms of discipline become more punitive and harsh.

Parents should ask themselves, "Does my disciplinary style advance the message that we can learn from mistakes, or does it punish and humiliate my children for their mistakes?" Also,

> *Parents should ask themselves, "Does my disciplinary style advance the message that we can learn from mistakes, or does it punish and humiliate my children for their mistakes?"*

examining the other side of the coin, consider whether your disciplinary style holds your children realistically accountable for their actions. Or do you rush in and excuse or "rescue" your children from mistakes they have made? We have worked with an increasing number of parents who have difficulty setting limits or allowing their children to fail in situations that do not pose issues of safety. The intentions of these parents may be good, but as we shall see, they are robbing their children of learning how to deal with hardship and develop self-discipline.

The Permissive Disciplinary Style

Many of the examples we have offered so far describe punitive or authoritarian parents, but we also wish to illustrate the overly permissive or overly protective parent's influence on children's psychological growth. Andi Hart, whom we described in Chapter 3, had difficulty setting limits for her fourteen-year-old daughter, Katie. Katie had no curfew and frequently stayed out all night. She became pregnant and had an abortion. In therapy she admitted with much honesty and insight that if her mother had tried to set a curfew, "I probably would have fought her tooth and nail, but at least I would have known she cared about me." The permissive style also can make it difficult for children to become more responsible and manage mistakes effectively, as in the following example.

The Silver Family: "I Don't Want to Lose His Love"

Anita and Darin Silver were the parents of eight-year-old Don and five-year-old Meryl. They had been encouraged to contact us by their children's pediatrician after the Silvers told the physician about their difficulties in setting limits and disciplining their children, especially Don.

In our first session with Anita and Darin, they recounted numerous examples of their children dictating what went on in the family. Their examples reflected their seeming inability to set limits or hold their children accountable for misbehavior.

Darin looked exasperated as he said, "Sometimes I feel Anita and I are the children and Don and Meryl are the parents. They tell us what to do, and we follow."

We asked Darin and Anita to give us a few examples so we could gain a sense of what was happening in their household.

Darin responded, "There are many. I'll start with bedtime. We put Meryl to bed at seven-thirty and Don at eight o'clock. Some evenings Meryl will go to sleep right away, but some evenings she won't. She'll say she's not tired and come out and demand we play with her. Every night is a battle with Don. He comes out constantly, says he's not tired, and insists we play with him. By the time he finally gets to bed most evenings, it's nine-thirty or ten o'clock, or even later. When he goes to sleep so late, it's often difficult getting him up in the morning."

We asked how they had tried responding to that problem.

Anita answered, "We spoke with our pediatrician, and she offered what seemed like sensible advice. She suggested that we ask the kids if they want a drink or have to go the bathroom, and then we spend ten or fifteen minutes reading to each of them. We tell them that when we're finished reading, the lights go out, and they have to remain in bed. She said if they come out and say they can't sleep or want us to read another book, we take them by the hand and walk them back to bed. She also said we might wish to keep a star system in which they receive a star for going to bed on time, which they could trade in for a privilege like staying up an extra hour on Friday or Saturday night or watching an extra thirty minutes of TV on the weekend."

We asked how this idea had worked out.

Anita said, "Not well. If they came out of their rooms, we found it difficult to take them back in. Don especially would spend an hour negotiating with us about why he shouldn't have to go to bed. He would actually tell us, 'If you loved me, you wouldn't make me go to bed.' Soon Meryl was using the same line."

We asked how the parents had handled their response.

Anita said, "We told them we loved them but they had to go to bed. When we said that, they would tell us that we didn't love them, and they continued arguing. It's hard to believe, but we soon fell into the trap of spending an hour or more trying to convince them that we love them. It's really crazy."

Darin interjected, "And it's not just about bedtime. Another thing that drives me crazy is how rudely they talk to Anita and me. If I ever spoke to my parents the way they speak to us, I would have gotten a good whack on my backside. I can't believe the lack of respect they show us. Sometimes I feel they treat us like servants. They tell us to get them things, and it's as if the words *please* and *thank you* don't exist."

We wondered how he and Anita reacted when their children directed them to do something without asking politely.

Darin replied, "Sometimes I do what they want, since I know they'll continue nagging. Sometimes I ask them, 'When you ask me to do something, what should you say?' When I do that, they might say 'please' and 'thank you,' but it's as if they say it just to get what they want."

We asked him if he reminded the children to say "please" and "thank you" all of the time.

He said, "I guess we should, but sometimes it seems that it makes no difference at all."

Anita added, "They can be so ungrateful. Don doesn't get much homework, but he often says he can't do it, so we end up doing most of it for him. And I can't believe what I did last week. He came home from school upset because he got five out of ten spelling words wrong. The teacher doesn't even put a grade on the paper or a minus sign next to the wrong answers. She puts a check mark next to the right answers and tells the class if there's not a check mark, then it's a word for them to study again. Anyway, Don asked me to call the teacher to say that he hadn't been feeling well the night before and didn't have as much of a chance to study. I told him that it wasn't necessary, that the teacher knows that sometimes kids are going to get spelling words wrong, and it just means they have to study them again. I also said that one of the reasons he got half of the words wrong was not that he hadn't been feeling well, but that he had insisted on watching TV." Anita paused.

We asked whether she had called the teacher.

"I hate to admit it, but Don kept nagging me so much that I eventually did."

We asked her first to tell us why she had called when she felt it wasn't the right thing to do. Then we asked her to share the teacher's response.

Anita answered, "I guess I called because I felt it would be easier to call than to continue hearing Don's nagging. I know it's not right."

As a way to encourage the Silvers to reflect on the possible consequences of their actions, we asked them why it hadn't been right to call the teacher.

Darin stated the problem clearly: "I think that each time we aren't firm, each time we don't set limits or consequences, Don and Meryl get the message that they can do what they want and that we will give in to all of their demands."

We agreed and then asked the Silvers what they thought would happen if they continued to let the children do what they want and didn't set limits.

Darin said, "The answer may seem obvious, but I think Anita and I really have to keep your question in mind. I think if we don't set limits on their demands and don't have consequences for their rudeness, they may grow up to be people who are not very responsible or caring and who feel they are due whatever they want. Also, getting back to Anita calling the teacher about Don's spelling test, if we keep making calls like that, our kids may not learn how to deal with mistakes. They may not learn how to accept responsibility for their actions."

We were impressed with how clearly Darin described the possible consequences of continuing a permissive disciplinary style. We praised his understanding of what might occur unless he and his wife began to change the ways in which they responded to Don and Meryl.

Darin commented, "I guess I may have a good understanding that what Anita and I are doing is not very helpful, but trying to change is difficult."

We empathized that such a change would not be easy. Then we advised the Silvers that, as we worked with them, we should all keep in mind what would be likely to occur if changes were not made.

Anita reflected, "You asked before what Don's teacher said when I called her. Her attitude was similar to yours. She was kind, but her message was firm. She said that it's important not to rush in and make excuses for Don, that he wouldn't learn to take ownership of his actions if we rushed in whenever he made mistakes or did something wrong. She also said something that was interesting, even though she said it might be hard for Don or any child to do."

We asked what the teacher was referring to.

"She suggested that I tell Don that if he felt there was a reason for the mistakes he made on the test, he should go up and speak with her directly. She said one of her goals is for students to take more responsibility for their own education, even students as young as Don."

We told the Silvers that we liked Don's teacher's philosophy. We asked Anita whether she suggested to Don that he speak with his teacher directly.

"Yes, but he immediately said that he wouldn't and that I should do things like that. I told him, 'In the future, you'll have to do it,' and he yelled that I didn't love him."

We commented that Don frequently seemed to accuse his parents of not loving him. Anita agreed.

Darin listened closely and then said, "I knew I shouldn't have done what I did the other day."

We asked what he was remembering.

"I had to buy a couple of shirts for myself, and Don wanted to go with me to the department store. Quite honestly, I thought the reason he wanted to go with me was that the department store is right next to a toy store in the mall. I told Don, 'You can come, but we won't be stopping in the toy store.' He said, 'That's OK.' I should have known better. I bought the shirts, and as we were leaving the department store, Don spotted a small guitar in the window of the toy store and told me how much he wanted it. I told him he couldn't have it. He said he wanted it. I should have just left the mall, even if I had to drag him out."

We guessed that he hadn't taken that route.

"Unfortunately not. He started crying and saying, 'You don't love me.' I said I did love him. He said I didn't. I said I did. Oh, well, you get the picture."

Given the regrets Darin had expressed a few moments before, we weren't surprised by his next comment: "I finally bought it for him."

We acknowledged that it can be frustrating when a child begs us for a gift and accuses us of not loving him. Then we returned to the earlier topic of consequences. We asked Darin to identify the consequences of buying his son the guitar. We asked what Don had learned and whether that lesson was worth the price of giving in to his demands. We explained that we were trying to make certain the Silvers understood that, when we asked such questions, we weren't trying to be critical, but rather to help them figure out more effective ways of disciplining their children. We wanted the Silvers to know we weren't being judgmental but would instead move forward on making changes.

Darin assured us that he understood we weren't being critical. Then he said, "The questions you're asking are important ones. Like Anita, I feel one of the reasons I give in to Don is that he, and to a lesser extent Meryl, can wear you down. But there's another reason. I have to admit that when Don says I don't love him, it really gets to me. I'm not sure why. Maybe it's because I never had a close relationship with my father. What I do know is that I don't want to lose his love."

Even in this initial session with the Silvers, several important parenting dynamics emerged. The Silvers were well-intentioned parents whose disciplinary style worked against equipping Don and Meryl to deal with mistakes and setbacks and to become increasingly responsible, caring, and self-disciplined individuals. On the positive side, these parents could articulate the negative consequences of their permissive, overprotective approach. On the negative side, they had difficulty assuming a more authoritative stance.

In the sessions that followed, we reviewed several key points and discussed specific changes they could make in their parenting style. We emphasized that a major goal of discipline is to promote self-discipline and a resilient mindset in children. This required that the Silvers set appropriate and realistic limits and consequences and enforce them consistently. We also reminded them that it was important for children to learn that setbacks and mistakes are likely to occur in their lives, but that in almost all instances, we can benefit by learning from these mistakes.

To handle Don's temper outbursts when he didn't get what he wanted, we advised that they should tell him (and Meryl if she acted the same way) that he could continue to scream and yell but it would not get him what he wanted—if anything, it would prompt them to remove him from the situation. We mentioned with some levity that some youngsters seem to be experts at having tantrums in public places such as malls or restaurants. We suggested that, if that occurred, the parent should take the child gently by the hand and lead him or her out. If the child resisted, which doesn't happen very often, the parent could let the child know that a privilege would be lost (e.g., television time) if the child did not comply with the parent's request.

We emphasized that each time a tantrum led to a reward such as a guitar, the Silvers were teaching the children that screaming and yelling would get them what they wanted. While neither parent desired this kind of negative mindset to develop in their children, they were reinforcing it each time they caved in to Don or Meryl's demands.

We also noted that when children get whatever they want by having a tantrum, they're unlikely to develop a sense of responsibility or self-discipline. Unfortunately, what they are likely to develop is a more self-centered attitude with little ability to learn to delay gratification. That kind of attitude would not serve them well as they faced different challenges and setbacks. When parents don't hold firm, they're actually doing their children a disservice.

In addition, we addressed Don and Meryl's accusation that they weren't loved when the parents failed to meet their demands. We stressed to the Silvers that most children learn early on that one way in which they can really tug at a parent's heartstrings is to utter the words *You don't love me.* In our experience, many parents give in, especially after becoming engaged in a long argument in which they try to convince their child that they do love him or her. Instead, it is best to say calmly, "I do love you. You may not believe me, but just because I say no to something you want doesn't mean I don't love you. You can continue to say I don't love you, but it won't get me to change my mind." We advised that if the nagging continued after this statement, the

Silvers could repeat the statement in a calm, even voice. And we urged them not to end up by giving in. In that kind of situation, we said, everyone ends up losing.

Another issue we addressed with the Silvers was their tendency to "rescue" Don from discomfort, as his mother did when she called his teacher after he failed a spelling test. This problem is hardly unique to the Silver household. In our practice, we are witnessing an increasing number of parents who rush in to protect their children from possible distress and from experiencing the consequences of their actions. Although we certainly do want parents to intervene if their child is in danger, we strongly recommend that parents hold their children accountable, so the children learn responsibility.

We asked Darin and Anita what message would be communicated to children if parents never allowed them to make mistakes or if the parents made excuses when the children made mistakes or engaged in inappropriate behavior. Restating the message to focus on the goal of discipline, we added another question: What message are parents communicating by not using disciplinary techniques that hold their children accountable?

Smiling, Anita said, "I know how Don and Meryl would answer. They would say that it showed we loved them and wanted to protect them."

Returning her smile, we acknowledged that she might well have guessed their answer. Then we added that we believe it is the responsibility of parents to teach kids a different message: that when we act in certain ways, we must learn to consider and take responsibility for our behavior.

We believe it is the responsibility of parents to teach kids that when we act in certain ways, we must learn to consider and take responsibility for our behavior.

We shared our experience that another message is communicated when parents don't hold children accountable or when they make excuses for their children. This behavior by parents seems to say, "We have to jump in and rescue you because we think you're too fragile or vulnerable to handle the situation."

Looking astonished, Darin said, "I never thought of that before. That's a valid point."

We responded that we want parents to deliver a message that says, "You will make mistakes from time to time, and we'll be there to help you figure out better ways of handling the situation in the future." We added that we think that's what children have to learn.

Anita reflected, "Based on what you just said, I think Don's teacher made a lot of sense when she told me that if Don has a question about a grade, he should speak with her directly."

We agreed, since that approach would place the responsibility on Don. We pointed out that the teacher's plan would teach Don that he must be responsible for his actions and his parents would not bail him out. That approach, we added, was actually a form of effective discipline.

During the sessions that followed, the Silvers considered our recommendations about being firmer, not giving in to Don or Meryl's demands, and communicating clearly that if the children insisted on crying or saying they weren't loved, their behavior would no longer lead the parents to change their minds.

As Darin and Anita prepared to apply their new disciplinary scripts, we warned them in a light voice that when they began setting the new limits and refusing to give in or rescue their children, they should not expect Don or Meryl to say, "Thank you so much. We see that you are becoming more responsible parents." As a matter of fact, we added that if the children did say that, the parents should be very suspicious. The Silvers laughed.

Becoming a little more serious, we cautioned Darin and Anita that it is common for children to become more demanding and angry when parents finally establish limits and consequences. We emphasized that children are great at testing our resolve.

Anita responded, "That we know."

In the following months, we were impressed with the Silvers' ability to stick to their new guidelines with only a few slip-ups, which are to be expected when trying a new disciplinary approach. Much to the parents' pleasure, Don and Meryl's demanding behavior slowly diminished. To help Don cope with the discomfort of mistakes, the Silvers used constructive, problem-solving comments such as, "You had trouble this time, but maybe you can figure out what you can do differently next time. We're here to help if you need it."

Darin and Anita Silver were able to shift from permissiveness and caving in to an authoritative approach that helped them manage their children's frustration and mistakes more effectively. And as the parents became more confident, their children benefited by learning self-discipline.

The Authoritarian Disciplinary Style

The Silvers illustrate the drawback of being overly permissive: This style doesn't allow children to test their mettle and to learn effective problem-solving and coping skills. Such children become easily discouraged by setbacks and failures. Overly authoritarian parents also deprive their children of developing these important problem-solving skills, responsibility, and self-discipline. They just do it in a different way.

The Wilkins Family: Learning to Encourage

In Chapter 4, we met Susan and Jack Wilkins, who described their fourteen-year-old daughter, Patty, as an easy, cooperative child. In contrast, they said their twelve-year-old daughter, Melanie, was irresponsible, demanding, and rude and constantly accused them of not loving her and not being available to help her with her work. These descriptions resemble the words used by the Silvers to describe their son, Don. However, while the Silvers gave in to Don's demands, the Wilkinses tended to be harsh and punitive with Melanie, especially as they constantly compared her unfavorably with Patty. Although these two sets of parents handled discipline quite differently—one falling under the umbrella of authoritarian and the other under permissive—they shared similar levels of success. Both discipline styles were counterproductive, working against the development of self-discipline and a resilient mindset in their children.

We could appreciate the Wilkinses' frustration and wanted to change the track this family was on. The family had cast Melanie in the role of the "bad child," and she knew it. When children are anointed with this label, it rarely motivates them to change their behaviors in a positive direction; all too often, they begin to believe the label and act in ways that confirm it. In response, parents typically become angrier and may resort to disciplinary practices that lessen their child's self-confidence and ability to handle mistakes and take risks.

We told Jack and Susan that they had good goals in wanting Melanie to persevere with challenging tasks and not constantly seek their help. Then, pointing out that what they had been doing had not helped them achieve their goals, we suggested they stick with the goals but consider other ways of reaching the goals.

> *When children are anointed with the label of the "bad child," it rarely motivates them to change their behaviors in a positive direction; all too often, they begin to believe the label and act in ways that confirm it.*

Jack answered, "I think we've exhausted all of our ideas. Each time we encourage Melanie to try something on her own, she tells us she doesn't know how. If we say she should keep trying, she accuses us of not wanting to help her and not loving her."

We agreed that this response could be frustrating. We reminded the Wilkinses that they had said they eventually would yell at Melanie, which was not accomplishing their goals.

Susan responded, "We know, but she's so frustrating. The other day, I was so annoyed by her behavior that I said some mean things I regret saying, but she seems to bring out the worst in us."

We asked Susan to share what she had said that was mean. We explained that her example might help us find other ways of handling the situation.

She answered, "Melanie asked me to help her with a school assignment. She was supposed to write a brief paper, just two pages or so, about someone she admired, telling what she admired about the person. Melanie told me she couldn't think of anyone to write about, that she was stuck. I told her I'd help her think of someone, but then she would have to write the paper. She said, 'Fine.'"

Susan continued, "We had recently watched a documentary about Amelia Earhart, and Melanie was fascinated by her life. After the documentary, Melanie commented how courageous Amelia Earhart was, and she wondered if we would ever find out what had happened to her when she disappeared while flying. Since Melanie seemed so impressed by Earhart's courage, I suggested that she might want to write about her. I even helped her find a couple of articles on the Web, so she could have a little more information. We discussed some of what she might say in the paper. But then Melanie resorted to her typical behavior."

We asked what happened.

"Melanie immediately told me she didn't know where to begin and basically wanted me to write the paper for her. I was firm and said I'd be happy to review the paper, but she had to do it. She began sulking but sat down to write. About an hour later, she showed me the paper. It was terrible. Since she used spell check, there weren't spelling mistakes, but it was poorly written, and she really didn't elaborate on why she admired Amelia Earhart. I told her the paper wasn't very good, that it seemed she hadn't even tried. Melanie was angry and said she had. I was so annoyed that I said, 'If you really tried and this is the best you can do, then you have a real problem, because a third-grader could do a better job.' Melanie became furious and screamed, as she often does, 'You don't love me! I hate you!' and stormed out of the room. I followed her and told her she couldn't be so disrespectful, and I grounded her for the next two weeks."

Before we continued discussing the specific incident, we mentioned to the Wilkinses that several of their examples of Melanie not trying or giving up had concerned school. We asked them whether Melanie had ever had an evaluation for any kind of learning problems.

Jack answered, "Back in fourth grade, her teacher wondered about that. The school did some brief testing, but the testing didn't indicate she had any learning disabilities. Why? Do you think she might have learning disabilities?"

We replied that we weren't certain but would be happy to review the school's testing and see if any new testing was warranted. We explained that sometimes kids have some learning problems that are not identified, and learning remains a real challenge for them. Some may seem to give up but only because they feel they aren't capable of succeeding. When adults aren't aware of the learning problems, they tend to expect more from the child than the child can deliver. Reassuring the Wilkinses that we were willing to look at this possibility more closely, we returned to the example Susan had just given. We observed that she had used the word *mean* to describe some of the things she said to Melanie.

She responded, "I think it was pretty mean to say a third-grader could do a better job. Saying something like that is like telling Melanie I don't think she's very smart. But I do think she's smart; I just don't think she tries hard enough. She gives up before she even starts."

We wondered why Susan thought she would do that.

Jack said, "She's just a quitter."

We asked him to explain.

"As we've said, she's so different from Patty. Patty sticks with things, and Melanie gives up."

Assuring Jack and Susan that we didn't want to make excuses for Melanie giving up and that we shared their goals of helping Melanie take more responsibility for her behavior and stop quitting, we encouraged them to pursue those goals by thinking about how Melanie perceives herself and her parents. We explained that we could use Melanie's perceptions as a jumping-off point in figuring out the best approach to use with her. Our goal was to steer the Wilkinses toward viewing Melanie with greater empathy.

Susan replied, "As we've mentioned, Melanie would say that we're not helpful and that we don't love her. I'm certain she also believes we love Patty more. I know we enjoy being with Patty more, since she's so much easier to be with."

We asked the Wilkinses to describe how they would like Melanie to describe them.

Susan said, "That's an interesting question. A quick answer would be 'In the same way that Patty would probably describe us.'"

We asked what that would be.

Susan answered, "I think Patty would say that we loved and supported her, but it's easier to love and support her."

Building on the theme of what the two girls perceived, we commented that siblings sometimes talk about the ways their parents treat them. Sometimes they complain that their brothers or sisters are treated better, but sometimes not. We asked whether Patty had ever talked about Jack and Susan's interactions with Melanie.

Susan said, "Actually, she has. We told you Patty is a great kid. In the past few months, she told me she thought some of the things Jack and I were saying and doing with Melanie weren't very helpful. As a matter of fact, Patty was in the next room when I made the comment that a third-grader could do better than

Melanie did. She also heard me blow up at Melanie and ground her. After that, Patty told me that she thought I was being tough on her sister and it was making matters worse."

We asked Susan how she had responded to Patty's remarks.

"I simply said that Melanie sometimes made me so angry that I say things that probably aren't very helpful. What I didn't tell you before—maybe because it's something I'm also ashamed of—is that after I told Melanie she was grounded, she cursed at me, and I slapped her and told her she couldn't talk with me that way. I hit her arm. It wasn't hard, but it was still hitting her."

We noted earlier that the Wilkinses were basically caring people who had difficulty responding to a more challenging child. Unlike Jules Upton in Chapter 4, who was harsh and punitive with his two sons and his wife, the Wilkinses had an authoritarian style that seemed less entrenched, and they were more open to making changes. The fact that Susan Wilkins expressed regret about her comments and her slapping Melanie signaled that she recognized the need for changes, even though she appeared to blame Melanie for the harsh words and actions by implying that her anger was triggered by Melanie's actions.

Although the Wilkinses were aware that their response to Melanie was making the situation worse, we thought it was important for them to understand fully the damage their disciplinary practice was causing to their relationship with their younger daughter and to her confidence and self-esteem. We wanted them to understand this negative impact so that they would be motivated to change.

We believe that describing our resilience model, the role of discipline in that model, and the tenets of attribution theory helps parents assume ownership for their behavior and encourage their children to do the same. The Wilkinses found attribution theory particularly intriguing in terms of their approach to Melanie. During the discussion, we asked them how they thought Melanie experiences mistakes.

Jack answered, "I'm not really sure. She spends so much time trying to avoid doing things that she often doesn't give herself a chance to make mistakes."

Listening intently to her husband's observations, Susan added, "I really hadn't thought of it before, but when Jack said Melanie avoids doing things, all I could think about was that she must believe that she will fail. With that attitude, it's not surprising that she wouldn't even try. It's what you just told us about attribution theory. She feels so pessimistic about succeeding that she must attribute mistakes to things she can't change."

As Susan spoke, her eyes filled with tears. She continued, "It's very upsetting for me to think about the things I said. Melanie already felt defeated, and I made her feel even worse. And to add to it, I grounded her. But what's just as upsetting right now is that I don't know how I should handle situations like that. I'm not sure what I should say or do when Melanie doesn't try or when she screams at us or says we don't love her."

We agreed that it was difficult to know what to do, because Melanie had an almost knee-jerk reaction to challenging tasks: running from them. We advised the Wilkinses that their goal should be to respond and discipline her in a way in which she would begin to believe that mistakes offer opportunities for learning. The goal would be to lessen Melanie's feeling of defeat and her fear of humiliation. We suggested that we begin by reviewing the situation Susan had just told us about and by considering other ways she could have responded. Since the situation was similar to many others, it could provide some guidelines for effectively handling Melanie's behavior in the future.

Susan agreed, "That would certainly be helpful to Jack and me."

Before beginning that exploration, we commented that whatever strategies we would develop together would be more effective if Jack and Susan avoided making comparisons between Melanie and Patty. We observed that the two girls probably sensed how much more their parents enjoyed being with Patty. Acknowledging that Patty was an easier child to raise, we explained that it would be difficult to change Melanie's perception of herself and her parents if she kept sensing the unfavorable comparisons Jack and Susan made with Patty.

Susan responded, "What you're saying makes a lot of sense, but it's hard to change."

We agreed but emphasized that the change was important and that we would be of whatever help we could. We explained that to help them make the changes, we would explore the situation that had occurred between Melanie and her mother and then discuss what Jack and Susan considered Melanie's strengths (the "islands of competence" introduced in Chapter 5). We wanted to help the parents figure out what gave Melanie satisfaction and what she believed her strengths to be, and then we would look for ways of reinforcing those strengths. We told the Wilkinses that, in our experience, children are less likely to exhibit behavior problems if they are involved in activities that spotlight their strengths and if they feel their parents appreciate those strengths.

Jack said, "I think I can speak for both Susan and myself when I say we probably haven't done a very good job of appreciating Melanie's strengths."

Acknowledging his concern, we returned to the situation involving Melanie's report about Amelia Earhart. We told the Wilkinses that we were fascinated when Susan mentioned that Melanie was drawn to Amelia Earhart because of her courage. Based on what they had told us about Melanie, it seemed unlikely that Melanie saw herself as very competent or courageous. Assuring the Wilkinses that we didn't intend to transform them into therapists, we suggested that when Melanie decided to do a paper about Earhart, they might have engaged her in a discussion about Earhart's courage, especially whether Earhart might have ever been afraid of things not going right and, if so, how she might have handled her fears. Often, we explained, children are more willing to talk about the challenges and anxieties of others than to admit their own, but by talking about others, they are really talking about themselves. If Melanie had been interested in such a discussion, it might have led to a dialogue about taking risks and managing fears.

With a reflective look, Susan said, "That's an interesting idea. I'm sorry I hadn't thought about it at the time."

We assured her that the opportunity was likely to arise again in the future, so it would be good to keep in mind. We continued by praising Susan's idea to help Melanie get articles about Earhart from the Web. We suggested that, in the future, it would be important that Melanie sit by the computer with Susan or Jack to learn how to do the research herself. For example, if they used a search engine to get the list of articles, they might retrieve one article and then ask Melanie to look at the list and select another to review. That approach would involve her more in the process.

Jack interrupted, "I think we can do that, but then comes the tough part—when she says she doesn't know where to begin and wants us to write the paper. If we refuse to do it, she has a tantrum. What then?"

We agreed that he and Susan had tried many things and acknowledged that what we were about to suggest might seem similar to their past attempts. We emphasized that success often depends on our tone of voice or the exact words we choose. We explained that when Melanie said she didn't know where to start, the reason might be that she really didn't know. Whether or not she really was capable, Jack and Susan would have to begin with her view of reality. As they had mentioned, Melanie might feel defeated before she began; if they pushed her, she might get angrier and more sullen, and they might react by being more punitive.

Jack asked, "What might Susan have said when Melanie said she didn't know how to start the paper?"

To answer that important question, we reminded the Wilkinses of their goal to have Melanie take more risks, do more on her own, and not be so afraid of making mistakes. With that in mind, we suggested that Susan might have told Melanie, "I know that getting started isn't easy. I can't write the paper for you, since it's your assignment, but maybe I can help get you started by our working on an outline." These words would tell Melanie she wasn't being abandoned but that she had to be involved in the work.

Susan asked, "What if she says she can't even do that?"

We advised that, instead of disagreeing, the parents needed to validate what Melanie said. "Validation" doesn't mean agreeing, but expressing that they understand the other person's feelings. We suggested that Jack or Susan could say, "I know you feel you don't know how to get started, but that's what I want to help you with." Then they could offer some assistance with the outline, being careful not to end up doing the work for Melanie. Acknowledging that this approach might sound similar to what Jack and Susan had done in the past, we repeated that the wording and tone of voice might make a big difference.

Susan said, "I can see that. But what happens if Melanie works on the paper and comes back with something that isn't very good and shows little effort? I know I shouldn't yell at her or mention a third-grader could do better or end up grounding her, but how should a parent handle that?"

Before we could respond, Susan smiled and added, "The more I think about it, the more I know what I did would not end up in a book about effective parenting."

Jack laughed and said, "Unless the book had examples of what not to do. A lot of my own remarks could be in that section."

We interpreted the Wilkinses' good humor as a sign they were enjoying this problem-solving dialogue with us and were beginning to believe that, in fact, there were less punitive disciplinary practices to use with Melanie. They seemed to have more of a sense of direction and control, lessening their own frustration.

We returned to Susan's question of what to do when Melanie showed her a paper that was not very good. We recalled that when Melanie showed Susan the paper, Susan had assumed her daughter was not trying. We asked her to consider how she might have responded if she thought Melanie really had tried but felt inadequate and defeated, so that her negative feelings contributed to the paper's poor quality. Our intent was to modify the negative mindset the Wilkinses had developed toward their daughter, a mindset that was contributing to a harsh, unforgiving approach.

Susan replied, "But I think she didn't try. She rushed through it just to get it out of the way."

We agreed that she might have done that but asked Susan to try interpreting Melanie's rushing through the work as a sign of how frustrated and defeated she felt. Perhaps Melanie had just wanted to get it out of the way because she believed that, even if she worked on it for another hour, she couldn't improve its quality. We added that we weren't asking Susan to make excuses for Melanie, but to understand her plight.

Susan answered, "I think I would have been more understanding and wouldn't have accused her of not trying. But I'm struggling with knowing what to say even if I become more understanding."

After listening intently, Jack volunteered, "I have some ideas. I don't know if they'd work, but as you've emphasized, if we don't change our negative scripts, it will be harder for Melanie to change hers. I think that when Melanie showed the paper to Susan, it might have been better for her to say, 'That's a start. There are places that need some revisions. Let's look where.' I think Melanie would be more receptive to that instead of Susan and me punishing her."

We assured Jack that his idea sounded excellent and might work. We added that Melanie might be more receptive to hearing that kind of comment if she felt her parents had been helpful right from the start of the assignment. We also reminded the Wilkinses not to lose sight of one of their main goals: that any forms of discipline or teaching should help Melanie feel more comfortable about making mistakes. She needed to believe that mistakes are experiences from which to learn, rather than feeling punished or judged. The session ended at this point, but we promised to continue the discussion at our next meeting.

Interestingly, at the beginning of the next session, the Wilkinses mentioned that Patty had told them that during the past week they had been nicer to Melanie. When they asked Patty what she meant, she explained that they had not been yelling at Melanie and punishing her and that they were talking in a "kinder" way. Jack and Susan had welcomed this feedback.

Jack and Susan offered examples in which they had spoken to Melanie in a more empathic, kinder fashion. They said that when they began seeing Melanie as a struggling girl who felt defeated, they became more understanding and more willing to help her with tasks, but without doing the tasks for her. During the week, they also did something that we had planned to suggest, but they did it on their own. They shared with Melanie some of their own struggles growing up. They told her about times that they had not felt very smart and had been discouraged. They told us they made certain not to come across as lecturing Melanie or giving her an "empty pep talk." They observed that Melanie seemed genuinely interested in their childhood experiences.

As we continued discussing effective ways of responding to Melanie's struggles and holding her accountable for her actions, we returned to the topic of her islands of competence, a theme we introduced in Chapter 5. We explained that children are less likely to engage in problem behaviors if they feel we appreciate their strengths. We told the Wilkinses that identifying and reinforcing a child's islands of competence is one of the most powerful forms of discipline available to parents.

As many parents do, Jack responded, "I'm not certain I understand why you say reinforcing islands of competence is a form of discipline."

We explained that we view discipline as a teaching process, and part of this process involves discovering and applying our strengths. When children experience success in their areas of interest, they are less likely to resort to negative behaviors. When they are involved in activities that bring them a sense of joy and accomplishment, they have less time to do things that invite parents' disapproval, anger, and punishment. We added that when children experience success in one area, they may be less hesitant to try things in areas that have been more difficult for them.

Jack answered, "It's certainly an interesting way of looking at discipline. I guess I've always thought of discipline as punishment, of getting kids to stop or modify certain behaviors. I actually like the way you envision discipline. It certainly seems more positive than the approach we've used with Melanie."

As we discussed islands of competence, the Wilkinses mentioned that Melanie had a lovely singing voice and liked to draw pictures and show younger children how to draw. Jack observed, "She inherited those 'islands' from Susan. My family tells me to lip sync when I start singing, and I think I'm still stuck at the level of drawing stick figures." After a pause, he added, "Patty takes after me in that regard. She's not a very good singer or artist."

We commented that Jack had seemed to be thinking about something right before he made his last comment.

He replied, "I was. I was thinking about something you said in our last session about how we always compare Melanie with Patty in an unfavorable way. I know we probably shouldn't compare our children to begin with, but I realized this was one of the first times I can remember that I emphasized something positive that Melanie could do but Patty could not."

Susan said thoughtfully, "It's important that we focus on Melanie's strengths."

We explored with the Wilkinses how they could highlight Melanie's islands of competence. Susan belonged to a community theater group and also taught Sunday school to young children. The theater group, which included some children and adolescents, often performed songs from musicals. With her mother's encouragement and a promise that she wouldn't have to perform a solo at least initially, Melanie joined the group. Her mother later told us, "Melanie has received many compliments about her singing." Melanie also began to help her mother in the Sunday school class, especially helping the children draw Bible figures and scenes. Reporting on that project, Susan remarked, "The kids love Melanie, and I love to watch the joy Melanie is having."

Other factors contributed to change in the Wilkins family. We held several family meetings in which we engaged in the problem-solving process described in Chapter 4. We also discussed with Melanie her concerns about how smart she was. We recommended some testing to assess the factors that might be contributing to her difficulty in school, especially with her writing assignments. During the course of the evaluation, Melanie revealed that she felt "very, very dumb." She offered a poignant comment: "Sometimes I wonder if there is something wrong with my brain that can't be fixed."

The evaluation indicated that Melanie was a bright child but had some learning problems, especially in the area of organizational and writing skills. She was reassured to learn that nothing was wrong with her brain and that there were strategies that she and her teachers and parents could use to strengthen these weaker skills.

Teaching Constructive Responses to Mistakes

Throughout our intervention with the Wilkins family, we communicated important parenting guidelines. Here are some of the key points:

- Discipline is a teaching process that should be free of parental actions that humiliate, cause the child to lose hope, or take away opportunities for the child to become more accountable for his or her own behavior.
- Discipline should be used to help children believe that mistakes are experiences from which to learn rather than feel accused or judged.

- When children believe they can learn from mistakes, they are less likely to engage in self-defeating behaviors that often elicit punishment from their parents.
- Parents must recognize that their mindset, including their interpretation of their children's behavior, will determine whether they respond to their children with understanding and empathy or with anger and resentment.
- As parents strive to modify problematic behavior, they must also reinforce and honor their children's interests and strengths.

Changing Mindsets and Attributions

As we have witnessed in the previous two chapters, your disciplinary style plays a major role in determining your child's mindset about successes and failures. Discipline should enhance a child's sense of ownership and responsibility, highlight and reinforce the child's strengths, and lessen the child's fears of making mistakes. If we keep these goals in mind, we will help our children develop self-discipline along with respect for themselves and others.

7

Helping Your Child Cope with Doubts and Disappointments

Some children seem to have a black cloud that follows them wherever they go. They lack confidence in themselves and doubt that others can soothe or comfort them. This ominous cloud, which may be partly a result of their inborn temperament, is often reinforced by life experiences that are themselves influenced by this temperament. These youngsters are easily disappointed in themselves and in the seeming lack of attention and affection they receive from adults. They begin to doubt whether parents, teachers, or friends generally care about and are interested in them.

Confronted by these feelings, they struggle to find different ways of coping. To manage the distressing feelings that they have let themselves down and cannot succeed, some children withdraw and isolate themselves. Others protect themselves against their discomfort by becoming sarcastic and resentful, blaming others for whatever discomfort, humiliation, or problems they experience. In response, parents who are already frustrated with their children's negative attitude and behavior are likely to become angrier, sometimes uttering demeaning comments or applying forms of harsh discipline that children interpret as confirming they are unloved or are a disappointment to their parents. A cycle of negativity and anger is in full force.

Discipline That Doesn't Bring Your Child Down

A key question for parents is how to respond to a child's pessimism and disappointment in a way that lessens rather than intensifies the child's negativity. In terms of this book's focus, we can pose the question in the following way: How can you deal with your own disappointment and anger as a parent so that you don't use forms of discipline that add to your child's feeling he or she is a disappointment and that you don't care about him or her? This question is difficult to answer. When faced with a negative child, parents can easily fall into the trap of becoming increasingly frustrated and negative themselves, resorting to an authoritarian style of discipline.

> *When faced with a negative child, parents can easily fall into the trap of becoming increasingly frustrated and negative themselves.*

The Elefson Family: "You Think I'm a Real Disappointment"

Their twelve-year-old son's pediatrician referred Dena and Garth Elefson to us. Despite above-average intelligence and good academic skills, Aaron was struggling in seventh grade, and the pediatrician and the school questioned whether he might have a learning disability or attention-deficit/hyperactivity disorder (ADHD).

Garth began, "We just don't understand Aaron's problem. The school and his pediatrician think he may have a learning disability or attention problems. But he did quite well in elementary school. I think his problems began in middle school. First we thought he was just overwhelmed with middle school, but now we think he may just be lazy and also distracted by other activities such as his music. He can spend hours playing his guitar or banging on his drums."

We asked Garth to explain what made him think his son might be lazy.

He replied, "Well, we know he's smart and capable when he sits down to do the work. When he does his work, it's not bad. But he's doing less and less work. Also, a couple of years ago, when he seemed to be having some problems completing some of his assignments, the school psychologist did an evaluation, and it didn't indicate any learning problems. Now the school and pediatrician think he may have learning problems that didn't show up in the earlier testing. Can someone just develop learning problems at a certain age?"

We replied that learning problems usually are present all along, but sometimes these problems become more apparent when the work at school becomes more demanding or requires the use of more advanced skills such as conceptual or writing abilities. We assured the Elefsons that we could look at that possibility more closely.

Garth replied, "I see, but Aaron still seems lazy to me and lacking motivation. Not only that, but in the past, he was pleasanter and more agreeable. Lately, he has become irritable and angry for no apparent reason. If you ask him to do a chore he's supposed to do, he reacts as if we were prison guards punishing him for not doing what he's expected to do."

Dena jumped in. "As Garth says, Aaron is definitely more irritable and angry. But I don't want it to sound as if Aaron was a happy-go-lucky kid before middle school. It has just gotten worse. He always seems to see the glass as half empty rather than half full. When I mention that to him, he gets even angrier and says we don't love him."

We asked what Dena mentioned to him that would get him angry.

She replied, "Sometimes I get so frustrated when Aaron complains that no one loves him or no one cares about him that I yell at him, saying he has a good life and should learn to see the glass as half full and not half empty. I've told him that when people see the glass as half empty, they will continue to feel miserable. I'm trying to help him learn that he shouldn't have a sour look on his face all the time, but when I try to tell him that, he yells back that I don't love him."

We asked how she responded when Aaron said she didn't love him.

"I tell him that we do love him, but when he acts the way he does, it's not easy to like him."

Garth followed with an intriguing statement: "When I tell Aaron he could do better in school if he weren't so lazy, he says, 'You think I'm a real disappointment.' I've never used the word *disappointment* with him, but actually that's how I do feel. I think Dena and I have been good parents, and it's disappointing to see your child not try things and just seem to give up."

We asked Garth how he usually responded when Aaron said he thought Aaron was a real disappointment.

Garth replied, "I don't think I respond very well. My first inclination is to tell Aaron that he *has* been a disappointment, that he could do better if he were more optimistic. I've never said that to him, because he'd take it as a criticism and as evidence that we didn't love him, just like when he accuses Dena of not loving him when she tries to tell him that unless he removes the sour look on his face and stops seeing the glass as half empty, he'll continue to be miserable."

Given that the Elefsons had not directly told Aaron he was a disappointment, we asked, what had they said? We explained that we were asking because sometimes even well-intentioned parents say things that have the opposite effect of what they want. In our work with parents, we try to look for other ways to say things, keeping in mind how a child may experience communications.

In part, we added, the Elefsons had already done some of that when they said they refrained from telling Aaron he was a disappointment, because he would take their comment as a criticism and a confirmation that they didn't love him.

In explaining these thoughts, we wanted to highlight the importance of empathy and effective communication in parenting skills and to reinforce the attempts Garth was already making to be more empathic. Just as children's strengths need to be encouraged, we find it important to identify the parents' existing mindset and actions that are already contributing to more effective parenting and disciplinary practices.

We repeated our question, asking how they typically responded to Aaron's negativity. We explained that the answer would help us in future meetings by giving us a sense of what had and hadn't worked and what modifications we could consider that might be more effective in helping Aaron to become more positive and optimistic.

With a smile, Garth said, "I try to tell him that I'm not disappointed in *him* but in his behavior and attitudes. The reason I'm smiling is that whenever my father said things like that to me, I often didn't even know what he was talking about. It wasn't very helpful at all, yet I say the same thing to Aaron."

We returned his smile as we assured him that many parents have lamented, "I'm saying things to my kids that I didn't like when my parents said them to me." We explained that parenting styles include the "scripts" we heard as children, even the scripts we weren't crazy about.

Dena asked, "But what else can we say when Aaron says we're disappointed in him? I was once watching a talk show in which a psychologist said that when kids say things like Aaron told us, we should ask them how it makes them feel to think that. I tried it with Aaron, and he rolled his eyes as if I were asking him the dumbest question he had ever heard. He sarcastically answered, 'It makes me feel great,' and then he said he knows I'm disap-

pointed in him. It seems like he has an answer to counter everything I say."

We empathized that this kind of situation can be perplexing
and frustrating. Then we assured her that, as we gathered more
information from them, we hoped to gain a clearer picture of
how she and Garth might respond so that Aaron would be better
able to hear how much they cared about him. We explained that,
in future meetings, we would offer more specific suggestions for
communicating with Aaron more effectively, but in the first session, we wanted to shift gears and return to an earlier topic that
would help us decide on the steps to take. We asked the Elefsons
to describe a little more of the history of Aaron's difficulties,
clarifying when the problems began.

Dena said, "Basically, the problems started in middle school,
but as I mentioned, there were signs even in elementary school.
But then things weren't as bad. Or, looking back, perhaps they
were as bad, but we just weren't aware of it."

We asked her to explain what kind of signs she had been aware
of. "Aaron's our only child, so we can't compare him with any
siblings, but we certainly see how our nieces and nephews and
our friends' kids act. Most of them seem more content or satis-
fied. Even when Aaron was younger, he didn't seem as happy. I
remember him telling us that we didn't love him when he was
four or five years old. He especially said it when we told him
he couldn't do something or we wouldn't buy him something.
Sometimes it was maddening. One time when he was about five,
he told us he wanted some kind of toy, I don't remember what.
We told him he already had a lot of toys. He started to cry and
accused us of not loving him. I told him he should enjoy all the
toys he did have. That comment certainly didn't help."

Garth added, "As we've said, Aaron can really be frustrating.
Sometimes Dena and I have wondered if we're too tough with
him, but at other times we wonder if we're too easy—that we

don't hold him responsible enough for his homework and chores. I think we should take his music away when we get these bad reports from school. But music is one of the things that bring him the most joy. Once when we received several warning slips about Aaron, we told him he couldn't play his guitar or drums unless his school performance improved. We thought that would motivate him to do his work, but it only made him angrier, and his school performance didn't improve. It's really confusing to know what consequences to use. It's like trying to figure out the best way to respond when he says we don't love him or that he's a disappointment to us. Even as I'm saying this to you, I'm feeling anxious about what to do next. I'm worried that we're not helping Aaron and, if anything, our relationship with him is deteriorating." Garth's word *deteriorating* was powerful, capturing the confusion and despair he and his wife were facing.

The Elefsons were experiencing some of the same feelings of frustration, disappointment, and anger as other parents we described earlier in this book. When children are disappointed in themselves and others, parents are often at a loss about what to do. As one parent said, "I want my daughter to stop feeling sorry for herself and to stop blaming us for her problems. If only she appreciated that she's leading a pretty good life, especially compared with most kids." Not surprisingly, though, when we tell our children this, they aren't going to say, "I'm so sorry for not seeing what a good life I lead. All of my feelings of disappointment and sadness are now gone."

We decided to see if we could help the Elefsons by using our strength-based model. Mentioning that Garth and Dena had told us a lot about Aaron's negative attitudes, we asked them to describe what brought Aaron joy and what he felt competent doing.

Dena replied, "Music is one of the few things that brings him satisfaction. He's pretty good with the guitar and drums. He also likes to draw cartoons. He's pretty good at that, too. If he could play his guitar or drums or draw all day long, he would feel he was in heaven."

We asked whether Aaron had an opportunity to play his guitar or drums in school or display his artwork in some way.

Garth said, "He plays drums in the school band and is quite good, but I'm not sure he realizes that he's a good musician. He often compares himself in a negative way with other kids in the band. Rather than enjoying his accomplishments, he tends to downplay them. It's another example of him seeing the glass as half empty."

We assured the Elefsons that as we worked together, we would try to figure out the best ways to capitalize on Aaron's interests and strengths. We explained that if Aaron could begin to appreciate his strengths—his islands of competence—he could begin to feel less disappointed and pessimistic, and he might change his (and their) view that they were disappointed in him. Before continuing the discussion of strengths, however, we recommended that Aaron undergo an evaluation to assess whether he might have learning problems that were becoming more evident in middle school, which sometimes happens when the work becomes more demanding.

Dena asked us to clarify what we meant by evaluation and testing. We explained the different kinds of tests that would be involved and the importance of assessing Aaron's learning strengths as well as his weaknesses.

Interestingly, Garth seemed hesitant. He said, "If Aaron is found to have learning problems, he'll probably use that as an excuse. I can just see him saying that because he has a learning problem, he can't do the work, so we should get off his back, and if we don't get off his back, it just shows that we don't love him."

We thanked Garth for bringing up that concern, which is shared by many parents. We explained that when children are diagnosed with a learning problem, we address how to make certain that they never use it as an excuse to behave in ways that interfere with coping effectively. Rather, we can use the information to help children and their parents understand their learning strengths and vulnerabilities so that they can set more realistic expectations. Also, the information can be important for developing strategies at school to help the children succeed. The Elefsons nodded their understanding.

We added that we have found another benefit of such an evaluation. Many children with learning problems believe they aren't very smart, and some expect they will never learn. Deep down or maybe not so deep down, they're disappointed in themselves and feel they've disappointed their parents. Some express their feelings directly, such as when Aaron accused his parents of considering him a real disappointment or not loving him. Others become angry and irritable—behavior Aaron had also shown. However, when children gain a better sense of their learning problems and appreciate that they can be helped with these problems, they often become more hopeful. Not only that, an evaluation can help parents become more realistic and hopeful and can be the basis for learning to use more effective disciplinary practices.

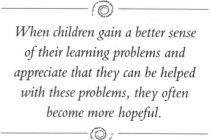

When children gain a better sense of their learning problems and appreciate that they can be helped with these problems, they often become more hopeful.

Finally, we assured the Elefsons that we would directly address the concern that Garth had raised. As the evaluation proceeded, we would discuss what to do if Aaron used any of the test results as an excuse for any of his negative feelings or behavior.

Dena asked, "What do we tell Aaron about coming in for testing? He has had testing in the past and seemed to believe it was being used to confirm that things were wrong with him. When the school psychologist did testing, Aaron told us we were having him tested as 'punishment' because we 'didn't love him.' We tried to explain that wasn't true, but I'm not sure he ever believed the school psychologist or us. He actually became angrier while being tested. I don't want to go through that again."

We agreed that we didn't want to see that either, and we agreed that testing certainly doesn't thrill most children. We shared that some feel as if they're being placed under a microscope and that we're looking for what's wrong with them. One boy told us he thought he had a "bad brain." We explained that, as a general approach, we want children to believe that the testing will help them and their parents and teachers. Also, we treat the evaluation as an opportunity for parents to share with their children any concerns they have about whether they've been too strict or have said things that were hurtful.

Garth asked, "Are you saying we should apologize to Aaron?"

We assured him that we weren't necessarily advocating an apology, although there's nothing wrong with an apology if it is deserved. Referring to Dena's earlier example of yelling at Aaron for seeing the glass as half empty and not enjoying life, we recalled that her intention was to change Aaron's negative outlook. But most likely, Aaron had perceived her remark to be criticism and reinforcement of his belief that he was a disappointment to his mother. Thus, we weren't suggesting that the Elefsons apologize to Aaron for specific things, such as what Dena said, but they might want to let him know in some way that they realized some of the things they had said might not have been helpful.

Garth replied, "It's interesting that you point out Aaron's perspective. It's what you mentioned before and what I've actually been thinking about. Most likely, when we've said things to him, he has felt that we're being mean and punitive, but we're just trying to help him be less negative and less pessimistic."

We again supported Garth's goal while reinforcing the importance of being empathic. We repeated that we shared the Elefsons' goal of helping Aaron be more positive and optimistic, and we explained that, in order to accomplish our goal, we would have to keep in mind Aaron's perspective and determine ways of talking to him so that he would experience words as helping rather than accusing him. We pointed out that Garth had already begun to do this in his earlier remarks that he had wanted to tell Aaron he was a disappointment but had realized that his son would experience those words as criticism that would only lead to more anger. Because of the chance of being misinterpreted, we advise that when parents say or do something with their children, especially if it involves correcting their children's behavior, they should first consider what they hope to accomplish and then ask themselves, "Am I saying or doing it in a way that my kids can really hear what I have to say and respond constructively?" In the case of preparing for an evaluation of Aaron, we counseled the Elefsons that the way they explained the testing to Aaron could actually create an opportunity for Aaron to begin feeling that they loved him and wanted to help him.

This last comment touched a chord in Dena. She tearfully replied, "I'd love for Aaron to feel that way. I'd love for him to know how much we love him, but I'm certain right now, as Garth just said, he sees us as mean and punitive."

We shared our hope that our suggestions of what to say to Aaron would give Dena and her husband a sense of how parents can be firm but less punitive, so that children will become more cooperative and less sad. Garth assured us that they were ready to listen.

We suggested that he and Dena might begin by telling Aaron that they believed they had said some things to him that might have led him to think they didn't love him and were disappointed with him. Most likely, he would agree. But whether or not he agreed, they could say, "Right now the most important thing is for you to realize we do love you and want you to know we're on your side." We added that they could empathize by saying, "We know that, except for playing in the band, school has not been the happiest place for you, but we think you would like to be happy and succeed."

Dena interrupted, "But what if Aaron says he just doesn't care about how he does in school?"

We agreed that Aaron might say something like that. But we added that we thought he did care. When children believe they aren't very smart and can't achieve in school, they often protect themselves by saying they don't care. Therefore, if Aaron said he didn't care, it would be important to avoid getting angry and saying things like "You *should* care" or "You're never going to succeed unless you begin to care." We advised the Elefsons to be careful not to get into an argument, but simply to say something like, "You may not care as much now, but who knows? Maybe in the future you'll care a little more." These words would introduce the possibility that his perspective might not be cast in stone and could change. And if Aaron replied that he wouldn't care in the future, the Elefsons shouldn't pursue the point.

Their next point, we suggested, should be to say that they believe they and the school could be more helpful, especially if they had a better idea of his strengths and learning style. They should emphasize that all children are able to do some things well, as he is a very good musician and artist, but most children also have trouble with certain areas. They could tell Aaron that some children find reading or writing easy but can't play a musical instrument or draw. Other children are great artists but may have some difficulty with reading.

Garth said, "I don't know if we've ever spoken with Aaron that way before. We usually just criticize his negative attitude."

We asked Garth and Dena how they thought Aaron might respond if they began to speak with him in the way we had suggested.

Garth replied, "I'm not sure, but what you're suggesting sounds better than what we've said to him in the past."

We continued our advice by saying that even if Aaron remained skeptical after they had said the things we suggested, it would be important for Garth and Dena to begin talking specifically about the evaluation. Since Aaron had undergone testing in the past and said it was used to find out what was wrong with him and to punish him since they didn't love him, we thought the parents had to bring up those feelings.

Dena asked us to explain what we meant they should say.

We suggested that she and Garth tell Aaron that they thought there was something that could help all of them figure out the best way for Aaron to learn and succeed in school, but they realized that when it had been done in the past, Aaron felt it was a punishment. They should emphasize that testing was not meant as a punishment at all, but rather as a way of helping. We predicted that when Aaron's parents mentioned the testing, Aaron would most likely balk at the suggestion. We advised them to respond simply by saying they had set up an appointment for him to meet us and that we would be able to explain the reasons for the testing and ways the testing could be used. They could emphasize that the testing wasn't a punishment but rather a way of making certain he would get help in school if he needed it. Finally, reminding the Elefsons that Aaron might dismiss what they said, we encouraged them not to give up.

Garth wondered, "What if Aaron says he won't come to see you?"

We acknowledged that many children respond this way. Although we don't want children to feel that they're being forced to see us, we suggested that the Elefsons firmly tell Aaron that he must come in and that we would explain the testing to him and wanted to hear his views. We wanted Aaron to begin feeling like a vital part of the evaluation and to know that we would welcome his input. We added that the Elefsons could also let Aaron know that after the testing, we would explain his strengths and the areas that need some reinforcement and would suggest specific ways to provide this reinforcement. By offering these comments, we emphasized that a key ingredient in our approach was for Aaron to feel in control of his life, a vital feature of self-discipline and a resilient mindset (see Chapter 3).

Dena replied, "What you're suggesting makes a lot of sense, but I'm concerned that at this point, Aaron sees us in such a negative way that he'll reject almost anything we say."

We agreed that he might but reminded her of her desire to change his negative perception. We counseled her that the sooner she and her husband began, the better. After all, the situation wouldn't improve on its own. Aaron wouldn't change his perception until his parents changed what they said and did with him. We emphasized that we weren't blaming Dena and Garth for the tension in their home; rather, we wanted to convey that they could have a large influence in lessening that tension, including Aaron's feelings that he was a disappointment to them and to himself.

These last few comments are ones we offer many parents. We try to offset their own feelings of helplessness and inadequacy about changing their relationship with their children and modifying their disciplinary approach.

In this initial meeting with Dena and Garth Elefson, we tried to empathize with their frustration, so they wouldn't perceive us as judgmental of their parenting efforts. Also, while we acknowledged their anger toward Aaron, we emphasized the value of adopting a more empathic stance, trying to see the world through his eyes. We highlighted instances in which they had already shown empathy, demonstrating that they had already taken several positive steps. In addition, one of our goals was for them to think about ways in which we might use Aaron's interests and islands of competence (music and art) to counteract his feelings of unworthiness. Our questions were intended to encourage the Elefsons to reflect on their disciplinary practices, and we hoped they would not continue to punish Aaron by prohibiting him from engaging in his islands of competence. Some parents might contend that the only time their children listen to them is when the parents threaten to take away a favored activity. However, in our experience, this kind of "high-stakes" discipline all too often backfires, fueling greater anger and resentment.

We will return to our work with the Elefson family in the next chapter, when we highlight a mindset that burdens a number of children—namely, the feeling that things are unfair and life has dealt them a bad hand. Like Aaron, many children do have several overlapping negative mindsets and don't fall neatly into one category. In this chapter, we will offer suggestions about what parents might say and what forms of discipline they might use to counteract children's feelings that they are a disappointment to their parents and to themselves.

Discipline with Acceptance

As we have emphasized in our previous books, to discipline effectively and nurture a resilient mindset in children, parents need to love their children unconditionally. That means we parents must accept our children for who they are, not necessarily what we want them to be. We have found that, when children believe they have let themselves and others down, contributing factors include parents' failure to appreciate the children's unique temperament and learning style and parents' unrealistic expectations for what their children can achieve. In such situations, parents often punish children for not meeting unrealistic expectations. This punishment promotes anger and self-doubt, rather than confidence and resilience.

Acceptance and unconditional love do *not* mean allowing our children to do whatever they want, without any limits on their behavior. If anything, when children feel accepted, they are more receptive to fulfilling our requests and respecting our consequences. They experience our requests and limits in an atmosphere of love and support. For example, Paul and Lilly Breem, whom we met in Chapter 5, were able to accept their son Wade's interest in theater although they and their other son, Phillip, shared interests in

When children feel accepted, they are more receptive to fulfilling our requests and respecting our consequences. They experience our requests and limits in an atmosphere of love and support.

academics and sports. In contrast, Mitchell and Paige White, also in Chapter 5, openly conveyed their disappointment in their son, George, who was shy and had learning problems. Earlier in this chapter, the Elefsons struggled to accept their son, Aaron. Once they had decided Aaron's problems were rooted in "laziness," they became less empathic and more punitive, failing to appreciate and reinforce his strengths. The result was a boy with anger, low self-esteem, and a strong sense that he was unloved.

In our discussions about acceptance and realistic expectations, parents often ask us what we consider to be realistic expectations for children of different ages. Our best answer to this question is, "First tell us about your child, and then we can provide an intelligent view of appropriate goals and expectations for that child." Although certain guidelines apply based on developmental principles, our goals and expectations should not be predicated on a child's chronological age. As we have noted, children are very different from birth, and we must take these differences into account when we consider appropriate expectations and disciplinary practices. If parents do not align their expectations with acceptance and appreciation of their child's unique qualities, then the stage is set for family stress and anger and the use of punishment that reinforces children's feelings of letting themselves and their parents down.

The Cerano Family: "We Can't Take Larissa Out in Public"

For a portrait of unrealistic expectations, we have a relevant example in the parenting style of Travis and Beverly Cerano, a family we introduced in our book *Raising Resilient Children*. Given the theme of this chapter, we will expand upon our earlier book's description of the Cerano family.

Travis and Beverly Cerano consulted us about their six-year-old daughter, Larissa. Some parental descriptions leave a lasting impression on us. This was certainly one of them. Beverly immediately told us, "We can't take Larissa out in public. Trips to supermarkets or department stores are a nightmare. The first thing that happens is that she wants us to buy things. If we refuse, she gets upset and eventually has a tantrum. She screams that we don't love her. Once she even said she knew we were going to give her back."

We asked what Larissa meant when she said her parents would "give her back."

Beverly replied, "We wondered the same thing, so we asked her. Her response was unbelievable, especially since the first time she brought up 'giving her back' was a little before her fifth birthday. She said she knew we didn't love her and we'd give her back to the hospital where she'd been born. If she believed in the stork theory of birth, she probably would have accused us of planning to give her back to the stork."

We asked whether the Ceranos had had a chance to ask Larissa why she thought they would give her back to the hospital.

Beverly responded, "We did. And again I couldn't believe that such a young child would think this way. She said we didn't love her, we didn't give her what she wanted, and she actually said that she knew we had wanted to exchange her for another baby in the hospital."

We asked Beverly what she felt when her daughter said that.

"I felt very sad to think that Larissa thought we wanted to trade her in for another baby. I tried to explain that we did love her, that we did not want any other child but her. When I said that, Larissa wondered, 'If you love me, why do you yell at me so much?' I tried to tell her that sometimes we got angry because of her screaming, but we did love her."

Travis stepped in. "I often thought Bev was spending too much time trying to reason with Larissa, which only made her tantrums worse. Then Bev would become more upset at Larissa, so she'd yell or spank her. I learned my lesson, though. When

I took Larissa to the store, even when I threatened a spanking before we even entered the building, she still was too demanding and started crying after a few moments. She screamed that I didn't love her. To be honest, I wasn't sure if she said that just to win my sympathy and get her way or if she really felt that way."

Beverly noted, "Sometimes it's so difficult to know what's the best way to deal with Larissa's tantrums. Based on the recommendation of a friend, we went out and bought a book on preventing tantrums. The book suggested that we prepare Larissa in advance by telling her that we're going into the store but we're not going to buy anything and please don't ask. Even when she agreed, we still had problems."

As we listened to the Ceranos' description of Larissa, we felt sure that, at that point, she had limited capacity for self-discipline and was quickly overwhelmed when enticing materials were placed within sight. The lure of seeing many items that she desired soon eclipsed her promise not to make requests. Therefore, despite the advice of the parenting text, Larissa and her parents would be caught up in lengthy arguments in the store, which routinely triggered the expected negative script, featuring Larissa's escalation of her requests, a spanking that confirmed to Larissa she was not loved, and everyone's leaving the store in distress.

Beverly told us that a neighbor, trying to be helpful, offered another strategy that had worked with her child: "She suggested we tell Larissa in advance that if she asks to buy something, we will immediately leave the store."

On the surface, this approach seemed sound. It appeared to lessen the likelihood of a screaming match, spanking, and frustration. To the Ceranos' dismay, however, Larissa began to cry and scream after leaving the store, and she could not be soothed.

Travis admitted, "We were so frustrated that we told Larissa we would buy her one item of her choice as long as it wasn't too expensive. Well, that didn't work. Larissa's idea of inexpensive just didn't match ours. Once again she ended up demanding and crying." Although we didn't say so at this moment, it is questionable whether most six-year-old children would understand the definition of *inexpensive*.

As we have done with many families, we began by confirming for Larissa's parents that the strategies they had tried were good ones for some children but by themselves would likely not be effective with Larissa or other children with her temperament. We discussed the concept of temperament and the importance of learning to understand and accept Larissa's temperament. We emphasized that acceptance did not mean giving in to Larissa's demands, but rather discovering more effective ways of responding to these demands. We gave the Ceranos reading material that describes how poor impulse control and a seemingly insatiable style affect children's behavior and how to discipline such children effectively.

At our next session, to make certain that the Ceranos understood the material we had given them, we started by discussing what they had read.

Beverly said, "We really weren't aware of how different kids' temperaments could be. I wish we had known more about it when Larissa was first born."

We agreed that if parents were more aware of temperaments, they might have fewer problems and use less punitive methods of discipline. We then explained that, given Larissa's temperament and impulsivity, she wasn't ready to enter a supermarket or department store with them. We emphasized that in those situations, she was likely to experience problems. With empathy, we explained that their expectations for Larissa did not match her temperament and learning style.

Travis said, "Even though I've read the material you gave me and understand temperament better, I still think that a six-year-old should be able to control herself. She has friends the same age, and they don't seem to have these problems."

We agreed that his point was understandable but commented that any child with Larissa's temperament would likely experience difficulty at Larissa's age in a similar type of setting.

Beverly noted, "Like my husband, I used to believe that Larissa could control herself if she wanted to. I felt that because she was so demanding, it must mean we'd spoiled her, given in to her, so she wasn't going to behave. But after reading the material you provided, I'm beginning to think I was wrong."

We acknowledged that many six-year-olds can show more restraint than Larissa, but Larissa's inability to do so was part of her temperament, not the result of their spoiling her. We emphasized that it was important for the Ceranos to understand that their difficulty in accepting their daughter's temperament had prompted expectations that Larissa couldn't meet, even though other children of her age could. In effect, they were punishing her for behavior over which she had little, if any, control. Their yelling and screaming were contributing to her belief that she was not loved, just as Aaron felt unloved by his parents.

Beverly said, "But not being able to take Larissa out to a store would be difficult. It's not always convenient for one of us to stay home or to arrange for a baby-sitter."

Agreeing with Beverly, we asked her to consider how often her outings, particularly shopping, had been disrupted by Larissa's behavior. We also suggested that the disruptions to her relationship with Larissa because of these outbursts were far more inconvenient and disabling than having one parent stay home or arranging for a baby-sitter. We reminded Beverly and Travis that the anger and frustration resulting from these situations contributed to Larissa's feeling that she was unloved and that her parents wanted to trade her in for another child. Although it was certainly inconvenient to make arrangements to have someone watch Larissa while they shopped, that effort would ease the tension in their home and improve their relationship with Larissa. We added that the pattern of negative behavior between them

and their daughter reflected more than just an immediate problem; it was setting up many future conflicts in all areas of family
life.

Beverly replied, "I can understand what you're saying, but how
will Larissa ever learn self-control if she doesn't have experiences
in which we set limits?"

Acknowledging that her concern was valid, we added the
qualification that learning often takes place within safe limits.
Using analogies to sports, we pointed out that when you're learning to swim, you would swim in the shallow end, and when
you're learning to bowl, you might want to put bumpers in the
gutters. You would do that because your goal is not only to learn,
but also, in the process, to feel safe, successful, and happy. In the
case of Larissa, taking her into a large supermarket or store at
that time would be beyond her toleration, so it wouldn't be the
best way to teach her limits. We pointed out that Travis and Beverly had discovered that, even with preparation, their shopping
trips with Larissa generally led to conflict and convinced Larissa
that she had let them down so much that they preferred she not
remain with them. Therefore, we concluded, these experiences
of going into stores were overwhelming for Larissa and couldn't
help her learn new skills.

We suggested that the Ceranos start with small, realistic steps.
We recommended that one step would be to take Larissa into
a more manageable convenience store, a place they could leave
rapidly. We encouraged the Ceranos to continue incorporating
choice but to be more specific and less open-ended. For example,
they might tell her, "You can have ice cream or a chocolate bar,"
rather than, "You can have something that isn't expensive." We
explained that offering Larissa realistic choices was a disciplinary
approach that nurtures important attributes of a resilient mindset:
a feeling of control of her life and the belief that she can begin
to solve problems and make decisions (see Chapters 3 and 4 for
details).

We also encouraged Travis and Beverly to use a strategy that they had tried inconsistently. Before entering a store, they should remind Larissa of the conditions they had set and the consequences that would follow if a problem arose. For example, after informing Larissa of her choice, they should remind her that if it was difficult for her to do what they requested, they would leave the store, and crying or screaming would not help her.

We suggested a number of strategies to apply within the home as well, guided by a process that would help Larissa develop self-discipline by becoming a more active participant in solving problems. We reviewed the problem-solving sequence outlined in Chapter 4. We recommended that Beverly and Travis select a couple of problem areas at home, such as Larissa failing to put her toys away or arguing about going to bed. We suggested that they talk to Larissa about why those behaviors were a problem and then enlist her input in how best to resolve them. As we described in earlier chapters, we've used that approach successfully with many other families, including the Burns family (Chapter 2), the Heath family (Chapter 4), and the Berkshires (Chapter 4).

At first the Ceranos were skeptical about involving Larissa in solving problems, believing that she was too young and impulsive to engage in this process. They also worried that her solution to problems would be "to get her way." Travis said, "From our discussions with you, I can see that we've been too inconsistent and sometimes too harsh with Larissa. I know we have to be more consistent and watch that we don't come across as ogres. But I think we can be consistent and tell her what to do without getting into a discussion with her and asking for her input."

We replied that the two things he mentioned weren't mutually exclusive. Acknowledging that it would help to be more consistent and less harsh and that the parents should be the main adults to set limits and consequences, we explained that we were suggesting an additional measure: as they became more consistent and less punitive, they should look for ways of involving Larissa in solving some of the problems. The more she learned to stop and think and the more she could appreciate that rules and limits weren't created to make her life miserable, the more she could develop self-discipline. We described our philosophy about the goals of discipline: If we always tell children what they should or shouldn't do, we may end up raising obedient or compliant kids. However, the major goal of discipline should not be to make children obedient or compliant, but to develop self-discipline in children so that they can reflect on what they do and understand why rules and limits are essential. Also, children tend to feel more respected and loved when parents include them in helping to solve problems.

Beverly said to her husband, "I wonder what would happen if we asked Larissa what would help her to remember to put away her toys or not scream."

He replied, "I bet she would either say she doesn't know or tell us it isn't important to her."

We agreed that those replies were quite possible and offered some responses that could be helpful. If Larissa said she doesn't know, they could simply say, "That's OK; we'll try to figure it out together." If she said it isn't important to her, they could validate what she said by noting, "We're glad you could tell us you feel it's not important," but then add, "It might not seem important, but it can lead to less arguing and yelling in the house, so it *is* important to figure out what to do about it." In deciding what to say, the parents would have to consider Larissa's cognitive level and involve her in a realistic way, but we encouraged them not to get thrown off track if she didn't immediately respond positively to their requests.

Beverly wondered, "What if Larissa tries to take advantage of us and says we should clean up her toys or that it's OK to scream?"

We advised that there were different things they could say. We reminded the Ceranos that it was their responsibility not to permit Larissa to take advantage of them and get her way. For example, if Larissa said she didn't want to put her toys away, they could tell her she had a choice: either they would help her put the toys away, or she could put them away by herself. Then they could state the consequences: if the toys aren't put away, they won't be available for her to play with the next day. They should emphasize to Larissa that it is her choice. Also, later, at a calmer time, they could say that some kids may forget to put their toys away, and they don't want to nag her to do so, so they wonder if she could suggest how they might remind her to put her toys away if she forgets to do so. (As we emphasized in Chapters 3 and 4, if your goal is to use discipline techniques that promote self-discipline and resilience, you must actively involve your children in considering solutions to disciplinary problems. And you'll often be surprised that they can come up with good ideas.)

We also addressed the Ceranos' concern that Larissa interpreted the limits they set as indications that they didn't love her. We explained that Larissa would be less likely to arrive at that interpretation if they also began to give her positive feedback about things she did well. We often advise parents, "Catch your child doing something good." We admitted to the Ceranos that when we're frustrated with our kids, it can become easy to overlook the many times they cooperate.

Beverly said, "I think we do catch Larissa when she does good things."

We declared that this meant they were already partway to their goal. We explained that we had raised this point so that she and her husband would praise Larissa as consistently as possible. We added that we hadn't yet spent much time discussing what they saw as Larissa's strengths, her islands of competence (see Chapters 5 and 6). We asked the Ceranos what Larissa enjoyed doing.

Beverly responded, "The first thing that comes to mind is that she likes to cook and bake. She's always asking me if she can help make cookies or a cake. Actually, when she helps me, she's much more focused and seems to really like what she's doing."

We asked Beverly to describe how she felt when Larissa was helping her.

"It's interesting you should ask that. At first I was concerned she would spill things all over the floor, but she didn't. When we've made cookies together or baked something, I've felt very close to her. It's something I should really do more often with Larissa."

We observed that, from her description, it sounded as if Larissa enjoyed baking with Beverly.

"Definitely. Larissa is delighted when we take the cookies out of the oven and even more delighted when we eat them."

We asked her what she said to Larissa at those times.

"I tell her what a good job she has done."

Travis interrupted. "As we're talking, I realize something. I also tell her how delicious the cookies are and what a good job she has done, but I'm not certain I tell her that enough. With all of her negative behavior, I'm not certain I tell her enough how much I love her and how much I appreciate the wonderful things she does like make delicious cookies. Perhaps if I did, she would be less likely to think we wanted to trade her in for another baby."

We acknowledged that when we're really struggling with our kids, sometimes focusing on their strengths or telling them what they mean to us takes a backseat to criticisms and yelling.

Following our discussions with them, the Ceranos began assuming a more proactive, empathic, problem-solving approach in which they learned to accept Larissa's basic style and temperament and then worked to accommodate to that style, within reason. Though Larissa's response was not always what they wished for, the Ceranos became better prepared to handle any setbacks that occurred. In addition, they focused on reinforcing her islands of competence. Their willingness to accept Larissa gave them strength to maintain their chosen course of intervention calmly when she challenged them. Initially, Larissa sometimes had tantrums and fell back to her negative way of responding or her negative scripts about being traded in for another child. When she had these outbursts, her parents learned to handle them firmly but calmly. Their calm response, in turn, led to fewer such outbursts.

When the Ceranos asked Larissa how they might remind her if she forgot to do something, she amazed them by saying that if they reminded her ten minutes before the time the toys had to be put away, it would be easier for her to pick them up than if they told her to put them away immediately. This simple strategy was successful, partly because Larissa herself had suggested it.

In the meantime, her parents continued to take her on short trips to small stores. Within several months, Larissa successfully made what her parents termed the "big jump" into larger stores. As important as the accomplishment of this "big jump" was, it reflected a more significant change—modifications in the mind-set of each member of the Cerano family.

Travis and Beverly shifted from perceiving Larissa as a self-centered, inconsiderate child who always wanted her own way to a child who happened to have been born with an inflexible, insatiable temperament. This shift of perception prompted a shift in disciplinary practices from being overly punitive and harsh to assuming a more authoritative, calm, problem-solving stance that still held Larissa accountable for her actions while reinforcing a sense of control and responsibility. The Ceranos also paid closer attention to reinforcing Larissa's strengths.

Larissa's mindset also underwent a transformation, in great part because of the changes demonstrated by her parents. As they replaced their punitive approach with a more tolerant, loving style, Larissa's feelings that she had disappointed herself and her parents lessened. In addition, their attitude that she could participate in solving problems reinforced her self-respect, self-acceptance, and self-discipline.

Self-Acceptance Supports Self-Discipline

In our clinical practices, we have worked with many children and adults who disliked themselves and felt their parents didn't accept them and love them unconditionally. When self-loathing dominates self-acceptance, children (and adults as well) are likely to engage in impulsive, self-defeating behaviors that generate further criticism and rejection. As you raise your children to develop responsibility and self-discipline, you therefore need to do so in a manner that does not assault their self-dignity but rather maintains a loving relationship with them in which they begin to trust themselves and you.

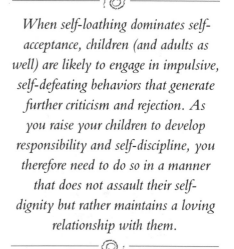

When self-loathing dominates self-acceptance, children (and adults as well) are likely to engage in impulsive, self-defeating behaviors that generate further criticism and rejection. As you raise your children to develop responsibility and self-discipline, you therefore need to do so in a manner that does not assault their self-dignity but rather maintains a loving relationship with them.

As we have seen with several families in this book, this loving relationship is a foundation for the emergence of self-discipline.

8

Responding Constructively
When Life Seems Unfair

Parents frequently complain that their children all too often utter the words "It's not fair!" The following statements illustrate the kinds of examples parents have given to describe their children's beliefs on the theme of unfairness:

- "Every time I tell my teenage daughter that she can't spend the day with her friends at the mall, she screams that I'm not being fair. Then she says all of her friends' parents let their kids meet at the mall."
- "My thirteen-year-old son says the reason he doesn't have any friends is that he's not very good-looking. He says his older brother got all of the good looks in the family and wishes he looked like my husband's side of the family rather than mine. He sees my husband and his family as being more handsome than people in my family."
- "Whenever we tell our eight-year-old daughter she can't have something, her first comment is, 'Why can't I? All my friends get the things they want. You're not fair.' I told her life isn't always fair, but that doesn't seem to help."

■ A poignant comment was offered by parents of two sons, one fifteen years old, the other thirteen. The fifteen-year-old had significant learning problems, while his younger brother was in the gifted program at school. After an especially stressful day at school, the fifteen-year-old told his parents that his younger brother "had already forgotten more than he would ever learn." He added, "Why was I born with a hole in my brain? It's just not fair."

Sometimes children's words about unfairness refer to actions parents or other adults have taken that youngsters believe are unreasonable, while at other times, children are bemoaning their situation in life. Such feelings overlap with themes found in earlier chapters in this book, especially in Chapters 3 and 6. However, so many children complain about unfairness that this issue deserves to be considered separately.

When Life Seems Unfair

When children perceive their life as unfair, they experience various feelings. These feelings prompt different behaviors, many of which do not ease their pain but rather intensify their belief that they are unloved. They often see the world through the lens of "unfairness" and are quick to interpret all actions by parents and other adults as a confirmation of how unjust people are toward them.

Some children wallow in sadness, constantly complaining about their lot in life. They may believe that things cannot change, so they don't try any positive action to remedy the situation. Their passive position may resemble that of a martyr who entertains little hope that things can improve. They offer many excuses for their inaction, including the common refrain "I don't care."

Other children lash out at whomever they feel has wronged them. They yell at parents, accusing them of treating their siblings better. For example, at a workshop, one mother reported,

"When I gave each of my two kids a glass of water, my daughter pushed her glass against her brother's glass to see if he had more water than she had. I was so frustrated and told her, 'It's just water from the faucet; I can give you more.' She said, 'If you loved me as much as my brother, you wouldn't give me less water.' I just blew up and told her that she was being ungrateful." This child's father observed, "It's like our daughter is poised to see things as unfair and that she's not getting enough compared with her brother. It's difficult to stay calm with her."

Still other youngsters develop an attitude of thinking, "If they won't treat me right, I won't cooperate." They may not scream at others, but they simply display a defiant attitude, often refusing to help or cooperate with the requests of their parents or other adults. They often believe parents possess overly demanding expectations of them, and they moan, "You're always on my back; you always want me to do more than my brothers or sisters (or the parents of my friends). Well, I don't want to!" At one therapy session, a teenage boy held up his hand and gave his father a "Heil Hitler" salute, yelling that his father could have been an SS trooper.

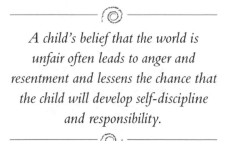

A child's belief that the world is unfair often leads to anger and resentment and lessens the chance that the child will develop self-discipline and responsibility.

A child's belief that the world is unfair often leads to anger and resentment and lessens the chance that the child will develop self-discipline and responsibility. To prevent or reduce these problems, parents need to use disciplinary techniques that minimize a child's perception of unfairness.

Unrealistic Parents, Unsatisfied Children

In Chapter 7 we mentioned that some children have a temperament that predisposes them to believe a black cloud perpetually hangs above their head. Similarly, from birth, some children seem to possess the attitude that the world is unfair. Parents observe that these children are harder to please or soothe. They sometimes label these children "insatiable" to capture the fact that whatever one does for them is not enough. One father said of his five-year-old daughter, "If I buy her a new toy, she's happy for a little while but soon complains that she wants another new toy." He then offered a poignant statement: "Her pleasure is so brief. Nothing seems to counteract her unhappiness. She always wants more and more, but when she gets what she wants, rather than being happy, she starts to think of what she doesn't have. To be honest, my wife and I really feel for her, but she also drives us crazy."

While some children from birth appear to be predisposed to perceive the world as unfair, such perceptions can also be triggered by parents' attitudes and behaviors. In the previous chapter, we discussed the importance of parents having realistic expectations and learning to accept their children for who they are, rather than what they hoped they would be. In earlier chapters, we witnessed firsthand the ways in which unrealistic expectations or the favoring of one child over another interfered with discipline and lessened the development of self-discipline. For example, the Wilkinses in Chapters 4 and 6 constantly compared twelve-year-old Melanie unfavorably with her fourteen-year-old sister, Patty.

Perhaps the most dramatic illustration of differential treatment was that of the Whites, whom we described in Chapter 5. They adored sixteen-year-old Linda, who was successful socially, academically, and athletically, while being disappointed in and harsh with George, their thirteen-year-old son, who had learning, social, and motor coordination problems. It was obvious to George that his parents were less understanding of him, and he reacted by setting a controlled fire in school—not to burn the school down, but more as a cry for help.

While most children will sometimes accuse their parents of being unfair, it is incumbent on parents to reflect honestly about their attitudes toward and interactions with their children. Parents must assess whether there might be any validity to their children's perceptions of unfairness and determine whether they should adjust their expectations and discipline. Parents need not alter their parenting style each time a child says, "You're not fair," or "You treat my brother or sister better than you treat me." However, parents need to take such comments seriously, especially if children offer them regularly and intensely. Also, parents can learn to respond to these accusations effectively and with empathy, regardless of how valid the accusations are. Although you may believe your child's perception has no basis in reality, the perception is your child's reality, so it is where you must start when you want to make a change.

> *Although you may believe your child's perception has no basis in reality, the perception is your child's reality.*

The Amherst Family: "Why Should I Clear the Table?"

Susanna Amherst, a divorced mother of two, was distraught when she came to see us. Her ex-husband, who lived thousands of miles away, saw his children only during one holiday season each year and three weeks during the summer. Susanna felt "alone and with little support" in raising the children. She described her position as an administrator at a local college as "challenging, gratifying, and tiring."

She noted, "Now that my kids are old enough to help in the house, I expect them to do so, but I get very little help from my twelve-year-old daughter, Jill." A red flag went up when Susanna added, "It's tough for my thirteen-year-old son, David, to help a lot, since he has learning problems. He needs more time to finish his homework each night and is exhausted by the time he does. I wish Jill would be more understanding."

Susanna provided more background about the family: "Their father left me about eight years ago for a younger woman, and while he provides some financial support, we really need my income to make ends meet. I like my job, but I wish I didn't have to work the long hours I do." Then, unsolicited, she offered a lengthy discourse about her life: "I'll be honest; even after all these years, I still feel a lot of anger toward my ex-husband. It's not just that he left me unexpectedly, but if we were still married, I probably wouldn't have the financial worries I do and probably could have a job that was satisfying but with fewer hours. I think it would be easier if I remarried, but who knows, that could add more problems. Also, I just haven't met anyone I'd want to be married to. I have two sisters, both of whom are in good marriages and have much more flexible schedules. Maybe I shouldn't say this. I'm happy for them, but sometimes I envy them. I don't want to sound envious, but maybe I am. I have to be careful that I don't fall into a martyr's role and feel that life has treated me unfairly."

She suddenly stopped and smiled. "Sorry! Sometimes I can get on a soapbox, especially when I'm feeling stressed out, which seems to be happening more and more lately. I feel like I have a motor mouth that doesn't stop."

We empathized that she had evidently experienced a lot of pressure as a single mother. We added that when people feel pressure, they often wonder about what might have been or compare themselves with others.

Susanna replied, "I appreciate your saying that. Sometimes I get angry at myself for feeling sorry for myself, which makes me feel even worse."

We told Susanna that we appreciated her honesty and her effort to come in to consult us. We expressed our desire to help her figure out ways to ease some of the pressure she'd been feeling.

She again responded, "I appreciate that."

We turned the conversation to Susanna's children, asking to hear more about them, including her concerns and questions about them.

Susanna replied, "Very honestly, I'm feeling stressed about both kids, but for different reasons. As I briefly mentioned before, it would make life so much easier if Jill would help out with some of the chores, like preparing dinner, clearing the table, or cleaning up, but I constantly have to remind her. When I remind her, she loves to tell me that I'm not being fair, that I don't expect David to do these things. I tell her that David can't do as much because of his learning problems and the pressure he feels about his schoolwork. I've said, 'Instead of thinking things are unfair, you should be happy that you don't have learning problems.' Last week I was so annoyed with her attitude that I told her, 'If anyone should think things are unfair, it's David, since learning is so hard for him.'"

We asked her to describe Jill's response when she made those statements.

"The usual. She said I never listen to her and that I love David more. In a belligerent tone, she said, 'Why should I clear the table? You never ask David to help, and he's a year older than I am. All he has to say is that he has a lot of homework to do, and you let him off from doing what he's supposed to do. You treat him like a king and me like a servant.'"

We commented that Jill's words were rather strong and asked Susanna how she had handled the situation.

She replied, "I guess not very well. When I tell Jill that she should be grateful that she doesn't have learning problems, she seems to get angrier. What makes things tenser is that David sometimes says he can't stand the arguing. I've resorted to taking things away from Jill, such as TV or phone time, and even grounding her. My feeling is if she doesn't have time to help out, then she doesn't have time to watch TV or speak with her friends. But rather than improving her behavior, she seems to dig her heels in even more."

Susanna began to cry, observing, "It's not a very happy household, and I feel stymied about how to make things better, especially since I'm so exhausted and overwhelmed. I feel like a failure as a mother."

As we listened to Susanna's words, several thoughts emerged. Unfairness was a dominant theme in the family. Susanna obviously felt that, compared with her sisters, her situation in life was not very fair, because her husband had left her and she had to work long hours to meet the family's financial needs. She saw David's learning struggles as unfair, considering that learning came easily to many children, including Jill. Yet her empathy did not spill over to Jill. She had difficulty accepting Jill's perspective that her mother had different expectations for and treatment of her and David. Of course, Jill's anger made it more difficult for Susanna to appreciate Jill's viewpoint. That difficulty did not excuse Susanna's actions, but it helped us understand her seeming lack of empathy toward Jill and her harsh discipline.

Susanna's frustration, exhaustion, and lack of empathy also contributed to her failure to communicate with Jill in a way that validated Jill's feelings. We believed such validation could serve as the basis for developing an authoritative disciplinary style that incorporated a problem-solving approach for addressing the tension and feelings of unfairness that pervaded the Amherst home. We recognized that, in offering suggestions to Susanna, we had to demonstrate the support, empathy, and validation of feelings that we were going to encourage her to show toward Jill.

Acknowledging that Susanna had been under a great deal of pressure for a number of years and had experienced a lot of friction between herself and Jill, we observed that she wanted a much better relationship with her daughter. We told Susanna that we had some ideas about improving the relationship. We asked that, as we began to share our ideas with her, she would let us know if she found any of the ideas to be unclear or if she thought we were misreading the situation or criticizing her. We assured Susanna that we didn't want her to feel we were being critical or unfair.

We used the last word purposefully, since unfairness was a central theme in the family. We also intended our choice of words to model an empathic approach that we hoped would help Susanna be more comfortable and receptive to hearing our message. Finally, we were trying to display a style of communication that she might use with Jill.

Susanna replied, "I *have* been stressed out for a while, and I know that sometimes I've been harsh with Jill. I know that when she says I treat David better than I treat her and that I'm unfair, it's a red-hot button for me. I'd love to hear your ideas about what I might do differently."

We shared our observation that Susanna's description suggested she got upset with Jill whenever Jill accused her of being unfair. Acknowledging that no parent likes to hear a statement like that, we asked Susanna why it might be such a hot button for her.

She replied, "I've thought about that, especially when I've yelled at Jill for being ungrateful. I feel terrible afterward, but I keep doing it. I know it doesn't help the situation."

We commented that when people have a hot button, they continue to do things that they want to stop. We asked Susanna to share any thoughts she might have about why being called "unfair" by Jill had been such a charged issue.

With noticeable emotion, Susanna replied, "As I mentioned a little while ago, I've told Jill that if anyone should think things are unfair, it should be David. He really struggles with learning. But, to be honest, there are times when I've wanted to shout, 'You think things are unfair! I'll tell you what's unfair. Being deserted by your father and having to struggle to make ends meet. That's unfair! And if you would help out, things could be a little better.'" Sadly, she added, "I've never said that to Jill. I would never say it. Even when I say it to you, it sounds like it's coming from a terrible, selfish person."

We assured Susanna that her words seemed to us to be coming from someone who felt as if things hadn't been very fair and who had been experiencing a great deal of stress. We added that she had helped us understand why the topic of fairness was such a hot button for her and why she had been strict with Jill but much more understanding toward David. As part of our treatment approach, we then asked Susanna some questions that we often ask parents in order to help them view their children with greater empathy. First we asked Susanna to describe each of her children in a few words.

She paused for a few moments before answering. "In describing Jill, I think I would use words like *uncooperative* and *ungrate-*

ful. For David the first word that comes to mind is *struggling*. Learning is a struggle, making friends is a struggle, athletics are a struggle."

Next we asked her to consider whether Jill and David had an accurate idea of how she would describe them.

"Yes, especially Jill, since I've used words like *ungrateful* with her. I think David also would have a sense of the main words I would use to describe him, since we've often talked about his struggles."

We asked her how she thought each of her children would describe her.

She replied, "Wow! That's quite a question. I'm certain Jill would say I'm not fair, that I punish her for no reason, that I love David more than I love her. I know she might say those things, but they're not true. She might feel that way, since I come down harder on her than David, since she's so uncooperative. If Jill were nicer and helped out more, I wouldn't have to yell at her or punish her."

In thinking about how David might describe her, Susanna said, "I think he would say I'm supportive and I appreciate the struggles he has with learning. I think I am more supportive with David than Jill, since, even with his struggles, David acts more respectful toward me than Jill ever has."

The session was nearly over, so we suggested that we continue this discussion at our next meeting. To help with the next discussion, we asked Susanna to think about one more question: How would you like both of your children to describe you?

She responded, "That's an intriguing question."

We agreed, adding that when we had a good sense of her answer to that question, we could begin to suggest steps she might take so that Jill and David would be likely to describe her in the way she wished.

At our next session, Susanna wasted little time sharing her thoughts about the last question we had raised. "I thought a lot about how I would want Jill and David to describe me. The entire process was upsetting, especially as I thought about Jill."

We wondered what had made the process so upsetting.

"What upset me was the fact that the way I'd like Jill to describe me is so different from the way she would describe me, and I'm not sure what to do about it. I think she has such a definite image of me that it won't change unless I tell her she doesn't have to help out or she can use the phone as much as she wants and watch TV all day long."

We responded by asking Susanna what words she would want Jill to use in describing her.

"Probably the words most mothers or fathers would want to hear. Words like *loving, caring, a good listener, patient, funny*. I doubt if Jill would use these words. As I told you last time, she'd probably say I'm unfair and that I really don't love her. I just don't know how I can get her to change and how she can become more cooperative."

Susanna's comments were revealing. While she wanted a more positive relationship with Jill, she believed that this would occur only if Jill took the initiative to make changes in her attitude and behaviors. But as we highlighted in Chapter 3, when people seek their happiness by waiting for someone else to change first, they may wait a long time and never be happy. In that chapter, we noted that when parents discipline their children, one of their goals should be to increase a sense of responsibility and personal control. We knew that we would have to help Susanna examine what she could do differently in her relationship with Jill so that Jill might change her perception of her mother. We also knew Susanna would have to realize that her different ways of responding to Jill and David and her relatively harsh methods of discipline contributed to Jill's feeling that her mother was uncaring and unfair.

We commented that the more Susanna described her relationship with Jill, the more we could see how frustrating it was for both of them. Based on everything she had told us, we said, it was obvious that Susanna wanted a more loving relationship with Jill and wanted Jill to describe her with kinder words.

Before we could finish the rest of our thoughts, Susanna said, "I would love to have that kind of relationship with Jill."

We responded that we shared the same goals but might have different ideas about the best way to reach those goals. We pointed out that what Susanna had been doing wasn't working, and that meant we had to think of another approach. Assuring her that our words were not meant as criticism and that we didn't expect her to make all the changes without Jill taking any responsibility, we explained that we had to focus on what Susanna could do differently. Perhaps, without intending to do so, she had been reinforcing Jill's belief that Susanna treated the two children very differently and had been much more demanding and harsh with Jill.

Susanna didn't reply at first. Then she said, "I know you're not being judgmental and want to help, but as I think about what you just said, it feels like you're saying I'm to blame."

Insisting that we weren't interested in assigning blame, we explained that we were interested only in her assuming responsibility for change. In our experience, we said, positive change is more likely to occur in a family when parents take the initiative to change their ways of responding that have not been effective—what we call their "negative scripts." We emphasized that when we say we want parents to take the initiative, we aren't blaming them, but rather empowering them.

Susanna looked perplexed. "Empowering them?"

We explained that it's empowering to identify what she had control over and could change, rather than constantly waiting for others to change first.

She said, "I can understand that. I have a question, and I really would like an honest answer. Do you feel I've treated Jill unfairly, especially compared with David?"

Smiling, we replied that we didn't want to play what some people refer to as the "shrink game" by merely asking, "What do you think?" So we promised to answer, but only after Susanna told us how she would answer that question.

Returning the smile, Susanna said, "Ah, you *are* playing the shrink game. If you had asked me that question about fairness a couple of weeks ago, I would have said I think I'm treating them fairly, since they have different needs. But now, thinking about the questions you asked about how I would describe them and how they would describe me, I'm not as sure anymore."

We responded that when Susanna mentioned her children having different needs, her point was important. For us, fairness is not treating each child exactly the same way, which is impossible to do anyway. Rather, it's treatment based on each child's unique temperament. However, if we acknowledge that parents treat their children differently, then they are obligated to ensure that the children know they're trying to be fair. If not, the children may develop a strong belief that parents are unfair, and if they do, they're likely to become angry and defiant. In turn, parents become angrier and more punitive. The result is a vicious cycle, with harsher forms of discipline being used.

Susanna said, "I know that's been happening in our home. I have to remember that Jill is only twelve years old and has been through a lot, especially with her dad leaving when she was only four. I think I've asked her to do more than a lot of parents ask their kids to do, but I need more help than many parents do."

Answering her earlier question, we told her that, based on her descriptions, we believed she might be expecting too much from Jill. However, we added that Jill might be more willing to help out than Susanna realized. We added that we hadn't talked about David as much, but we sensed that he might feel distress from witnessing the arguments between his mother and sister.

Susanna immediately agreed. She said she could see that she had to make some changes and asked for suggestions. We discussed several of the ideas conveyed in earlier chapters in this book. We encouraged her to develop a problem-solving approach, including a discussion of the issue of fairness. We advised her to ask for help without using a negative or threatening tone, to look for opportunities to thank Jill when she cooperated, and to lessen the use of punishment that only stirred up Jill's anger and resentment.

More specifically, we recommended that Susanna discuss with both children that there had been too much tension in the home and that she recognized she had contributed to some of this tension. We advised her to explain that she had felt stressed out and really could use some help but wanted to get help in a way that everyone agreed would be fair. By acknowledging this issue, she would make it more manageable. If she felt comfortable doing so, she could also say that she had expected a lot from Jill, and even though David has learning problems, perhaps he could contribute to the household responsibilities. We suggested that Susanna list some of the daily or weekly duties and ask Jill and David how they thought they could help. We commented that, in our experience, when children are invited to help solve problems, they often rise to the occasion. Also, when they come up with solutions, they are more likely to think the solutions are fair and are more likely to follow them, since they feel some ownership of the ideas.

After listening closely, Susanna responded, "What you're suggesting sounds reasonable, but I'm concerned that Jill might say something nasty like, 'It's about time you realize how unfair you are.' Then I'm likely to get angry, and soon we'll be back where we started."

Expressing our appreciation for that important point, we agreed that this kind of conversation doesn't always go as planned, so we advise parents to be prepared for the possible obstacles. We suggested that if Jill said, "It's about time you realized how unfair you are," Susanna could reply, "I'm just sorry it took me so long to realize, since it caused a lot of friction between you and me that I wish weren't there."

Smiling, Susanna replied, "I wish you could be there invisibly when I speak with Jill and David. You could give me prompts when I'm not sure what to say."

We replied that doing more preparation during counseling would help the conversation go more smoothly. We returned to discussing the family meeting we had proposed that Susanna hold with Jill and David. We suggested that Susanna tell David that she knew he had difficulty helping out on school nights, since homework took him so long to do. Then she could say that she wanted to figure out with him and Jill what he might do during the week and on weekends that would take some of the pressure off of his sister. We added that it would be very important for her to tell the children directly, "All three of us must contribute, but I also want everyone to feel that the solution is fair."

We also reviewed the "safety net" we recommend that parents establish when devising strategies—that is, to recognize the possibility that parents or children might forget to meet a certain responsibility, so they needed to decide in advance how best to remind each other. As we have highlighted earlier in this book, anticipating possible obstacles helps to defuse disappointment, frustration, and anger.

Before our next session, Susanna called to report on her meeting with Jill and David. Although she had anticipated that Jill might not wish to sit down for a "family meeting," Jill didn't need much convincing once her mother had told her the purpose of the meeting: to make certain that responsibilities in the household were distributed fairly. Jill had responded, "It's about time you're trying to figure out how to be fair." Jill had said this in a negative tone, but wisely, Susanna didn't respond in kind. Instead, she simply told her daughter that she didn't want any of the family to feel that things were unfair. She also told Jill that she thought some of the consequences she had imposed on Jill were too harsh and wanted to find a more effective way of responding. According to Susanna, Jill enthusiastically accepted her mother's assessment.

Susanna began her meeting with David and Jill by acknowledging that she felt there was too much friction in the house. She told them she was certain there were steps all three of them could take to ease the arguing and tension. She said that, given all of the pressure she had been experiencing as she tried to balance her work and home responsibilities, she hadn't carefully thought through her expectations for herself and for them. She admitted that she might have been arbitrary in defining responsibilities for them.

As Susanna shared with us what she had told David and Jill, she said, "I was surprised by how attentive they were, especially Jill. I expected her to offer a sarcastic remark, but she didn't. Maybe it was because I was trying to do what you had suggested."

We asked her to remind us what our suggestion had been.

"To be more empathic and to validate what Jill was feeling."

We commented that it sounded as if she had done a pretty good job.

Susanna thanked us and continued to describe the meeting with her children. She said she had made a list of the main responsibilities she felt had to be met for the household to run smoothly. She asked David and Jill whether they wanted to suggest any modifications to the list. They offered a few. Once the three of them had agreed on the initial list, they discussed which of the responsibilities could be done by any of them and which by just one of them. They also identified tasks that could be rotated each month so that no one had a tedious or boring task for too long a period. In addition, Susanna brought up David's learning problems, noting that some responsibilities might be more difficult for him to do on a weeknight because of homework requirements but more manageable on the weekend, when his time was more flexible. Susanna commented, "I learned something that I didn't expect. David seemed eager to accept responsibilities. I think he felt that he wasn't pulling his load. Also, by making excuses for him, I might have been sending the wrong message."

We asked her to say what that message was.

"That I didn't think he was capable of handling things. He actually said that he felt there were ways he could help out."

We reinforced Susanna's important point by observing that sometimes when parents try to protect their children and make things easier for them, the parents may be doing the children a disservice. If we're too protective, we may unintentionally communicate that we don't have faith in our children's abilities to handle challenges. We never want to put children in ten feet of water if they can't swim, but we certainly can encourage them to begin to get their feet wet. We added that excusing one child from meeting certain responsibilities because that child is struggling with learning problems will lead to resentment in the family's other children if they feel too much is expected of them. We suggested to Susanna that one of the reasons David had been upset by the battles she was having with Jill was that he knew responsibilities could be handled more fairly. We told her that we have known children in David's position who feel a little guilty about that kind of situation, because they believe they've been the cause of some of the problems.

> *If we're too protective, we may unintentionally communicate that we don't have faith in our children's abilities to handle challenges.*

Susanna responded, "A few weeks ago, I wouldn't have thought David felt that way, but now I can see that he might have." Smiling, she added, "And I was proud of how David and Jill said some jobs like taking out the garbage were so boring that they should probably be rotated every two weeks, not once a month, and we worked out a schedule. Also, I'm glad you brought up the importance of deciding how we should remind each other if one of us forgets to meet our responsibilities. Since we put all of the responsibilities on a list, I told them the best way to remind me would be just pointing to the list. Guess what? They said I could do the same if they forgot to do something."

We originally had planned to schedule some family meetings with Susanna, David, and Jill to reinforce the positive changes that were taking place, but given David and Jill's response to their mother's new parenting practices, she believed the family meetings they were having at home were accomplishing the goals we would have addressed in our office. We viewed this as a sign that Susanna was feeling more competent and assured in her role as a mother. In our sessions with her, we continued to discuss her parenting skills and also explored in greater detail her feelings of dissatisfaction and anger about the situations that had occurred in her life, including her husband having left her.

Although Susanna had originally contacted us about the problems she was experiencing with Jill, eventually she began to confront issues related to her own life, issues that influenced her parenting practices. As we discussed strategies for helping Jill and David feel more empowered, Susanna recognized the extent to which she had adopted a martyr role, believing that she had been dealt a poor hand in life and that she couldn't do much to improve the situation. Interestingly, the more she removed herself from this role, the more effective she became as a parent, shifting from an authoritarian to an authoritative position. Power struggles with Jill decreased, replaced by a problem-solving approach that nurtured self-discipline.

Respect Your Child's Feelings

We have worked with many parents who are frustrated by their children's complaints that things aren't fair. At one of our workshops, a father said, "It drives me crazy when my twelve-year-old son says things aren't fair, that he gets too much homework, that we don't buy him the kinds of sneakers his friends have, that his best friend has a fifty-inch TV screen while we only have a thirty-two-inch screen. The other night, I told him, 'If you think things aren't fair now, wait until you get into the real world and have to work for a living. Stop complaining about things being unfair. You have it pretty good, and you should start appreciating what you've got.'"

We asked the father whether his words had helped.

"It helped me get some feelings off my chest, but I don't think it changed his mind. Quite honestly, I didn't know what to say."

We acknowledged that it can be hard to know how to respond, and we shared what we have learned from experience. Trying to talk a child out of feeling that things are unfair rarely works. Instead, it's often helpful to validate what your children are feeling and, as much as possible, to engage them in problem solving.

The father asked, "What do you mean?"

We suggested that he might say to his son, "I'm sorry you feel so many things aren't fair. You might not be able to change some things, but maybe you can change some other things. I don't know if teachers will give you less homework, but if you want the more expensive sneakers that some of your friends have, I'll give you the money I would have paid for a regular pair of sneakers, and we can figure out how you can earn the rest."

The father said, "I'm not sure that would work."

We agreed that it might not but suggested that it was worth a try. In our experience, the combination of validating a person's feelings and helping to solve problems tends to be more effective than for a parent to tell a child to appreciate that he or she has it good. Even though from our perspective our children often do have it good, telling children how they should feel or what they should see typically fuels their resentment.

Trying to talk a child out of feeling that things are unfair rarely works. Instead, it's often helpful to validate what your children are feeling and engage them in problem solving.

As we finished explaining this idea, a mother at the workshop stated, "It's interesting what you just said about validation. My daughter is eleven years old and has to take growth hormone shots. The shots are painful, and I know her self-esteem suffers, especially when she is teased about her size. A couple of years ago, she was feeling down and started asking me why she was the one who had a growth hormone problem and no one else at her school. I was careful not to immediately say she shouldn't be feeling sorry for herself or wishing that someone else had the problem. I told her doctors really don't know why different kids may be born with different problems."

The mother continued, "I said I could only imagine how distressing it was for her to have this problem, but at least there were treatments that might help. I think it helped that I could validate her feelings and then offer a comment about possible treatment. In fact, she has been diligent about taking her shots, and she is growing."

Thanking the mother for her story, we clarified that validating our children's feelings doesn't mean we necessarily agree with our children, but rather that we hear what they have to say. We think children are less likely to have discipline problems when they believe their parents are listening and trying to be fair, even if the parents end up disagreeing with them. But all too often, a vicious cycle gets set in motion when parents get angry with their children in response to negative attitudes and behavior. The children react by getting angrier, the parents become more punitive, and their actions reinforce the children's belief that the parents are unfair and unfeeling. In contrast, validation and empathy short-circuit that negative cycle or keep it from developing in the first place. This sets the stage for solving problems rather than intensifying problems and punishing children.

When we finished this explanation, the mother whose daughter had a growth hormone problem smiled and said, "Wow! I didn't realize I was doing all of that with my daughter."

Unfortunately, we have seen what happens in families where feelings of unfairness and anger make it harder for the family to practice empathy and problem solving. Let's return to the Elefson family, whom we met in the previous chapter.

The Elefson Family: "My Brain Feels like It's Exploding"

In Chapter 7 we described the issues raised by Dena and Garth Elefson, whose twelve-year-old son, Aaron, was struggling with learning problems in school. They consulted us because Aaron's educators and pediatrician were concerned about a possible learning disability or attention problems. His difficulties seemed to have intensified in middle school but were apparent in his elementary school years.

During our initial conversation with the Elefsons, they described a negative component of Aaron's mindset: his belief that he had let himself and others down. He coped with his psychological pain and shame by avoiding schoolwork and found pleasure only while playing his drums or guitar or drawing cartoons. When Aaron failed to fulfill his school requirements, his parents responded by becoming angry and telling him he should meet his responsibilities and give up the "sour look on his face." Understandably, Aaron interpreted their words and actions as a sign that they didn't love him and that he was a disappointment to them. Garth and Dena acknowledged to us that Aaron was a frustrating child and, in fact, did disappoint them. Their frustration prompted more punitive discipline, which included withholding one thing he really enjoyed and excelled in—his music. Withholding Aaron's music became the Elefsons' main form of discipline, and this approach backfired by confirming for Aaron how angry and disappointed his parents were. He seemed not to perceive his contribution to the family's state of affairs.

In many families, a child is burdened by two or more overlapping negative mindsets, each reinforcing the other and adding to the child's misery. As we evaluated Aaron's patterns of thinking, feeling, and behaving, we learned that his feeling that he let himself and others down was sitting side by side with a belief that was not readily apparent to his parents, since he had hesitated to share it with them. This unstated belief was that life had dealt him an unfair blow in the form of something being wrong with his brain. In our initial meetings with Aaron, he revealed his feelings of sadness and helplessness.

Not surprisingly, given Aaron's earlier negative experience of testing by the school psychologist, he informed his parents that he didn't want more testing, that "you're just trying to punish me and find out how dumb I am." Following our advice, Garth and Dena described the testing as a way to get a clearer picture of Aaron's struggles in school. They emphasized to Aaron that they were concerned they might have been too harsh with him because they didn't understand what was interfering with him succeeding in school. As we recommended, they also highlighted Aaron's islands of competence, his music and artwork.

Although Aaron didn't say, "I can see your point of view and am eager to be tested," he was at least willing to meet with us. As he entered our office, he had a scowl on his face but a look of sadness in his eyes. He immediately announced that testing was "stupid" and he didn't want any tests.

We replied that we appreciated his telling us how he felt about testing. We added that many children tell us they don't want tests, and we expressed our belief that children should not be tested until we have clearly explained the reason for each test and the ways the tests can be helpful. We invited Aaron to ask us any questions he had. With these comments, we empathized with Aaron, let him know that his feelings were normal, minimized possible power struggles, and helped him to feel he was an active participant in the evaluation process.

We asked him about his previous testing, and he rolled his eyes, offering the opinion that the tests were "dumb" and didn't help him. However, he couldn't say how he had hoped the tests might help. He also said no one had given him feedback about the results of the tests.

We explained that all children learn differently and that the tests could point out his areas of strength and the areas of learning that needed support.

He replied, "School stinks. The work is boring,"

We asked him whether there was any part of school he liked.

After providing the obligatory answer, "recess," he said band was pretty good but not much else. This led to a discussion of his enjoyment of playing the drums. After learning more about his love of drums, we switched topics and told him that his parents had said he was a pretty good cartoonist.

Aaron replied, "I like to draw cartoons."

We asked whether he drew a particular kind.

"Not really."

We asked whether there were any favorite characters that he drew.

Given Aaron's situation, his answer was fascinating: "Yeah, I like to draw Pressurehead."

Observing that "Pressurehead" was an interesting name, we asked Aaron what had led him to give his character that name.

Aaron responded, "I call him Pressurehead since he always walks around feeling pressure."

Sticking with this metaphor, we asked him to describe the kind of pressure his character experienced.

"You name it: pressure about having friends, finishing his homework, dumb demands from his parents like making his bed every morning."

We told Aaron his character sounded interesting and invited him to draw us a picture of Pressurehead so that we could have a better idea of what he looked like.

"Sure, why not?" Aaron proceeded to draw an impressive caricature of a boy whose brain was exploding.

We looked at his detailed drawing and praised him as a skillful artist.

"Thanks," he replied flatly. Then he announced with a smile, "Sometimes the pressure really builds up, and look what happens."

We asked him to say what was happening.

"His brain is having a bad day." Aaron had a sense of humor, if macabre.

After confirming his observation, we asked whether Pressurehead ever had a good day. Since Pressurehead seemed to be a representation of Aaron, we thought we could learn more about Aaron by asking about his alter ego.

Aaron said, "Not often, especially when he gets hassled, which happens a lot."

We asked what Pressurehead got "hassled" about.

"You name it—about school, chores, almost anything."

We asked whether Pressurehead got tired of having so much pressure on him.

Aaron was growing enthusiastic about this dialogue. He said, "Yup. He doesn't know how much longer he can take it."

We asked what Pressurehead was feeling.

Aaron's response was revealing. "Pressurehead keeps thinking, 'My brain feels like it's exploding. Why me?'"

We asked him to clarify what he meant by "Why me?"

"There aren't too many kids like him in the world who always feel like their brain is going to explode, so he wonders why he had to be one of them. Other kids don't walk around worrying about things like that."

We told Aaron he was a creative storyteller and then asked him to consider whether Pressurehead might think anything could help him. "Do you think anything could help you?" is a question we typically ask youngsters when we're seeing them for an evaluation or in therapy. Our goal is to assess whether they believe things can improve.

Aaron said, "Pressurehead's not sure."

We wondered whether Pressurehead had any parents.

"Yes."

We asked whether those parents knew how pressured he was feeling.

"No."

We asked whether he had ever told them. This is another question we often ask; our goal is to evaluate whether a child has taken any initiative to seek help.

"Not really. He tried once, but they thought he was just making excuses, and they ended up putting more pressure on him by punishing him. They told him he should just get rid of the pressure in his head and look happy. Didn't they know he wanted to feel happy but didn't know how he could? Pressurehead knew they were disappointed in him. That's why Pressurehead felt things were unfair and probably wouldn't change."

As we were conversing, Aaron drew a few more pictures of Pressurehead, each notable for the lack of a smile. In one striking picture, Pressurehead was bent over, balancing a board on his shoulders. A globe of the world was in the middle of the board.

We commented that he had made another amazing drawing and asked him to describe what was going on.

"Oh, he's carrying the world's problems on his shoulders."

This was one of the most remarkable first sessions we have had with a child. The power of metaphors and storytelling was very apparent, giving us a wealth of information about Aaron. When it was time for the session to end, Aaron said, "But you didn't give me any tests. I thought you were doing testing."

We replied that we would do testing at our next session but first wanted to get to know him and what he liked to do. We reminded him that we were impressed with his drawings.

Aaron thanked us and added, "I'll see you for the testing."

We felt we had established the beginning of a positive relationship with Aaron. We hoped it would provide a basis for Aaron to feel more comfortable when we administered tests, especially since in the past testing, he had felt he was under a microscope.

The next day Dena called us and said Aaron had told her the session was OK and that he would come back. She said the description "OK" was actually very positive.

Aaron began the next session by showing us some other drawings he had done and gave us a couple to keep. We thanked him for his thoughtfulness. We next explained the purpose of the testing. We said the tests could help him and us understand his strengths and weaknesses. We emphasized that this understanding could help us figure out the best possible school program for him. We reminded him that if he had any questions about the purpose of any of the tests, he should just ask us, since we wanted to make certain that everything we did was clear to him. We were hoping that our description of the evaluation, including the importance of his input, would offset his previous negative image of testing as punishment or as a confirmation that things were wrong with him.

Aaron was basically cooperative during the evaluation. On a few occasions, when faced with a challenging task, he would make comments like "This is a stupid question" or "How is this going to be helpful?" We responded to his questions and comments by thanking Aaron for letting us know how he felt and then discussing the purpose of specific test questions. One of our goals was to help him to experience a sense of control and ownership in the evaluation process.

The testing revealed that Aaron was a bright child but did have some learning problems. The most evident was his difficulty in organizing and expressing his thoughts on paper. He had ideas he wanted to convey in his writing, but something was lost in the translation when he tried to express his ideas via the written word. Obviously, this difficulty interfered with successfully completing assignments and became even more noticeable in middle school, where the number and complexity of writing assignments and book reports increased.

Aaron's discourse about Pressurehead suggested that he was concerned that he had something wrong with his own brain that interfered with learning. Intensifying his distress was his belief that he was a disappointment to himself and others (see Chapter 7) and that things were unfair and wouldn't change. Aaron's seeming lack of motivation to fulfill school requirements was rooted in his perception that he had a defective mind that couldn't learn. His anger and sense of hopelessness were further fueled by his perception that his parents thought he was lazy and became angry when he tried to communicate his unhappiness to them. In addition, his parents had punished him by briefly taking away the activity that brought Aaron the greatest sense of accomplishment—his music.

After the evaluation, we asked Aaron to choose whether we would go over the results with him and his parents in separate meetings or together. He opted for a third choice: separate meetings plus the possibility of a joint session with his parents after the individual meetings. He explained his concern that if the first meeting were with him and his parents, his parents would be upset with him no matter what the testing revealed, and their reaction would make it harder for him to understand what we said. We explained that in family meetings, we always try to lessen anger and disappointment and teach kids and parents how to work together more closely. Even with this explanation, Aaron said he would still prefer separate meetings at first. He emphasized, "If I'm not there, it might be easier for you to explain things to my parents without them getting upset with me."

We did request his permission to share with them his drawings and accounts of Pressurehead. As we have learned from the many children and adolescents we have seen in therapy who have expressed their feelings through stories and metaphors, we didn't need to tell Aaron that we thought Pressurehead was really a representation of himself. Although we were certain that was the case, we have found that when we state this kind of direct comparison, children often become less willing to continue using stories and characters to express their feelings. Aaron agreed to let us show his parents any of the drawings he had made.

We reviewed the test findings with Aaron, specifying his strengths as well as his difficulties. We described the different tests to help him to understand more precisely why he was struggling in certain subjects at school. We tried to help him to appreciate that these difficulties did not mean he had a defective brain but meant he needed reinforcement in particular areas of learning. We explained that we would work with his school to make certain that such reinforcement was made available to him.

Most importantly, we talked to him about his mindset or assumptions about himself and others. We felt that we could do this comfortably, since a trusting relationship had developed during the evaluation. We told Aaron that as we figured out the best way for him to be more successful in school, we were concerned about a possible obstacle to his success. When many children have faced similar kinds of frustrations and problems, we said, they begin to feel that nothing will help, and they may even become sad. Some feel very disappointed in themselves and believe they have let others down. Some feel that things are unfair. We added that, although we understood why children would have all of those feelings, we were concerned that if the feelings remained, they could interfere with trying new things that might help.

Aaron wondered, "Well, if some kids have these feelings, how do they get rid of them?"

We cautioned Aaron that changing feelings is not always easy, especially when people have had the feelings for a while. We explained that it helps for children to believe that they can begin to do better with the right kind of teaching approach and that there's not something wrong with their brain that will keep them from learning. It also helps if children know their parents and teachers don't believe they're lazy, but instead offer encouragement and support. We added that this was the reason why, as we help children, we always like to work closely with their parents and teachers.

Aaron readily jumped at this explanation. "Will you be going over the things you told me with my mom and dad?"

We told him we planned to do that, because it would be very helpful. We asked him whether there was anything we had said to him that he wouldn't want us to discuss with his parents or teachers.

Aaron said, "Not that I can think of."

We returned to discussing our plan to hold a meeting with Aaron's parents and then with all three of them. We asked Aaron whether he still wanted us to do it that way or would prefer to be at the next meeting with his parents to discuss the results of the testing. We offered this choice again, so that Aaron would have options and would feel like an integral part of the evaluation and treatment process.

After thinking for a moment, Aaron said, "I think you should meet with my parents first, and then we can have a family meeting. I just think that would work out better."

We agreed. Before the testing, Garth had voiced concern that if we discovered that Aaron had a learning problem, Aaron would use it as an excuse for not doing his work, but Aaron never offered such an excuse.

In our meeting with Garth and Dena Elefson, we reviewed the evaluation findings, highlighting the areas in which Aaron was struggling and his strengths, including the two they had mentioned to us—his music and art. We showed them his drawings of Pressurehead, which they had not previously seen, and described our dialogue with Aaron about this character's view of himself and the world. We voiced our belief that Pressurehead was Aaron's representation of himself, explaining that many children use stories and metaphors in this way. We also emphasized that Aaron had not resorted to telling us that he should be excused from school requirements because of his learning problems. If anything, we had already started to discuss ways of remedying and coping with his problems.

Both parents listened intently. When we finished, Dena said, "What you're telling us is very helpful. I also want you to know that, since the evaluation began, Aaron has seemed less uptight and sad."

Garth countered, "That may be, but I haven't seen an improvement in his homework."

We reminded him that we shared their goal of enabling Aaron to accomplish his schoolwork, but we explained that we would have to achieve another goal before Aaron would be more successful in school.

Garth queried, "What's that?"

We predicted that it would be easier for Aaron to meet school requirements if he became more hopeful that he could succeed. We explained that Aaron would have to begin changing his attitude—his mindset about himself and others.

Garth asked, "How do we do that?"

We replied that although there isn't one easy answer, there are steps we could begin to take. We advised that, in the family meeting with Aaron, they should communicate to him that they had gained a better idea of why he has been struggling in school. If they felt comfortable doing so, they should even acknowledge that they regret having been annoyed with him when he felt depressed and having punished him by taking away his music.

Garth quickly raised a question he had posed in our first session: "Are you saying we should apologize to Aaron?"

Recalling that Garth had asked the same question in our first meeting, we replied that we weren't sure that what we were suggesting was really an apology. But, we added, even if it were an apology, what would be wrong with that?

Garth pondered the question and then said, "I'm not really sure." He then offered a perceptive observation, reflecting a significant shift in his mindset: "When I saw Aaron as lazy and unmotivated, I didn't see any reason for me to apologize or say I wish I had handled things differently. However, after hearing the test results and knowing he has some learning problems, I'm more willing to acknowledge that perhaps I could have dealt with things more effectively, including not taking away his music as a punishment."

Observing that what Garth had said was very important, we told him we thought Aaron would feel reassured to hear from his father that he understood Aaron's struggles and appreciated his strengths. We predicted that if Garth were to tell Aaron he was impressed with his son's artwork and music, those words would be very meaningful.

Garth objected, "But in the past when we've complimented him, Aaron has basically dismissed our compliments."

Acknowledging the truth of this, we suggested that when the climate at home was more positive, Aaron might be more willing to accept the compliment or at least not reject it.

Garth said, "I guess there's no harm in letting him know we appreciate his strengths."

We agreed but warned Garth not to get upset if Aaron didn't immediately accept his compliments. Learning to accept a compliment could take time. Continuing with the theme of Aaron's strengths, we advised Garth and Dena to consider another step. We recommended that they stop taking away Aaron's strengths as a form of punishment. We reminded them that the technique had not been very effective; if anything, it had added to Aaron's frustration and resentment. We explained that taking away children's islands of competence not only invites them to become angrier, but also lessens their chance to do things that make them feel good. It increases their sense that the world is unjust and unfair.

Garth asked, "But what if he wants to do music and art all day long and nothing else?"

Impressed with this question, we explained that although we recommended that he and Dena not take away these activities as a punishment, they could certainly set a limit on how much time he spends with each activity. This limit could be a topic for us to discuss at our family meeting. We added that we viewed the family meeting as a forum for reviewing the evaluation findings, for the parents to express some of the ideas we had just recommended, and for all of us to engage in a problem-solving conversation.

Dena asked, "What do you mean by a problem-solving conversation?"

We replied that the term means we would identify a couple of key problems, such as school and homework requirements, and ask Aaron what he thought would help. We explained that he was likely to be willing to think about effective solutions if he believed his parents were on his side and that there was hope.

Dena said, "That seems to make sense."

We added another piece of advice. Dena and Garth should find opportunities to let Aaron know how much they cared about him and loved him. We told them we believed he felt starved for their acceptance, and we reminded them of our goal to change Aaron's attitude that he had let himself and them down and that the world was unfair. Finally, we reassured them not to worry if he rejected their comments at first or seemed indifferent to them. We explained that Aaron might not know how to handle their new script.

In this session with the Elefsons, our goal was not only to review the test findings, but also to offer concrete suggestions of how to begin improving their relationship with their son and changing their punitive disciplinary style. We emphasized that these changes were essential if Aaron was to give up his negative outlook and self-defeating ways of coping and adopt a more hopeful attitude that would result in more effective responses to his problems.

In the family meeting, we began by briefly reviewing the test findings. We were pleasantly surprised when Garth jumped in and said, "Before we go on, I want to say something."

Aaron looked at his father apprehensively, perhaps expecting the negative comments he had grown so accustomed to hearing.

Garth said, "Aaron, this testing has really helped me to understand things more clearly. I must admit that I have been annoyed with you and thought you could do better if you would get rid of your negative attitude and buckle down. Now I appreciate that you would like to do better, but there are things you need help with, rather than a lecture from Mom or me. We'll do whatever we can."

Aaron looked amazed at his father's words. There was more to come. Garth continued, "I also don't think we've told you often enough that even though we've gotten angry with you, we think you have some real talents in music and art. We saw the pictures you drew of Pressurehead and thought they were incredible. I guess we haven't told you enough how proud we are of you and how much we love you."

Aaron was so stunned by these comments that all he could do was nod in appreciation.

Dena reinforced her husband's words by saying she agreed with him, especially his statement of how much they loved Aaron.

While Garth had basically conveyed feelings we had suggested he express, his manner was far from mechanical or rote. It was evident that he and his wife had done much thinking about what we had recommended, and his words were genuine.

We held several more family meetings during the next few months, and all three of them attended several school conferences. Aaron felt he should attend the meetings, since "it's my school program." Not unexpectedly, they encountered some obstacles along the way, especially when Aaron struggled with his schoolwork and resorted to the belief that he had "hit a brick wall and things wouldn't improve." However, with the empathy, encouragement, and support of his parents and teachers, these negative attitudes appeared less often and with less intensity.

In addition, instead of his parents taking away his music and art as a punishment, they suggested that the school increasingly highlight these islands of competence. He continued to play in the school band, and his drawings were frequently displayed in the hallways. He entered a contest to select artwork that reinforced the message that students should not use drugs. Interestingly, his drawing was of Pressurehead's brain exploding and was titled "What Drugs Can Do to Your Brain." He won second prize. His parents proudly displayed Aaron's medal in their home.

Our work with Aaron and his parents illustrated that when parents replace discipline emphasizing punishment with practices that fall under an "authoritative" rather than "authoritarian" label, a more hopeful, resilient mindset and behaviors are likely to follow.

When Life Deals Us Difficulties

Our friend and colleague Mark Katz wrote a wonderful book about resilience, titled *On Playing a Poor Hand Well*. As Dr. Katz expresses it, we are all dealt different hands when we enter the world. Some youngsters will face more challenges and adversity than others. If parents respond with frustration, anger, and harsh discipline, then their response will confirm for children that the world is unfair and that their situation isn't likely to improve. However, as we witnessed with the Amherst and Elefson families, a shift in the parents' approach can help children feel more accepted and respected and show them they can play a poor hand with confidence and self-assurance.

9

Encouraging Your Child to Make a Difference

The behaviors of many children and adolescents invite angry responses from adults, yet some of these children keep doing what draws the angry response. The reasons for this are complex. Some children come into the world with what has been referred to as a "difficult temperament," meaning they are hard to soothe or satisfy, feel that people are unfair and arbitrary, are rigid and unable to compromise, and quickly lose their temper. Other children have experienced emotional or physical abuse, so they mistrust adults, expecting the worst even from those who are trying to help.

Not surprisingly, youngsters with difficult temperaments are more likely to provoke parents and other adults. Their ongoing challenging behaviors test the understanding and patience of even the most empathic parents. When parents finally show their frustration and annoyance, it confirms to these children that they are not loved and that adults are unkind. They experience the world as being angry at them. While some recognize to a certain extent that their behavior provokes this anger, others don't seem to understand their role in their treatment at all.

Whatever the reasons for the development of this unfortunate scenario, it often becomes an entrenched family pattern in which anger is met by anger. When this occurs, positive comments from parents become less and less frequent. Authoritarian forms of discipline become the rule rather than the exception. The goal of teaching children to be effective problem solvers and more caring, reflective, self-disciplined individuals recedes to the background as parents adopt a disciplinary style in which they react to problems instead of preventing them. Many of these children assume a "poised for attack" stance to protect themselves from a world they perceive as angry and unforgiving. Parents tell us that using constructive, positive forms of discipline with these youngsters seems to take on Herculean proportions. However, what we can learn from disciplining children who possess this kind of angry, mistrustful, negative mindset can be used with all children. To see how children with this mindset can learn resilience and self-discipline, consider the difficult case of Nathan.

Nathan: "Programmed to Throw Chairs"

In our practices, as we've worked with many angry children and their families, we have witnessed the spiraling impact that anger has on a family's life and discipline style. Yet we have also learned that parents and other caregivers can implement certain discipline strategies that not only reduce their own and their child's anger but also reinforce compassion and cooperation in the child. The first author (Bob) saw this more than thirty years ago while serving as the principal of a school in a locked-door unit of a psychiatric hospital. All of the students were inpatients at the hospital,

> *Parents can implement certain discipline strategies that not only reduce their own and their child's anger but also reinforce compassion and cooperation in the child.*

and many had been admitted because of violent episodes. The staff constantly debated the most effective forms of discipline and behavioral systems. Based on their different opinions, staff members used inconsistent approaches that only added to the tension in the unit.

Nathan, a ten-year-old boy admitted to the hospital, showed the value of a strength-based model of discipline, the model we have been exploring in this book. Nathan was admitted for violent outbursts toward his adoptive parents, his teachers, and any adults who attempted to set limits. He had also engaged in several incidents of sadistic acts toward animals, including breaking a bird's neck. The policy of the inpatient program required that children attend school on the day following their admission. Each child was placed in a classroom with two teachers. These teachers would visit newly admitted children on the inpatient unit (a building adjacent to the school) to introduce themselves prior to the first day of school. Nathan's teachers, following the policy, went to introduce themselves but remained only a few minutes because Nathan greeted them with obscenities and had to be restrained from kicking them. It was hardly an auspicious introduction! After the encounter, one of the teachers half-jokingly (or perhaps half-hopefully) said, "Maybe we won't have to worry about Nathan. Maybe he'll refuse to come to school and stay on the inpatient unit."

Nathan came to school accompanied by two child-care workers. I greeted him at the door and offered to spend a few minutes with him in my office, telling him about the program. Almost every child and adolescent accepted this invitation. Not Nathan. He simply shouted, "Where's my classroom?" and the two child-care workers showed him. Within a couple of minutes, he abruptly picked up a chair and hurled it at one of the teachers, just missing her shoulder and face. He was restrained and escorted back to the quiet (time-out) room on the inpatient unit, where he spent the day as his angry behavior escalated. His teachers visited him in the afternoon, but once again, he hurled obscenities at them.

The next day at school was a repeat of the first day. Within a couple of minutes, Nathan picked up a chair and hurled it at his other teacher. This time his aim was more accurate, and the chair hit the teacher on the arm and shoulder. Given this violent action, he was once again restrained and taken back to the quiet room on the inpatient unit, where he spent most of the day.

I carefully reflected on the information I had been given about Nathan. He had been adopted as an infant, and recently, in light of his dangerous outbursts, his adoptive parents had basically given up. They believed a state agency should take custody to provide whatever services were necessary. When Nathan last saw his adoptive parents, he told them he hated them and they had always been mean to him. Besides having these problems with his emotions and relationships, he had been diagnosed with both receptive and expressive language disorders, as well as other learning disabilities. Nathan's school record was filled with anger and failure. He reportedly had few, if any, friends.

At an emergency meeting about Nathan, the staff discussed this information. The group considered the likelihood that Nathan felt rejected by two sets of parents (biological and adoptive) and his difficulty trusting others. Also, he had just been placed in a locked-door facility and then was told he must spend the day in a school, a setting that had proved so frustrating to him in the past. In addition, children's anger and outbursts are often worse when they have language disorders, because they have trouble understanding what people say to them and expressing their feelings other than through physical actions.

Some staff members disapproved of our attempt to understand Nathan's behavior by being empathic and seeing the world from his perspective. One teacher expressed what others felt: "We shouldn't make excuses for Nathan's problem. The bottom line is that he is a violent kid who seems to show little remorse. If he continues to act in ways that lead him to the quiet room, then that's where he may end up spending his time. That's up to him. He can't keep acting the way he's been acting. He has got to learn to conform to our rules."

I responded, "In trying to understand Nathan's actions, I'm not condoning what he's doing, nor am I suggesting that there shouldn't be consequences. I'm just wondering if there are other things we might do besides placing him in the quiet room."

The teacher replied, "Maybe after a few more days in the quiet room, he'll see that we mean business and that we won't tolerate his throwing chairs or trying to hurt people."

Another teacher offered an interesting observation: "I understand the reasons for sending Nathan to the quiet room when he throws a chair, but I'm bothered by something. Nathan doesn't like school, and we end up punishing him by kicking him out of school. Is that really an effective punishment? Maybe he's getting exactly what he wants."

The first teacher said, "I hear what you're saying, but if he decides to act the way he has acted the first two days, I don't think he can remain in the classroom. His behavior frightens the other kids and disrupts any kind of teaching we try to do. It's tough enough to teach kids in a locked-door unit. We have to minimize any disruptions."

A third teacher said, "It's really difficult to know what to do. Nathan won't allow us to talk to him. We can't get to know him, and he can't get to know us."

Everyone at the meeting seemed exasperated. Another teacher interrupted the silence with a comment that at first appeared almost comical, but in fact was profound. Her comment would provide the foundation for a major shift of mindset from a punitive stance with Nathan to one that nurtured his dignity and resilience. It also taught the group the importance of both empathy and a preventive approach to disciplinary issues. What she said was, "I think that Nathan is programmed to throw chairs."

I asked, "What do you mean by 'programmed to throw chairs'?"

She replied, "I think that, given Nathan's difficulty trusting others and given his suspiciousness, when Nathan feels threatened such as in a school, he knows only one way to respond, and that's through violent acts. I know he may act violently at other times, but I think when he's feeling vulnerable or threatened, he only has one way of coping, and that's to act out aggressively. He knows no other way. That's what I mean by 'programmed to throw chairs.'"

With that explanation, the group realized a simple fact with far-reaching implications. Nathan might have been programmed to throw chairs, but another group was equally programmed. The staff. They responded to his behavior the same way each time: by placing him in the quiet room. When we had identified this dynamic at the meeting, a couple of the staff members became a little defensive, arguing that the so-called programming of the staff was actually a staff being consistent and holding Nathan accountable for his behavior.

The teacher who had introduced the notion of Nathan being "programmed" answered, "We should be consistent, but maybe with a different approach. If you look at what has been attempted with Nathan in the past and even in just two days here, the focus has been on how to punish him, rather than how to teach him to be more responsible."

The discussion became livelier as another participant said, "Maybe if Nathan is in the quiet room long enough, he'll learn what he shouldn't do."

I said, "That might happen, but for a moment, let's look at what we might do to change our program. We can still be consistent, but perhaps there's another way of disciplining Nathan that will be more effective. Maybe the best way of breaking the programming cycle is for us to do something different from what Nathan is expecting."

At that moment, some levity entered the discussion. One teacher jokingly said, "Let's remove all of the furniture and other objects from the classroom. Then Nathan won't have anything to throw."

Another laughed and said, "Then the classroom will look just like a quiet room."

Another chimed in, "Maybe they have Nerf chairs. Then if Nathan throws a chair, no one could get hurt."

It was interesting to note that as those in the room began to reflect upon new programs or scripts, the atmosphere became lighter and more conducive to considering different approaches.

The group eventually developed a new strategy. Some staff members had questions about it, wondering if we were giving in to Nathan. Yet there was a recognition that past interventions had been unsuccessful, so there wasn't much to lose by implementing a new strategy.

The next day, just as Nathan was entering the school building with the same angry expression on his face, I startled him by glancing out the door and exclaiming, "I don't believe this! It's very upsetting—really upsetting!"

Nathan was taken aback and turned to look in the direction I was facing. All Nathan saw were trees.

He said, "What's upsetting?"

I replied, "Oh, you don't see it; that's good. You won't be upset."

Nathan looked puzzled, perhaps a little distracted from the usual "program" he was prepared to follow. He asked, "Upset about what?"

His attention was increasingly riveted on me, and I responded, "Well, since you don't see it, I'll tell you, but I hope it's not too upsetting for you."

"What is it?"

Having won Nathan's undivided attention, I was ready to follow through on the rest of the plan we had devised at the meeting the day before. I said, "I have a home to go to, you have a place here at the hospital, but all of the birds at the hospital are homeless. There's not one birdhouse on the grounds of the hospital." (The theme of homelessness was specifically selected as a possible motivating force in light of Nathan's own possible feelings of homelessness, having been given up by two sets of parents.)

I didn't know if Nathan would reject what I said and head for his classroom to throw another chair or if he would respond with interest. Fortunately, the latter occurred. Nathan asked, "There's not one birdhouse at the hospital?"

I answered, "Not one. Now can you understand why I'm upset? What if a bird wanted to get food or stay at a birdhouse?"

Nathan, who previously had not considered the issue of homelessness in birds and in the past had actually broken the neck of a bird, challenged me, "Well, what are you going to do about it?"

"What do you think we should do?"

Nathan replied, "Get a birdhouse."

I said, "I have a better idea. What if you and your teacher *built* a birdhouse? This way you could build the exact kind you want."

"I don't know how to build things."

"I'm sure your teacher can help. Let's go speak with your teacher [the same teacher Nathan had hit with a chair a day earlier] and see what he thinks."

As we approached the teacher and he noticed the less angry, more excited look on Nathan's face, he sensed that the new program might be working. Nathan and I explained the desire to build a birdhouse. The teacher said he had never built a birdhouse, but he was certain there were books he could get to help with the project. He added that he would look for books after school and then invited Nathan into the classroom. No outbursts occurred throughout the school day.

During the next couple of weeks, Nathan's school activities centered around the birdhouse project. He became involved in reading about birds and birdhouse construction, measuring the dimensions, buying wood, accepting help while engaged in the building, waiting a day for the paint to dry, making a peanut butter ball with seeds, and then hanging the birdhouse on a tree by the entrance to the school.

These different components of Nathan's project served multiple purposes. For a child accustomed to failure, it invited him to demonstrate mastery and competence and then to feel comfortable displaying his finished product (his island of competence, as we've discussed in several places in this book) for all to see and admire. For a child hesitant to read or engage in learning, it provided the motivation to discover the benefits and excitement of absorbing and using new information. Also, almost every phase of the work required him to learn to plan and refrain from acting impulsively, a challenge for a child with his temperament. In addition, for a child who was on guard and suspicious of others, the project gave him a chance to interact with others in a trusting way. This foundation established a stay at the hospital that was marked by greater cooperation and compromise on Nathan's part than any of us would have predicted based upon his first two days.

Learning to Contribute

While Nathan benefited noticeably from the birdhouse project, the impact on the mindset of the staff was almost more significant. In many of my workshops, I share the birdhouse story as a turning point in my own thinking and therapeutic approach. The experience with Nathan prompted me to realize that engaging children in helping others not only nurtures a more compassionate, responsible attitude, but, in fact, is a preventive form of discipline. When children are involved in what we now call *contributory activities*, they are less likely to engage in negative or antisocial behavior. Some might say it is a feature of a time-honored disciplinary technique—distracting children or redirecting them away from negative, "programmed" behaviors.

As we have emphasized in our previous writings, children appear to come into the world with a desire to be helpful and valued. While parents are mowing the lawn, three-year-olds will eagerly approach and ask if they can help. They show interest in helping us cook, rake leaves, build with our tools, and even sweep the kitchen. We believe children have an inborn need or drive to help and to make a positive difference in the lives of others. While most children can sometimes appear self-centered, placing their own needs first, they also receive pleasure from reaching out and being helpful. For this pattern of caring and helpful behavior to emerge and be maintained, parents need to nurture it.

> *While most children can sometimes appear self-centered, they also receive pleasure from reaching out and being helpful.*

In our book *The Power of Resilience: Achieving Balance, Confidence, and Personal Strength in Your Life*, we offer clinical material and research findings to indicate that this drive to be helpful is present throughout life and is an integral component of a resilient mindset. When children feel they have contributed to the welfare of others, it reinforces the belief "Because I am on this earth, it is a better place." Such a belief adds meaning to one's life regardless of one's age. We have observed that helpful behaviors promote self-dignity, responsibility, and compassion.

Psychologist Emmy Werner, one of the world's foremost researchers in the area of resilience, captured the value of contributory activities when she wrote:

Self-esteem and self-efficacy also grew when youngsters took on a responsible position commensurate with their ability, whether it was part-time paid work, managing the household when a parent was incapacitated, or, most often, caring for younger siblings. At some point in their young lives, usually in middle childhood and adolescence, the youngsters who grew into resilient adults were required to carry out some socially desirable task to prevent others in their family, neighborhood, or community from experiencing distress or discomfort. (p. 511)

Linda Weltner, a *Boston Globe* writer, conveyed a similar message:

Dr. Janice Cohn suggests [in her book *Raising Compassionate, Courageous Children in a Violent World*] that kids need genuine accomplishments in order to develop a healthy sense of self-esteem. Empty praise, she says, has a destructive effect upon children's character. In contrast, when kids help others, they come to feel truly competent, powerful, and proud of themselves. Cohn cites studies which show that those with a commitment to caring for others not only have higher levels of self-esteem, but perform better academically and socially, and are at lower risk of suffering from depression or anxiety disorders. It turns out that those who are involved with something beyond themselves are most likely to report high levels of well-being and life satisfaction. (p. E2)

Research that we conducted supports the observations of Werner and Cohn and offers evidence that children are excited about and welcome the opportunity to contribute to the well-being of others. We asked a large group of adults to tell us the most positive and negative memories they had from when they were students. We asked specifically about positive experiences that included something a teacher said or did that enhanced self-esteem and motivation. The most common theme reflected a child being given the opportunity to contribute in some form to the school environment. Here are a few of their responses:

- "As a first-grade student, I had the responsibility of raising and lowering the coat closet doors because I was one of the taller boys in the class. This made me feel so good because I was so self-conscious about my height."
- "In a one-room school, the teacher had me sit and do spelling with the second-graders, once I had shown some ability in this subject."
- "My English teacher asked me to tutor a senior who was in danger of not graduating because she was failing English grammar. I was in tenth grade."
- "In the third grade, I was chosen to help get the milk and straws."
- "In the eleventh grade, my art teacher asked me to paint a mural in the school. I still correspond with her."

These responses validate psychologist Urie Bronfenbrenner's observation that part of every child's curriculum at school should be a "curriculum for caring" in which students receive instruction in and opportunities for taking care of others. In our view, a curriculum for caring should extend beyond the grounds of a school to the child's home and community.

Help Your Children Feel They Make a Difference

Enlisting your child's help really can lessen the child's anger. A by-product of the improved behavior is that the child is less likely to perceive that others are constantly angry with him or her. In fact, the more helpful a child is, the less likely it is that others will be angry with the child. The following suggestions will help you put this principle into practice in your own family.

Choose Words That Say Kids Matter

The label that many parents use to describe responsibilities they want their children to fulfill is one that unfortunately has taken on negative connotations. That label is *chores*. We often tell our children, "Remember to do your chores." In addition, in many children's minds, chores often become linked with homework, another unwelcome activity in many homes. We have yet to interview a child who tells us, "I am so fortunate to have chores and homework to do." In fact, we warn parents to be suspicious if their child ever utters such sentiments. When we ask parents at our workshops, "How many of you love to do chores?" rarely is a hand raised. However, when we ask, "How many of you like to help others?" almost all hands go up eagerly.

Can a label such as *chores* make a difference in a child's perception of what is being requested and the extent to which he or she will cooperate? We believe it can. Of course, removing the word *chore* or similar ones from the English language wouldn't magically motivate children to be more responsible. However, when parents have tried to convince us of their children's lack of responsibility, they typically mention a failure to complete household chores. When parents are preoccupied with day-to-day chores, it is easy for them to lose sight of the many areas in which their children *are* responsible. While it may be evident to parents why certain chores have to be done, it is not necessarily evident to the children. We are struck by how many parents angrily discipline their children for failing to do their chores. These children may eventually comply with their parents' requests in order to stop the reminders and punishments, but the result is that, rather than promoting responsibility in their children, these angry reminders create resentment.

We have found that when parents say, "We need your help," children are more likely to respond cooperatively, since they are less likely to interpret the parents' request as an imposition. We aren't suggesting that each time you say to your child, "We need your help," he or she will eagerly reply, "Thanks for asking me to help, Mom and Dad!" However, we believe that asking children for help is much more effective than telling (ordering) them to do things. Requests that are cast in terms of helping out tend to nurture compassion, responsibility, and resilience.

> *When parents say, "We need your help," children are more likely to respond cooperatively.*

The Leopold Family: "We Appreciate Your Help"

We witnessed this in our work with the Leopold family, whom we met in Chapter 3. The parents, Mona and Lawrence, were concerned about their three children: twelve-year-old Liz, ten-year-old Madison, and eight-year-old Manny. The parents complained that all three children were "rude," frequently calling their parents derogatory names. The parents responded with their own negative statements, such as "You always act like brats" or "You'll never learn how to act in a kind way."

In our interventions, we encouraged Mona and Lawrence to think about the impact their words had on their children, to develop realistic expectations, limits, and consequences for their children, and especially to provide positive feedback when they "caught their children doing something good." It is very interesting to observe the inordinate amount of time many parents, such as the Leopolds, spend reprimanding their children in comparison with the time they spend complimenting them. Even more intriguing are the explanations some parents offer to explain this difference. One father told us, "The reason I spend more time reprimanding my kids than complimenting them is that they spend more time being uncooperative than being cooperative." Unfortunately, this father failed to realize that his feedback was reinforcing his children's negative behaviors.

We advised Mona and Lawrence to apply several strategies that would help them become more effective disciplinarians. Some of these were described in Chapter 3, and given the theme of this chapter, we wish to emphasize another strategy here. This strategy addressed our impression that Liz, Madison, and Manny didn't understand the ways in which their cooperation would benefit the entire household. They lacked this understanding in part because their parents didn't show appreciation to their children when they were cooperative.

To remedy this situation, the Leopolds began by telling the children they wanted to speak with them. Later, when the parents recounted the situation to us, they explained the children's reaction by saying the children were accustomed to criticism. Liz had blurted, "Not another lecture! Why don't you stop nagging us?"

Lawrence told us that he responded, "No, not another lecture. Mom and I think we already nag you too much." As Lawrence recalled this, he smiled and said, "You know what I wanted to add, but I didn't." We agreed that we could guess. He continued, "I wanted to say that the only reason we had to nag them was that they were irresponsible, and if they were responsible, we wouldn't have to nag them."

We smiled and asked him what had held him back.

Laughing, he replied, "I thought you would nag me about it not being a good idea."

We joined in the laughter and assured him that we would never nag, but rather ask him to think about what he had said. On a more serious note, we pointed out that when Lawrence had held back from saying what he might have said in the past, it showed us that he was thinking about how his words were coming across to his children. We asked Lawrence what he had said to the children next.

"We told the kids we were really tired of lecturing and nagging. We actually told them that we thought our constant reminders were only making things tenser in the house. When we told them this, they looked stunned, not sure what was going to follow. To use your words, we changed the script, and I think it threw them off a little—not knowing what would come next." Turning to his wife, Lawrence asked, "Would you agree with what I've said so far?"

She answered, "Yes," and added, "Larry then said to them, 'What we really want to say is how much we need your help with different responsibilities in the house and how much we appreciate that help.'"

They both laughed, and we asked them why.

Mona replied, "I bet we're both thinking about Liz's response." Her husband nodded. She continued, "Liz said, 'Uh-oh, what are you looking for? What do you want?' And Larry was great. He said, 'We just want all of us to get along better and to help out in the house.'"

This beginning exchange about the important contributions that the Leopold children could make to the household was in accord with the other changes the Leopolds were making in their parenting style, especially involving their children in problem-solving activities and expressing appreciation rather than disapproval.

At one point, we emphasized to the Leopolds that the improvement in their children's behavior was significantly linked to the changes in their parenting and discipline style. We wanted to highlight their contribution to their home's more cooperative atmosphere. The significance of our compliment was not lost on them.

Lawrence replied, "Thanks for that kind of feedback. It's a nice feeling to know that you're making a difference in the lives of others, in this case in the lives of your children."

The Leopolds had learned a great deal about the characteristics of a self-disciplined and resilient mindset. We were gratified to see the whole family benefit.

Become a Charitable Family

We often ask parents, "Have your children seen you involved in activities in which you are helping others?" and "Have you and your children been involved in such activities together as a family?" These questions are based on the belief that it is easier to teach responsibility and caring when we serve as models for these behaviors and when we actively engage our children in contributory activities.

Obviously, we wouldn't want children to say their parents are out every evening performing different community activities. That level of activity would mean the parents are sacrificing valuable time with their children as they help others. However, we're always pleased when children report that their parents serve on a town committee, coach a youth team, or help raise money for a favorite charity.

Not only should children observe parents engaged in bettering the lives of others, but in addition, from an early age, they should be involved in these kinds of activities themselves. Even preschool children can help in differ-

> *Not only should children observe parents engaged in bettering the lives of others, but in addition, from an early age, they should be involved in these kinds of activities themselves.*

ent ways. For example, if parents plan to volunteer at a homeless shelter, they can assist their parents by preparing bags of toiletries before the visit.

A "charitable family" nurtures a tradition of involving the entire family in helping others. In so doing, parents reinforce in their children the belief that they are important, can help others, and truly make a difference. A child who develops this mindset is acquiring a sense of responsibility and compassion, as well as self-discipline. In our experience, charitable families typically use an authoritative style of discipline.

Returning to the Leopolds, they became active in supporting breast cancer research. This cause appealed to them because

Mona's mother and aunt had undergone mastectomies. Together, the Leopold family participated in charity events for breast cancer research, and the children were eager to support this cause.

Be Fair About the Boring Jobs

As a practical matter, even if we are careful to express to our children that we need their help for the household to run more smoothly, many responsibilities still seem boring or tedious. How many of us are eager to clean our room, clear the dishes, or take out the garbage? These are the kinds of activities that result in procrastination or "forgetting," which leads to nagging and punitive forms of discipline. Parents often ask, "What can we do so that our kids complete these chores without our nagging?" There are steps you can take to help to get things done and prevent discipline problems:

1. Talk about why the tasks have to be done. Discuss with your children why certain activities are important and what would occur if they weren't done. One couple emphasized this point by informing their three children that if their dirty clothes were not placed in the hamper, they would not be washed. When the older son in the family, a fourteen-year-old, discovered one morning that he had no clean pants or shirts to wear, he quickly learned the consequences of not complying with his parents' request. Initially, he tried to blame his parents, arguing that he didn't know they had done the wash the day before. They calmly informed him that he had a choice: he could remember to place his dirty clothes in the hamper, or he could do his own wash. To their surprise, he chose to do his own laundry and from that point did his own wash and even his own ironing. Obviously, not many adolescents make the same choice, but it worked for him.

2. Have a family meeting about what needs to be done. Sit down as a family, and list the household responsibilities. Often differences of opinion arise about what responsibilities are important. These differences can serve as the basis for further dialogue among family members. Some chores judged important at one point may later be discarded. Once a list of responsibilities is complete, your family can review which items must be done by certain members of the household and which can be done by any family member. This decision typically depends largely on the children's ages and skills. You wouldn't expect a four-year-old to clean leaves out of the gutters, but that child could help rake.

3. Figure out who does what, when, and for how long. When your list of responsibilities is done and prioritized, your family can develop a system for how these responsibilities should be delegated and for what length of time. Some responsibilities are more tedious than others. Many families design a rotating schedule so that chores among family members change every week or every month.

4. Agree on a way to remind everyone of chores. Even with the aid of a written list and rotating chores, children (and even parents) may forget to meet their responsibilities. Discuss what the family should do if anyone, including parents, neglects to fulfill a responsibility. In our experience, many families come up with simple reminders in the form of brief, nonaccusatory comments such as "You forgot to clear the dishes" or "You left the family room without putting the games away." Other families place a chart of the specific responsibilities at key places around the house, and when a responsibility is not met, family members point to the chart.

Whatever strategy you use, involve your children in understanding why everyone in the family needs to help and how the work can be distributed fairly. While parents can reserve the final say, children will appreciate their role in family life if they believe their views are being heard. When this occurs, they are more likely to be cooperative and responsible, and you will have helped to develop self-discipline.

The Joy of Accomplishing and Contributing

In this chapter, we have emphasized the importance of recognizing that discipline is far more than just punishment and must be understood as a process of teaching—teaching your children to be more thoughtful, compassionate, and responsible. Youngsters such as Nathan illuminate the important point that even very angry children can learn alternative ways of interacting with the world and trusting others. This change in mindset results not from authoritarian dictates in which the child's anger is matched by the anger of a parent or other adult, but rather from engaging children in activities that teach them the benefits of helping others. Such a positive approach to discipline prevents anger and behavioral problems from emerging, and it teaches important values and skills.

The Laramies: "Pied Piper of the Neighborhood"

Jackson and Annika Laramie consulted us about their fifteen-year-old daughter, Laurie. Laurie had difficulty making friends with children her age and demonstrated a "lack of responsibility" in various areas of her life. Her parents' description of her development indicated that she was socially immature and felt ill at ease with her classmates. They also noted that Laurie often appeared sad and angry, and she would plaintively ask, "Why does everyone always seem angry with me? Why doesn't anyone like me?" As the Laramies identified Laurie's difficulties, they also disclosed that Laurie's perception of people being angry with her was true.

Jackson said, "We know Laurie is sad and struggling with many issues in her life, but Annika and I sometimes feel there is more she can do for herself, that she often comes across like a 'victim' who feels nothing can improve her situation in life. I know we both get frustrated and have yelled at her. We tell her to invite kids over. When she responds that no one wants to be with her, instead of being more understanding, we get more frustrated and angrier. Then Laurie says, 'Everyone is angry at me,' and she gets mad at us and says we don't love her. I know we have to find a better way of dealing with her."

We responded that it might help for them to tell us about Laurie's strengths—her islands of competence. We explained that building on a child's islands of competence often can help the child deal with his or her worries and vulnerabilities.

Annika immediately replied, "It's a pleasure to watch Laurie with younger children. She has such a gentle style and is very patient with them, so they love to be with her. The other day, three eight-year-old neighbors came by to see if Laurie was available to teach them a game. Her entire face brightened when she saw them. She's so much more talkative with them than she is with kids her own age. She's the Pied Piper of the neighborhood."

Jackson agreed but noted that while Laurie could seem so responsible with these younger children, she often demonstrated a lack of responsibility in her day-to-day life.

We asked for examples.

Annika jumped in without hesitation. "She often forgets to make her bed or put her clean clothes away, so they're stacked on the floor. Sometimes we're not sure what's clean and what's been worn. We also think she should take more responsibility for getting ready in the morning. She sets her alarm, but sometimes she falls back to sleep, and we have to go in and wake her up."

Jackson added, "Annika and I wonder whether Laurie will become a responsible person or will have to rely on others to get things done."

It was obvious that the Laramies were feeling stymied by their daughter. They expressed their frustration with angry comments, which unfortunately confirmed for Laurie that people were angry with her. This intensified her own anger. We determined that her parents needed to shift from a punitive disciplinary style to one that relied on Laurie's strengths.

Our recommendations involved reinforcing Laurie's sense of responsibility by highlighting her islands of competence, feeling of contributing to the welfare of others, sense of ownership, and feeling of control over her life. We advised the Laramies to take advantage of Laurie's evident strength in relating to younger children. Fortuitously, a neighbor had recently asked her to baby-sit for her five- and seven-year-old sons two afternoons a week. Laurie's mother was available in case there were problems, so her parents encouraged her to accept the job, which she did. We also recommended that Jackson, Annika, and Laurie together decide on other ways in which Laurie could assume more responsibility in her life. We suggested that they ask Laurie to think about what would help her remember to fulfill these responsibilities as well.

The baby-sitting job provided experiences that boosted Laurie's self-esteem and sense of responsibility in several ways. First, the very act of taking care of the two brothers conveyed to Laurie that she was a capable person. In addition, her ability to solve problems was strengthened as she talked with the parents about what kinds of activities she could do with their sons while baby-sitting. The Laramies frequently spoke with Laurie about her baby-sitting activities, which gave them many chances to praise her for the wonderful work she was doing and her responsible behavior. She received equally positive feedback from the parents of the boys. Her success with the boys, together with the praise she received, helped to lessen her feelings that others were disappointed in her or angry with her. Laurie was becoming a more responsible adolescent as she developed a self-disciplined, resilient mindset.

This mindset was further reinforced by her concentrating on assuming greater responsibility in other areas of her life. One of those areas was getting ready for school in the morning without constant angry reminders. We had introduced the idea that Laurie might find it easier to be at school if she expected to be involved in an appealing activity, especially one that involved her helping others.

The Laramies consulted Laurie's guidance counselor, who pointed out that the high school was located next door to a nursery school and that several high school students earned credits by helping in the early morning. Laurie happily agreed to do the same. Since Laurie knew that the children at the nursery school depended on her, she made certain to be ready on time, earlier than she previously had awakened for school. Her parents were willing to drive her to school a half hour earlier, especially since this new responsibility created a calmer, less angry atmosphere at home.

This activity produced additional benefits. With the help of her guidance counselor, Laurie wrote an article for the school newspaper about her experiences working in the nursery school. As Annika observed, "When Laurie saw her name in print, it was worth several years of therapy."

Create Paths for Success

Once children are engaged in activities that are productive and benefit others, they are more likely to develop responsibility and compassion. At the same time, they generally experience less anger, and so do the adults in their lives. That was the experience of an assistant principal who attended one of our workshops and later sent us the following e-mail message:

> Your work has helped to save a family. Jerry's (not his real name) mother sat in my office this fall, crying. Jerry had given her difficulty for a few years but had recently become physically violent with her. We had started to see the same thing at school. On the

day that Jerry ended up in a physical restraint here, his mother came in and confessed that she hated her own son, then began to sob. She told me that she was thinking about seeing if he could live in a group home because she couldn't take it anymore.

I talked to Jerry and told him that I had a problem and thought he might be able to help me. We simply did not have enough custodial help during lunchtime. He agreed to help me by wiping down tables and sweeping the floor for a half hour at the end of lunch each day. Our custodians (who are awesome and child-centered) thanked him profusely and gave him authentic compliments about the work he had done. Jerry has not been in trouble since he started his new job three months ago. He is no longer physically violent or disruptive during class.

As we read this intervention, it reinforced our belief that in disciplining children, especially those who are angry and provocative, we must consider ways to prevent the anger from emerging. We can do that by providing opportunities for children to be successful and to contribute by helping others.

The same assistant principal told us about a second example:

Last week I set it up so that a fourth-grader (who has major organization problems, rarely brought in his homework, and is feeling pretty lousy about himself) started helping a second-grade class get their things ready at the end of the day. He helps them write down their assignments and pack their backpacks. The first day that he started, I caught him smile three times (normally we see three smiles in a week). He has consistently remembered to go to the second-grade classroom each day, and according to the second-grade teacher, smiles the whole time. He has been great about bringing in his homework ever since.

This creative, caring educator thanked us: "These are just two examples! Thanks again. Please keep your message out there. You have no idea how many children you are saving."

In actuality, this assistant principal deserves the compliments. She demonstrated the courage to change the negative way many adults relate to children. Instead, she initiated a course of action that helped prevent problems and enhance the self-esteem of at-risk youngsters. Her interventions embraced the true meaning of the word *discipline*, that is, a teaching process.

The Taunton Family: "A Child with Joy"

In Chapter 5 we met the Taunton family, including ten-year-old Jeremy and eight-year-old Lucille. Jeremy's parents and his school counselor described him as an angry child who bullied others and had much difficulty accepting any compliments or positive feedback. He had problems with reading. At home and school, he had temper tantrums during which he threw things. The counselor noted that Lucille had told her teacher she was scared, since her parents yelled at and spanked Jeremy when he was naughty. Jeremy also was a boy who didn't seem to find joy even in things he did well; his parents reported that he didn't seem to believe compliments he received.

In Chapter 5 we examined Jeremy's behavior through the lens of attribution theory—that is, what he thought were the reasons for both his accomplishments and his setbacks. His parents reported success as they shifted their discipline style from an authoritarian, punitive approach to giving Jeremy choices and keeping discipline focused on consequences for his choices. At the end of our discussion of the Tauntons in Chapter 5, we raised the question of what might be the best way for the Tauntons to communicate with Jeremy so that he could begin accepting acknowledgment of his accomplishments. We predicted that Jeremy's negative attitude and behavior would improve if he began to experience the joys associated with realistic achievement.

During an individual session with Jeremy, we asked him what he thought he did pretty well. He quickly replied, "I don't know." When we reworded the question and asked what he enjoyed doing, we received similar answers. We simply responded, "That's OK. It takes many kids several weeks to figure out what they enjoy doing or what they're pretty good at."

During an individual meeting with Lucille, she confirmed what her parents had said about her brother's islands of competence—that Jeremy was a good artist and good in sports. When we asked her what her brother liked to draw, she said, "He draws a lot of scary-looking monsters. He even did one of a monster eating a girl and told me that the girl was me. I know he's only kidding. Sometimes he likes to try to scare me."

We asked whether there were other things Jeremy liked to draw.

"Yeah. He draws great pictures of cars and planes. He also draws great pictures of kids playing sports. Sometimes he copies them from magazines, but sometimes he does them without a magazine in front of him." She then offered an example that helped us consider strategies to use with her brother: "Last week I told Jeremy he was a great artist and that I wished I could draw like him. He asked me what I wanted to draw, and I showed him some dolls in a magazine."

We asked her to tell us what happened next.

"He showed me how to copy them. He was really nice when he showed me."

We asked whether she had copied the dolls.

"Yes. And then Jeremy told me my drawings were very good, and he helped me hang them up on my bulletin board."

We wondered whether Jeremy seemed to enjoy showing Lucille how to draw the dolls.

"Yeah. He was very nice."

When we met with Luke and Meredith Taunton, we asked them about Jeremy showing Lucille how to draw.

Luke recalled, "Lucille was ecstatic. She immediately wanted us to see her drawings. The moment we complimented her, she told us how helpful Jeremy had been and that he had shown her how to draw. I must be honest—I was hesitant to compliment Jeremy, since I thought he would just get angry and do what he usually does, reject our compliments. But I told Jeremy he did a great job teaching his sister how to copy the dolls. Much to Meredith's and my surprise, Jeremy actually said, 'Thanks.' Just one word, and what a difference it made to us."

We asked the Tauntons to consider why they thought he had accepted that compliment and even said thanks.

Meredith answered, "We thought about it, but we're really not sure. We've also noticed that his temper outbursts have gotten less in the last couple of weeks."

Admitting that we weren't sure of all the reasons why Jeremy could accept his father's compliment or why he seemed less angry, we suggested that the changes might be a result of the Tauntons' hard work. We observed that what they had been saying during the past few meetings suggested that they had been much less angry and punitive with Jeremy. They had apparently stopped spanking and yelling at him. We suggested that those changes helped Jeremy begin to realize his parents weren't angry with him, and in turn, he became less angry with them. We told the Tauntons that we have always been impressed by the improvement in children's behavior when their parents begin using a more positive approach. The Tauntons' efforts to change their negative scripts set the stage for Jeremy to begin changing his.

We continued with praise for Lucille, who obviously loved her brother. We told the parents that we had learned something from her description of Jeremy teaching her how to draw. We explained that we could use that information to help Jeremy feel better about himself and less angry.

Meredith asked, "What's your idea?"

We reviewed the concept of contributory activities and the therapeutic value of enlisting children to help others. We emphasized that it was essential to give praise for realistic accomplishments, and when Jeremy had difficulty accepting the compliments, it was important to avoid getting into a debate aimed at convincing him that he should accept compliments. After all, as the Tauntons had experienced, it's easy for parents to get angry when their children reject the praise they've offered. Instead, we advised the Tauntons to think about ways for Jeremy to help others, just as he helped Lucille. Based on his willingness to accept his father's compliment about helping Lucille—even saying thanks—we predicted that the experience of helping others would be effective in helping Jeremy feel more satisfaction.

Meredith said, "It would be wonderful to see that. It's hard to explain our pleasure when he thanked us for complimenting him about Lucille. For most parents, hearing the word *thanks* would have been nice but nothing extraordinary. For us, it was a very special moment."

Just as the Laramies did with their daughter, Laurie, earlier in this chapter, we enlisted the assistance of Jeremy's school counselor and teacher. They arranged for Jeremy to go to a first-grade classroom once a week and demonstrate to the students how to draw. To support this activity, the school's art teacher gave Jeremy a book that showed how to draw different animals step by step. She helped Jeremy prepare a "lesson" in teaching the first-graders how to draw animals.

The first-grade teacher observed, "The first-graders think Jeremy is the next Picasso. They think he is the greatest artist in the world. And they are so happy when they finish their drawings. I've asked Jeremy to help them put up their drawings around the classroom, and he has really been helpful. This is my first year in the school, so I really didn't know Jeremy in the past, but he seems like an entirely different child than I heard he had been."

In a conversation about a week later, the first-grade teacher said, "I was told Jeremy has had problems accepting compliments, but when I complimented him about what a difference he has made in the classroom, he accepted it without any difficulty."

His school counselor told us, "Jeremy seems much more relaxed and much less angry. We haven't had any incidents of bullying in weeks."

The Tauntons were friendly with the owner of the local bookstore in their town. They asked the bookstore owner if Jeremy might draw something that could be displayed in the bookstore. Their friend suggested that Jeremy draw a poster for children about the importance of reading books. She sent Jeremy an e-mail indicating that his parents had told her what a wonderful artist he was and that she would love to meet with him about the possibility of his doing a poster for the store. The theme of encouraging reading had special meaning for Jeremy, given his reading problems.

Jeremy met with the bookstore owner and then drew a poster. She insisted that he sign his name at the bottom and placed the poster in a window near the entrance for everyone to see. Jeremy's island of competence was prominently displayed.

A few days later, when Jeremy, Lucille, and their parents were walking by the bookstore, Luke said to his son, "What a great poster. I don't think I could draw anything as good as that." According to both parents, Jeremy beamed. In the session during which Luke reported this event, he told us with much pride and relief, "He is now a child *with* joy."

Our work with the Tauntons continued for almost a year. We had some individual sessions with Jeremy, meetings with the parents, and family meetings. We collaborated closely with the school counselor to ensure that Jeremy received the tutoring he needed to improve his reading skills and that he continued to have opportunities to be helpful in school. (He drew pictures for the offices of the school counselor and the principal.)

Not all of our interventions succeed as they did with the Taunton family. However, we have learned that children benefit when they are encouraged to help others. It is a simple fact that when they make a positive difference, they are less likely to make a negative difference.

The Wisdom of Serving Others

We hope you will carefully consider the positive form of preventive discipline we have outlined in this chapter. As you do, it may be helpful to reflect upon the sentiments offered by two renowned authors. Their words indicate that they appreciate the benefits of contributory activities.

Charles Dickens asserted, "No man is useless in this world who lightens the burden of it for anyone else."

Walt Whitman observed, "When I give, I give myself."

10

The Lessons and Power
of Self-Discipline

Our capacity for conscious self-discipline is in many ways what makes us human. Self-discipline underlies our ability to make choices and decisions, to plan and act responsibly. As author Martha Bronson notes in *Self-Regulation in Early Childhood*, "Self-regulation begins with life itself" (p. 2). What she calls self-regulation and we call self-discipline is the software driving the processes involved in attention, thinking, problem solving, and learning. These processes develop with age and maturity. Bronson explains the development this way:

> Especially in early childhood the nurturing of self-regulation requires an integrated approach that considers the whole child. Young children cannot separate their feelings, thoughts, and actions as older children and adults learn to do. The physical, social, emotional, cognitive, and motivational abilities and interests are intertwined. (p. 10)

She adds that, because of this development, discipline—what Bronson calls "support offered for self-regulation"—must be appropriate to the child's level of development in each of these areas.

Self-discipline has become a popular topic in our complex culture. A recent Internet search for the word *self-discipline* yielded over five million entries. A search using the phrase *self-discipline in children* yielded over one and a half million entries. Many of these websites promote ideas and strategies to help children develop self-discipline, which is seen to be a key task in early childhood. Most suggest that parents try to understand how to engage in this process. Some sites offer a behavioral approach, suggesting that rewards and punishments model and shape self-discipline. Other sites take a more empathic approach, suggesting that helping children appreciate and understand their feelings is the path to self-discipline. Finally, some heavily emphasize that children do what they see, so they guide parents to behave in self-disciplined ways, expecting that their children will follow their example. Regardless of the approach, it is apparent that helping children develop self-discipline is a major responsibility of parenting in our increasingly complex world. Raising a self-disciplined child requires a combination of all of these approaches, with particular emphasis on giving guidance rather than punishment.

> *Helping children develop self-discipline is a major responsibility of parenting in our increasingly complex world.*

Benefits of Self-Discipline

Self-discipline enables a child to consider and appreciate a problem, concentrate for whatever time is needed to find efficient and effective solutions to the problem, and enact those solutions to reach a successful resolution of the problem. Self-discipline is enhanced when a child learns several basic lessons:

- It is better to face difficult tasks than to avoid them.
- It is important to think and reflect before acting.
- We can divide larger tasks into smaller, easier parts so that reaching our goals is not overwhelming.
- We can appreciate, accept, analyze, and learn from our mistakes.

Many people offer easy excuses for poor self-discipline, rather than appreciating that the ability to appraise our decisions and their outcomes honestly and to learn from them is a key component to living a resilient, self-disciplined life.

Experienced teachers recognize the importance of self-discipline. Neil Abrahams, a mathematics teacher in the Houston School District, writes online at The Math Forum, "Teachers need to be able to count on students' self-discipline if they are to succeed. Yet America's youth culture and consumerism hinder the development of the self-discipline that is necessary for learning." Abrahams hypothesizes that self-discipline may be more responsible for differences in achievement than any other factor. We agree with him.

> *Self-discipline may be more responsible for differences in achievement than any other factor.*

Cordelia Fine, a research fellow at the Center for Applied Philosophy and Public Ethics at the University of Melbourne in Australia, describes research findings of Amelia Duckworth and Martin Seligman published in 2005 in the journal *Psychological Science*. Fine notes the authors' conclusions:

Underachievement among American youth is often blamed on inadequate teachers, boring textbooks and large class sizes. We suggest another reason for students falling short of their intellectual potential: their failure to exercise self-discipline. We believe that many of America's children have trouble making choices that require them to sacrifice short-term pleasure for long-term gain and that programs that build self-discipline may be the royal road to building academic achievement. (p. 10)

In the fall of a recent school year, Duckworth and Seligman evaluated 140 eighth-grade students in Pennsylvania. Each student completed an IQ test, and then they, their parents, and teachers answered questionnaires about self-discipline. For example, some questions asked, "Are you good at resisting temptation? Can you work effectively towards long-term goals? Do pleasure and fun sometimes keep you from getting work done?" The students also participated in a test of their ability to delay gratification. Each was handed a dollar bill in an envelope. They could choose either to keep it or to hand it back and get two dollars a week later. Each student's decision was carefully recorded.

In the spring of that school year, Duckworth and Seligman returned to this group of students and compared each student's grades with the data collected the previous fall. They wanted to identify the most important factors associated with school grades. By far, the best predictor of grades was self-discipline. Each student's capacity for self-discipline was twice as important as his or her IQ for predicting academic success. Self-discipline was also the most powerful variable in predicting which high school students would select, school attendance, hours spent doing homework, hours spent watching television (fewer hours with more self-discipline), and the time of day students began their homework (earlier with more self-discipline). The effect of self-discipline on final grades held consistently, even when controlling for grades from the first marking period, scores on achievement tests, and, as noted, scores on the IQ test. These findings support educators' belief that a major reason some students fall short of their intellectual potential is that they fail to exercise self-discipline.

Some people are simply more susceptible to temptation and distraction. However, all of us sometimes reach the limits of our willpower. All of us require practice and support to develop the self-discipline needed to live a successful, resilient life.

In this book we have tried to show how you can nurture and strengthen self-discipline in your children. Our approach is rooted in a model of resilience, since we believe that if children are to develop the skills and outlook associated with resilience, they must develop self-discipline.

> *View the teaching of self-discipline as a long-term process, and try not to become discouraged if the fruits of your labor are not immediately apparent.*

As is evident from the many families whose lives we have shared with you in this book, we recognize that the process of nurturing self-discipline in children can be very challenging, and the results of your efforts as a parent may not be immediately apparent. We suggest that you view the teaching of self-discipline as a long-term process and try not to become discouraged if the fruits of your labor are not immediately apparent. Some youngsters need more time to mature than other children. Remember, the seeds you plant when a child is young may not reach maturity until years later.

The Stockley Family: "When Is He Going to Grow Up?"

The challenges, setbacks, and successes associated with parenting and teaching self-discipline were poignantly, humorously, and dramatically captured with eleven-year-old Tyler Stockley and his parents, Julie and Craig. The second author (Sam) saw the family for the first time in the mid-1980s. Tyler was a pleasant though impulsive fifth-grader with learning disabilities and attention problems. Though his parents loved him, they struggled with poor self-discipline themselves, so they had difficulty serving as good models and consistent disciplinarians for their son. When I first evaluated Tyler and began working with him, I described a problem-solving model and used role-playing to help him understand.

"When you have a problem, how do you go about solving it?" I asked.

"I just do the first thing I think of," responded Tyler.

"Does it always work?"

"I don't know; I never thought about it."

"Well, from now on," I answered, "when you have a problem, I want you to stop, think about the problem, explain in your mind why it is a problem, think about a good solution, and then think about each step needed to reach the solution. Finally, I want you to ask yourself if the solution was effective. If not, go back and pick another one."

We diligently reviewed this problem-solving method. At the end of the session, I asked Tyler's mother to come in. I told her, "We need you to help Tyler remember to use his problem-solving method."

"Well, I'll try," answered Julie. "But sometimes I'm not such a good problem solver either."

"Then this will be a good method for both of you," I said encouragingly.

"OK," she responded.

"Have you noticed how Tyler goes about solving problems?" I asked.

Julie confirmed what Tyler had told me a few minutes before: "He just seems to do the first thing he thinks of. I think he learned that from his dad and me."

Laughing, Tyler said, "Remember last week when you got so mad when the car wouldn't start? You kicked it and hurt your foot."

Fortunately, Julie had a sense of humor and laughed, too. She added, "It still didn't start. That wasn't very good problem solving."

"How have you tried to teach Tyler to solve problems?" I asked.

Julie responded, "I guess I never really thought about it. I think I just assumed that children learn to solve problems by trying to solve them and learning from their experiences."

"Well, trial and error is one way to learn, but often a very hard way. We don't always know what to do differently in the face of failure."

"I never thought of that."

I continued, "Don't misunderstand; trial and error is an important part of the problem-solving process, but regardless of age, we all benefit from a guide to help the process along."

"Like that charisma guy you said I need?" asked Tyler. During earlier sessions, I had told Tyler and his mother about the importance of what we call a "charismatic adult" to help a child through tough situations. As described by psychologist Dr. Julius Segal, such an adult is a person from whom a child gathers strength.

"Yes, a charismatic adult is the perfect guide," I told him.

"Mom, will you be the charisma guide for me?" Tyler asked.

"I wouldn't have it any other way," she answered.

We patiently reviewed the problem-solving method and considered a particular problem Tyler had: getting up on time and being ready to leave for school.

"The problem is I'm tired in the morning," explained Tyler.

"Is that really the problem?" I asked, "Or is the problem that when it's time to leave for school, you're not ready?"

"That's the problem," said Julie. "I've told Tyler that if he's tired in the morning, it means he should go to bed earlier."

"But I don't want to go to bed earlier! I'm not a baby," Tyler quickly responded.

"Well, maybe there are other solutions we can think of," I said. "What else do you think we might do to help you be ready on time in the morning?"

"I could sleep in my clothes," answered Tyler. "Then I would be ready quicker."

"Well, you'll have to change your clothes sometimes," responded Julie, barely able to stifle a laugh.

"Maybe you could bring me breakfast into my room so that I could eat while I'm getting dressed," responded Tyler.

"That won't work, because it's not that you're slow getting dressed, it's that you're slow getting out of bed, and then you usually find other things to do instead of dressing," answered his mother.

This problem-solving discussion continued until the two of them reached an agreement that Tyler would take his clothes out the night before and get up ten minutes earlier, and his mother would provide a few more reminders in the morning. For the coming weeks, Tyler was ready more often, although his poor self-discipline continued to plague him, not just when getting ready in the morning, but in almost all areas of life. Julie agreed to continue using the problem-solving method with Tyler, reminding him when he needed to think about how to deal with different issues he faced. In fact, she wrote the problem-solving steps on a small card for him to keep in his pocket.

Tyler told her, "Sometimes I forget to take the card out of my pocket, so I forget what to do."

Two weeks after learning the problem-solving method, Tyler came to see me. His first words in the waiting room were, "I used that problem-solving plan and got in a lot of trouble. It's your fault."

I ushered Tyler into my office. "Tell me what happened," I asked.

What followed was a possible script for a movie. Tyler explained that he and a friend had been throwing a baseball. The ball went up on the roof and rolled into the rain gutter. Tyler continued, "I remembered what you told me. The problem is the ball is stuck on the roof. We need to get the ball. First thing I thought of was to get the keys to our motor home and move it closer to the side of the house."

"Why would you think that?" I asked.

"Because it has a ladder on the back. I can climb up, get on the roof of the motor home, and reach over and get the ball." Tyler answered. "But the motor home was too far from the side of the house, so I had to get the keys and move it."

At this point, I didn't know what to say, so I just listened.

"I remembered what you said about breaking the solution into parts, so I thought about how to move the motor home. I got the keys. I've watched my dad back it out of the driveway. You put the key in the ignition and start it up. You put your foot on the brake, put the motor home in reverse, don't touch the gas, just lift your foot off the brake slowly and let it roll down the driveway."

"So what happened?"

"Well, I was trying to move the motor home closer to the side of the house. I guess I turned too far. The motor home crashed into the side of the house."

"What did you do then?" I asked, realizing the gravity of the situation but trying not to smile at Tyler's explanation.

"Well, I pulled the motor home away and got out to take a look. The motor home had a hole in it, the side of the roof was crushed, and the ball was still on the roof," Tyler explained. "But Dr. Sam, I remembered what you said about sticking to one problem at a time. So my friend and I decided what else we could do to get the ball!"

At this point, I was again speechless.

"Our second choice was to get my little brother and maybe flip him up on the roof." Tyler's little brother, a mild-mannered, rather quiet seven-year-old, had once been accidentally set on fire by Tyler. When his brother saw Tyler and his friend coming toward him, he wisely ran away. Tyler continued, "So we decided to get a ladder."

"What a good idea," I responded.

"But we don't have a ladder."

"Who has a ladder?"

"The neighbor, but I'm not going to ask her."

"Why not?"

"Because if I ask her for a ladder, she'll call the police."

I didn't know why that would be, so I asked, "Why would she call the police?"

"Well, a few weeks ago, my mom sent me over to borrow some butter. Our neighbor wasn't home, so I went around back because her back door is always open. I know because sometimes she asks me to let her dog out in the afternoon. I decided to watch her big TV until she came home," Tyler explained.

"Well, then what?"

"She came home and was really angry. She told me that even though the door was open, I was a criminal because I broke into her home. She also told me that, in the state of Utah, you can shoot criminals in your home. I'm not going near her," Tyler explained firmly.

In light of this disaster, we decided to modify the problem-solving method. From then on, when Tyler thought about solutions, he should make a list of at least five and choose the third, fourth, or fifth but not the first two. I explained to Tyler that his first two choices were often impulsive and not well thought out. I also told Tyler that he had to think of the consequences even with the third, fourth, and fifth solutions. Tyler agreed.

When Julie picked up Tyler at the end of this memorable session, she immediately asked me if Tyler had told me about the motor home. I replied that he had. With an air of exasperation, she declared, "I just don't know how to help him make good choices when he solves problems."

"Mom," Tyler jumped in, "when I have a problem, I'm not going to do the first or second thing I think of. I'm going to do the third!"

"Who thought of that?" she asked.

"Dr. Sam."

"I think that's a good idea, but we need a strategy so you can remember," Julie said. Her suggestion indicated that she recognized the components of a problem-solving plan.

"Don't worry, Mom. I'll just remember how much I miss my allowance when I have to pay you back when I break something."

"Good idea, Tyler. Let's see how well that strategy works," I said as I scheduled Tyler for his next appointment.

A few weeks later, I received a phone call from a suburban police officer, asking if I knew Tyler. I explained privacy laws and permission, indicating that I couldn't tell the officer whether I did or didn't. Still, I asked to hear the story.

The officer said, "Tyler was at a swimming pool, and he almost seriously injured a young girl."

"What happened?" I asked.

The officer explained that Tyler and this girl got into an argument over a spot each had claimed in the grass along the pool. Tyler picked up his towel, put it around the girl's neck, and snapped it. Fortunately, she wasn't seriously injured, but she certainly could have been hurt.

The officer continued, "I saw what happened and took Tyler aside. He explained to me that 'Dr. Sam' had told him that when he had a problem, he shouldn't do the first thing he thought of. He told me that the first thing he thought of was to hit the girl. He then said 'Dr. Sam' also told him that when he had a problem, he shouldn't do the second thing he thought of. The second thing he thought of was to push the girl into the pool and jump on top of her. Tyler said 'Dr. Sam' told him to do the third thing he could think of—in this case, it was putting a towel around this girl's neck and snapping it."

I didn't know how to respond. Tyler had clearly failed to consider the consequences of his third choice. His lack of discipline had subverted the newly devised problem-solving method. Despite his best efforts, he once again found himself in trouble.

Tyler received a citation for aggressive behavior. Later that week, he and his parents came to see me.

"Tyler needs to be more responsible," Craig Stockley said. "We've got busy lives and lots of problems. We don't have the time to watch out for him. He's taking medication to help him. When is he going to grow up?"

Tyler was facing a lot of challenges. During an earlier visit, his parents had acknowledged that they both struggled with alcohol and had decided upon divorce but couldn't afford it. Adding to the family turmoil, Craig had just been laid off from his job. Still, Tyler's younger brother and older sister, who were going through the same experiences, did not appear to be struggling with self-discipline problems anywhere near as much as Tyler. The medication that Tyler was taking was in fact helping him perform much better in school, but pills will never substitute for skills developed through positive experiences.

"But you know, Tyler is a good kid," Julie added. "He just has to learn to control himself."

Tyler stared at the floor. He was clearly troubled and embarrassed, but when I asked what he thought would help, he didn't know what to say. I explained the importance of giving Tyler closer supervision and more opportunities to develop the self-discipline needed to succeed, not just on the playground but in school and all walks of life.

Shortly after that, the family moved. Seven and a half years went by before I heard from them. Craig called to tell me that Tyler had begun attending an electrician's training program. He asked me, "Can you write a letter explaining his learning disability so he can take some of his classes with help and take his tests untimed?"

"Certainly," I responded, then asked, "How is Tyler doing?"

"He's doing great."

Though I was pleased to hear this, my last encounter with Tyler had suggested that Tyler's limited self-discipline was likely to lead him into increasing problems. I asked, "Why is he doing so well do you think?"

His father said he didn't really know.

"It has been quite a while since we were last in touch. I'd like to hear what has happened to Tyler in the last seven years," I persisted.

Craig told me that he and Tyler's mother had been clean and sober over the past five years. They finally divorced, and both later remarried. Tyler lived with his father, and his two siblings decided to live with their mother. Tyler graduated from high school and was now in this electrician's training program.

"Why an electrician? Are you an electrician?" I asked.

"No, I'm not," Craig responded. "But it's an interesting story." According to Craig, during his junior year of high school, Tyler participated in a year-long vocational class in which youth help build a house. The electrical contractor for this class was a man who had done this for years but wasn't officially a teacher. He took a liking to Tyler, telling him, "You remind me of myself as a kid." He encouraged Tyler to consider becoming an electrician. He had no ulterior motives. In essence, he became a charismatic person for Tyler, offering him a full-time job in the summertime and a part-time job during his senior year. He sponsored Tyler through the electrician's union for an electrician's apprentice program. Most likely, given Tyler's history of learning disabilities and school problems, he never would have qualified for such a program without this type of sponsorship.

Needless to say, I wrote the letter supporting accommodations in the electrician's training program for Tyler. He successfully finished the program, and, three years later, I was delighted when Tyler called me.

"I'm really doing well," Tyler told me. "I like being an electrician. I've always worked well with my hands. I'm married. I love my wife, and we just had our first child. That's why I'm calling."

"Is the baby having problems?" I asked.

"No, not really problems," Tyler responded. "But he often wakes up crying and is hard to comfort. My mother said I was like that. I know how much trouble I had developing self-discipline. If my son is going to have problems, I want to get started early!"

What Tyler Taught Us About Self-Discipline

Tyler's journey in life teaches us that developing self-discipline and a resilient lifestyle is often a slow process. His journey also reminds us that we should never underestimate the power that any individual—whether educator, parent, or electrician—can have in serving as a charismatic adult. Such an adult can provide a model of self-discipline and guide the youngster to become more responsible and mature.

In addition, although Tyler's parents struggled with their own issues of self-discipline, the discussions they had with us may have helped to plant the seeds of Tyler's future success. Tyler's parents did not give up on him and were constantly looking for new strategies to help him be less impulsive and more thoughtful. And Tyler eventually found his island of competence in life as an electrician. As we noted earlier, sometimes the fruits of our labor with children are not evident until years later.

Gazing into Our Children's Eyes

In 2005, we edited an important scientific volume, *Handbook of Resilience in Children*. In our concluding chapter, we questioned how to go about predicting the future of today's children. What statistics should be examined? What outcomes should be measured? What formula should be computed? Despite a large, increasing, and valuable body of data, we don't possess definitive or precise answers to these questions. However, we examined the increasing number of risks facing children and observed that short- and long-term research (such as the study by Duckworth and Seligman described earlier in this chapter) repeatedly point to the importance of self-discipline as a powerful, protective resilience factor.

To gaze into the future of our species, we can simply gaze into the eyes of our children. Our future depends on the success or failure of our efforts to prepare our children to become happy, healthy, functional, and contributing members of society in their adult lives. But as you are well aware, the task of raising children and preparing a generation to take our place has become increasingly difficult. The complexity of our culture appears to increase the risks and vulnerabilities that have fueled the statistics of adversity—the growing number and severity of problems—for our youth. These statistics reflect the increasing difficulty of instilling in children the qualities necessary for health, happiness, and success. An absence of mental illness is no longer a guarantee of mental health and flourishing. We all must make a conscious effort to help children learn to use self-disciplined ways of thinking, feeling, and behaving, which will prepare them to cope effectively with the many problems and stresses they are likely to face.

> *Our future depends on the success or failure of our efforts to prepare children to become happy, healthy, functional, and contributing members of society in their adult lives.*

In a recent issue of the *American Psychologist*, Robert Weissberg, Karol Kumpfer, and Martin Seligman reflect on the growing interest in preventive discipline that applies what we know about resilience. Such discipline begins within families. Much research remains to be completed before we can fully understand the best way to promote this knowledge so that it becomes an integral part of raising children with a capacity for self-discipline. But by applying what we have learned so far, we hope this book will make a positive and important difference in your lives and the lives of your children.

Recommended Reading

Bernstein, J. 2006. *10 Days to a Less Defiant Child*. New York: Marlowe.

Bernstein, N. F. 2001. *How to Keep Your Teenager Out of Trouble and What to Do if You Can't*. New York: Workman Publishing.

Borba, M. 2004. *Don't Give Me That Attitude! 24 Rude, Selfish, Insensitive Things Kids Do and How to Stop Them*. San Francisco: Jossey-Bass.

Brooks, R., and S. Goldstein. 2001. *Raising Resilient Children*. New York: McGraw-Hill.

———. 2003. *Nurturing Resilience in Our Children: Answers to the Most Important Parenting Questions*. New York: McGraw-Hill.

Cline, F. W., and J. Fay. 2006. *Parenting with Love and Logic*. Colorado Springs: Pinon Press.

Coloroso, B. 2002. *Kids Are Worth It*. New York: Harper Collins.

Curwin, R. L., and A. N. Mendler. 1988. *Discipline with Dignity*. Alexandria, VA: Association for Supervision and Curriculum Development.

Edwards, C. D. 1999. *How to Handle a Hard-to-Handle Kid*. Minneapolis: Free Spirit Publishing.

Ford, E. E. 1994. *Discipline for Home and School*. Scottsdale, AZ: Brandt Publishing.

Goldstein, S., and R. Brooks. 2004. *Angry Children, Worried Parents: Seven Steps to Help Families Manage Anger*. Plantation, FL: Specialty Press.

Goldstein, S., K. Hagar, and R. Brooks. 2002. *Seven Steps to Help Your Child Worry Less*. Plantation, FL: Specialty Press.

Goldstein, S., and N. Mather. 1998. *Overcoming Underachieving*. New York: Wiley.

Griffin, L. 2007. *Negotiation Generation: Take Back Your Parental Authority Without Punishment*. New York: Penguin.

Hagar, K., S. Goldstein, and R. Brooks. 2006. *Seven Steps to Improve Your Child's Social Skills*. Plantation, FL: Specialty Press.

Kurcinka, M. S. 2001. *Kids, Parents, and Power Struggles: Winning for a Lifetime*. New York: Harper Collins.

MacKenzie, R. J. 2001. *Setting Limits with Your Strong-Willed Child*. New York: Three Rivers Press.

Mogel, W. 2001. *The Blessing of a Skinned Knee*. New York: Penguin Compass.

Nelsen, J. 1987. *Positive Discipline*. New York: Ballantine Books.

Samalin, N. 2003. *Loving Without Spoiling: And 100 Other Timeless Tips for Raising Terrific Kids*. New York: McGraw-Hill.

Shure, M. B. 1994. *Raising a Thinking Child*. New York: Henry Holt.

———. 2004. *Thinking Parent, Thinking Child: How to Turn Your Most Challenging, Everyday Problems into Solutions*. New York: McGraw-Hill.

Sornson, B. 2005. *Love and Logic: Creating Classrooms Where Teachers Love to Teach and Students Love to Learn*. Golden, CO: Love and Logic Institute.

Taylor, J. 2002. *Positive Pushing: How to Raise a Successful and Happy Child*. New York: Hyperion.

Zentall, S., and S. Goldstein. 1999. *Seven Steps to Homework Success*. Plantation, FL: Specialty Press.

References

Abrahams, N. 2006. Math forum discussion at http://www.mathforum.org/kb/profile.jspa?userid=41379 (information is no longer available online).

Baumrind, D. 1971. Current patterns of parental authority. *Developmental Psychology Monograph* 4:1–103.

Boston Globe. 1997. One more reason to be your own boss. July 25.

Bromhall, C. 2003. *The Eternal Child: How Evolution Has Made Children of All of Us.* London: Edbury Press.

Bronson, M. B. 2000. *Self-Regulation in Early Childhood: Nature and Nurture.* New York: Guilford.

Brooks, R., and S. Goldstein. 2001. *Raising Resilient Children.* New York: McGraw-Hill.

———. 2003. *The Power of Resilience: Achieving Balance, Confidence, and Personal Strength in Your Life.* New York: McGraw-Hill.

Covey, S. 1989. *The 7 Habits of Highly Effective People.* New York: Fireside.

Duckworth, A. L., and M. E. P. Seligman. 2005. Self-discipline outdoes I.Q. in predicting academic performance of adolescents. *Psychological Science* 16:939–44.

Edwards, C. D. 1999. *How to Handle a Hard-to-Handle Kid.* Minneapolis: Free Spirit Publishing.

Fine, C. 2006. Self-discipline: The road to academic success. *Australian,* June 14.

Goldstein, S., and R. B. Brooks, eds. 2005. *Handbook of Resilience in Children.* New York: Springer.

Goldstein, S., and R. B. Brooks. 2005. The future of children today. In *Handbook of Resilience in Children*, ed. S. Goldstein and R. Brooks, 397–400. New York: Springer.

Goleman, D. 1995. *Emotional Intelligence*. New York: Bantam.

Katz, M. 1997. *On Playing a Poor Hand Well*. New York: Norton.

Marano, H. E. 2004. A nation of wimps. *Psychology Today*, November/December. http://psychologytoday.com/articles/pto-20041112-000010.html.

Segal, J. 1988. Teachers have enormous power in affecting a child's self-esteem. *Brown University Child Behavior and Development Newsletter* 4:1–3.

Seligman, M. E. P. 1990. *Learned Optimism: How to Change Your Mind and Your Life*. New York: Simon & Schuster.

Shure, M. B. 1994. *Raising a Thinking Child*. New York: Holt.

———. 2000. *Raising a Thinking Preteen*. New York: Holt.

———. 2005. *Thinking Parent, Thinking Child*. New York: McGraw-Hill.

von Oech, R. 1990. *A Whack on the Side of the Head*. New York: Warner Books.

Weiner, B. 1974. *Achievement Motivation and Attribution Theory*. Morristown, NJ: General Learning Press.

Weissberg, R. P., K. L. Kumpfer, and M. E. P. Seligman. 2003. Prevention that works for children and youth. *American Psychologist* 58:425–32.

Weltner, L. 1997. Ever so humble: Kids need to give as well as get. *Boston Globe*, December 11.

Wen, P. 2001. Doctors seek insight into our outlook. *Boston Globe*, November 27.

Werner, E. 1993. Risk, resilience, and recovery: Perspectives from the Kauai Longitudinal Study. *Development and Psychopathology* 5:503–15.

Index